Digital Death

Mortality and Beyond in the Online Age

Christopher M. Moreman and
A. David Lewis, Editors

 PRAEGER

AN IMPRINT OF ABC-CLIO, LLC
Santa Barbara, California • Denver, Colorado • Oxford, England

Copyright © 2014 by ABC-CLIO, LLC

All rights reserved. No part of this publication may be reproduced, stored in a retrieval
system, or transmitted, in any form or by any means, electronic, mechanical, photocopying,
recording, or otherwise, except for the inclusion of brief quotations in a review, without prior
permission in writing from the publisher.

Library of Congress Cataloging-in-Publication Data

Digital death : mortality and beyond in the online age / Christopher M. Moreman and
A. David Lewis, editors.
    pages cm
Includes bibliographical references and index.
ISBN 978-1-4408-3132-4 (hardback) — ISBN 978-1-4408-3133-1 (ebook)
1. Death—Social aspects.   2. Information technology—Social aspects.   3. Internet—Social
aspects.   I. Moreman, Christopher M., 1974– editor.   II. Lewis, A. David, 1977– editor.
    HQ1073.D55   2014
    306.9—dc23   2014025699

ISBN: 978-1-4408-3132-4
EISBN: 978-1-4408-3133-1

18   17   16   15   14   1   2   3   4   5

This book is also available on the World Wide Web as an eBook.
Visit www.abc-clio.com for details.

Praeger
An Imprint of ABC-CLIO, LLC

ABC-CLIO, LLC
130 Cremona Drive, P.O. Box 1911
Santa Barbara, California 93116-1911

This book is printed on acid-free paper (∞)

Manufactured in the United States of America

Christopher would like to dedicate this collection to the memory of Kim Zarboni and Suzanne Timm, and to the Timm family.

David dedicates this collection to Robin Williams, the only Peter Pan, the only Genie, he ever believed in—and still does.

Contents

Part III: Virtual Worlds beyond Death

Introduction

A. David Lewis and
Christopher M. Moreman

In the BBC's award-winning police drama *Luther* (2010–2013), the title character, Detective Chief Inspector (DCI) John Luther, investigates the murder of internet troll Jared Cass. Accompanied by his junior partner, Luther learns that Cass "never went out. All he did was sit in that flat. He slagged off loads of people online. Any one of them would have killed him." Of all Cass's potential murderers, Luther must reluctantly suspect Ken Barnaby, a grieving father. Cass had insulted and angered so many online, yet what makes Barnaby their likeliest suspect is Cass's deeply personal digital assault—the desecration of Barnaby's daughter Cathy's online memorial.

Not only does Cass manage to have *Die U Slut!* appear on the screen of Cathy's memorial, but Cass also appropriates her image and voice. Barnaby explains to the detectives:

> It started with someone impersonating her online. Sending messages. "Help me, Daddy. It's so hot in Hell." Pictures of corpses, with her name written on them. Messages on Father's Day. Photos of a graveyard. "Wish you were here." And then, he started sending pictures. Cathy's face Photoshopped onto obscene images. My little girl. [. . .] We'd complain, the site would get taken down, but another would spring up. It—it just . . . It didn't stop. The taunts, the emails, the pictures. Horrible things.

Luther and his partner reluctantly arrest Barnaby when fingerprints confirm his involvement—though both sympathize with his motive for wanting Cass dead. But what did Cass do, exactly? He had no part in Cathy's death itself; the show suggests she died as a result of medical ailments. Moreover, Barnaby knows that the Father's Day messages and the

Photoshopped images are unquestionably fake, so it is not as though Cass is truly impersonating Cathy. As far as legitimate crimes go, Cass is likely guilty of vandalism, harassment, and perhaps some forms of digital piracy or identity theft. It is difficult to justify murder for such relatively minor crimes. Even the intensely disrespectful real-world funerary protests organized by the infamous Westboro Baptist Church inspired no more than contemptuous outrage.

Yet, the audience understands, along with Luther, how Cass's online actions could drive Barnaby, a grieving father, to take a life. Like the desecration of a cemetery or slander aimed at a deceased loved one, audiences are growing more accustomed to extending their sentiments for traditional mourning into digital environments—perhaps even more intensely. Of course, the audience spoken of here is a reasonably affluent one, a percentage of the world population with reliable computer and digital access to online sites or software; one cannot expect a citizen of a poverty-stricken country, one lacking in sufficient food, water, shelter, or hygienic plumbing, to share, necessarily, in this growing connection between the physical world and a virtual one—not yet, at least. But, speaking in terms of *Luther's* viewership, on both sides of the Atlantic as well as streaming online, this audience has enough of a developed relationship between the physical and the virtual, in all likelihood, to feel the Barnabys' pain.

This population of individuals who experience dying, death, mourning, grieving, and even mortality itself as a hybrid between the physical and the digital has grown in such number that it has become the focus of academic discussion. While not exclusively a religious matter—since it is as much a social, political, economic, philosophical, and psychological issue, among others—the intersections of mortality and digital existence caught our attention as members of the steering committee of the Death, Dying, and Beyond program unit of the American Academy of Religion (AAR). Building upon the ideas presented at our conferences, the two of us invited additional voices to expound upon some of the important questions raised by the complexities of navigating the age-old problem of mortality in the rapidly changing landscape of digital technology and virtual reality.

Of course, *Digital Death: Mortality and Beyond in the Online Age,* is not by any means the first work to treat this subject matter. Most notable among those books to come before include *Your Digital Afterlife,* by John Romano and Evan Carroll,[1] and *Death in the Digital Age* by Gabrielle Muse.[2] Romano and Carroll are less concerned about spiritual matters and more focused on pragmatic issues surrounding one's virtual, personal assets after death. In fact, the timely release of their work and the need for such information have led to their book being recognized as the go-to source for practical answers to how one might plan for dealing with one's digital legacy. Muse, on the other hand, addresses similar issues but from the perspective of the mourners, offering a short guide for dealing with the digital legacies of loved ones. The online community itself has also produced similar guides, including Vered Shavit's *Digital Dust*,[3] whose site grew out from the sudden death of her brother in a 2011 car accident and the difficulties that she faced in dealing with issues of digital legacy. Like Romano and Carroll, this encouraged her to aid and educate others on the complexities of online legacies and memorialization.

The above all take aim at the specific concerns of dealing with digital and online "property" after death, Carla J. Sofka, Illene Noppe Cupit, and Kathleen R. Gilbert, in their edited collection, *Dying, Death, and Grief in an Online Universe*, offer a range of perspectives to aid grief counselors and death educators deal with changing technology.[4] From these few examples, one can see that practical concerns have led the way in discourse and scholarship on the problems of death, dying, grief, and remembrance online.

Our *Digital Death*, as an early foray into this vast field of inquiry, is in no way meant to present itself as the final and definitive word on the phenomena of hybrid mortality. Quite the opposite, our hope is that this collection marks just the beginning of what we expect to be a growing experience. In fact, as this introduction is being written, the first Death Online Research Symposium has just recently concluded at the University of Durham, philosopher Eric Charles Steinhart has published *Your Digital Afterlives: Computational Theories of Life after Death*,[5] and the Johnny Depp film *Transcendence*[6] is arriving in movie theaters. Our topic, therefore, is easily regarded as an active and developing one. And one for which we look forward to further scholarship.

Given the novelty of the field, we sought a wide range of approaches to the topic, founded initially in the religious focus of the AAR but branching out more widely from there. As it turns out, many of the chapters naturally clustered around certain aspects of "digital death" and, in fact, provided either overlapping or distinctly different views on specific topics such as, digital cemeteries or Facebook memorialization practices. As *Digital Death*'s editors, we welcome this diversity, eager to expand the overall conversation rather than put early or artificial limits upon it.

Though the chapters were invited to consider the topic broadly, several of them came to share a number of similar elements. For some, this academic interest originated with a personal experience or loss, from Rebecca Moore's curating a site dedicated to the stigmatized dead of Jonestown (her own sisters included), to Erica Hurwitz Andrus's discovery of a virtual community of real-life mourners for a dearly loved, and yet entirely fictional, television character. Several authors, like Andrus, found themselves "cross-wiring" media, bridging television (as previously with the example of *Luther* and for Andrus with *Battlestar Galactica*), the novels of Vladimir Nabokov for Denisa Kera, and online gaming for William Sims Bainbridge, Stephen Mazzeo, and Daniel Schall. It seems as though for none of us is a consideration of "hybrid death" simply a mix of only two media, only two ingredients, but rather it is multimedial and cross-disciplinary, which is in itself worth noting for future discussions of just what the "online age" might mean.

If there was any one anchor—a current center of gravity—to the discussion of mourning and memorialization, it was easily the social networking site Facebook. Here, too, a number of other texts have already been written on the phenomenon of Facebook,[7] but little focused discussion has been given as yet to its effects on grieving and remembrance. And again, any news stories on the subject tend to focus on people's digital legacy or information privacy rights, not specifically issues of mortality. As such, we have chosen to give considerations of Facebook their own opening section in *Digital Death,* beginning with Erinn Staley's account of Facebook's recent policies and tools for memorialization as well as their "opportunities for religious innovation." Heidi Ebert and Ari Stillman then follow with their own individual accounts of Facebook's value for mourning "precisely because they were not designed to be used that way," and its propensity to essentialize human experience, respectively. Finally, Candi K. Cann asks how Facebook and similar memorializing platforms might, either accidentally or for intentional monetary motives, be promoting the increase of what she calls "the spectacle of mourning."

The second section applies the observations gleaned from Facebook and reaches out to consider Twitter, Pinterest, Instagram, QR codes, cyber memorials, digital cemeteries, dark tourism, and—related back to the story of *Luther's* Barnaby—digital vandalism. These four chapters—by Michael Arntfield; Bjorn Nansen, Michael Arnold, Martin Gibbs, and Tamara Kohn; Pam Briggs and Lisa Thomas; and Moore—demonstrate the breadth of perspectives that can be brought to bear on our shared topic. In truth, as their editors, we are excited to put these writings in dialogue with each other and encourage further consideration on questions like: How might Briggs and Thomas's concern for "thanosensitive design" impact the next generation of Mansen's digital cemeteries? Could Moore's concern for the disenfranchised grief of those touched by Jonestown result in a new destination for Arntfield's "dark tourism?"

The final section easily constitutes the "beyond" of our title *Mortality and Beyond in the Online Age*. While two chapters focus on the experience and effect of digital and online game playing, the other two locate themselves in terms of fictional narratives—of distinctly different varieties. Specifically, Andrus provides an account of real-life individuals coming together online to mourn, remember, and, in a way, provide an afterlife for the character of Laura Roslin from the 2003–2009 *Battlestar Galactica* television series. As her title notes, Roslin may have been fictional, but her fans' bereavement is both real and best expressed online. Conversely, Denisa Kera also deals with the real-world impact of fictional characters, yet hers both predate and prefigure online identity by generations, in considering the transhumanist implications of works by Nabokov and Diderot. Stephen Mazzeo and Daniel Schell and, separately, William Sims Bainbridge, connect these concerns for both a fiction's mortality and characters' reflection of our own hybrid identities into the worlds of digital gameplay—considering what might constitute "ending" in these worlds and what has, by financial necessity, already brought around such demise.

None of these chapters requires an *a priori* knowledge either of data or theory in order to be understood (even the ones on online game playing!), and we expect that readers will find interdisciplinary application to our discussions that can be usefully applied to nearly any field of social science or the liberal arts (perhaps even science and law, too). But, while this book has use for a wide audience, it is our genuine hope that the ideas, analyses, and meditations found in *Digital Death* will serve as a springboard for others to engage in explorations and considerations that we might never have thought possible. We, its editors, are limited, in truth—we have, albeit quite willingly, tied ourselves to the print medium for *Digital Death*, and, outside of its being transferred into an e-book or some such affiliated form, we remain in the lingering past of "the online age."

So, while we honor those who have helped and supported us to date, *Digital Death* is actually for the coming scholar who might recognize our humble attempt and will have the vision to take it further still. That is, we await the next set of thinkers to take us even further beyond.

Notes

1. John Romano and Evan Carroll, *Your Digital Afterlife: When Facebook, Flickr, and Twitter are your Estate, What's Your Legacy?* (San Francisco: New Riders, 2010).

2. Gabrielle Muse, *Death in the Digital Age—Managing Online Accounts When a Loved One Dies* (Riverview, FL: Idea Adapter, 2011).

3. Vered Shavit, *Digital Dust: Death in the Digital Era & Life after Death on the Net: Digital, Virtual and Online Aspects of Current Death* (2012–2014), http://digital-era-death-eng.blogspot.co.il/. Accessed May 25, 2014.

4. Carla J. Sofka, Illene Noppe Cupit, and Kathleen R. Gilbert, eds., *Dying, Death, and Grief in an Online Universe* (New York: Springer, 2012).

5. Eric Charles Steinhart, *Your Digital Afterlives: Computational Theories of Life after Death* (Basingstoke, UK: Palgrave, 2014).

6. Wally Pfister, dir., *Transcendence*, 2014.

7. See, for instance, Newton Lee, *Facebook Nation: Total Information Awareness* (New York: Springer, 2013); Alexander Lambert, *Intimacy and Friendship on Facebook* (Basingstoke, UK: Palgrave MacMillan, 2013); and Daniel Trottier, *Identity Problems in the Facebook Era* (Hoboken, NJ: Taylor and Francis, 2013).

Part I

Death, Mourning, and Social Media

Chapter 1

Messaging the Dead: Social Network Sites and Theologies of Afterlife

Erinn Staley

Introduction

"I keep wanting to call you," a Facebook user writes on one of her friend's profiles. "So many things to tell you that we would laugh about. I just have to keep trusting God on this one."[1] The user cannot reach her friend by phone, because he died five months earlier. Along with numerous other greetings, birthday wishes, and inside jokes, this message will receive no reply from its intended recipient. The senders of these greetings are not alone; experiencing the death of an online friend or acquaintance is not uncommon, nor is continuing to send electronic messages to the dead via social network sites.[2]

This chapter analyzes the widespread practice of using social network sites such as Facebook to send communication to deceased users, both immediately following the user's death and in the longer term. Dead users' profiles on the most popular social network site, Facebook, often persist, and many living users continue to post messages on them.[3] Studies of Christian social network users' communications to the deceased show that the messages often have theological content, indicating belief in heaven and expectation that the deceased is in heaven, where she or he is able to receive the electronic communication but unable to respond.[4] Current practices of sending messages to the dead perpetuate theological deferral of eschatology as future and other-worldly, but it is possible that user experimentation with social network technology may help create communities among the deceased's online friends in a way that offline rituals, such as speaking at a grave, typically do not.

Social Network Profiles of the Deceased

While the existence of Facebook certainly is familiar to most readers, its mechanics and policies regarding deceased users may not be. The fact is, Facebook users die, and their digital profiles endure in the absence of specific interventions. While the company does not publish the number of deceased users, one frequently cited source projected that 2.89 million users worldwide, including 580,000 U.S. users, would die in 2012 alone.[5] Even users who have given thought as to what should happen to their material goods upon their death likely have not made preparations for what happens to their digital existences, whether on Facebook or elsewhere online. The endurance of digital information that was created, owned, or once used by the now-deceased is a phenomenon that governments, attorneys, digital media providers, and digital media users are only beginning to address. While new laws, guidelines, and resources are emerging to help users make plans for the ownership, accessibility, and fate of social network profiles, email, photographs, and other digital possessions, laws and customs do not yet dictate a single outcome for social network profiles.[6]

At present, there are three possibilities for what happens to the Facebook profile of a deceased user. First, a third party can delete the account, either independently if she or he has the password or by requesting that Facebook remove the account, a process that requires proof, such as a death certificate and evidence of the requestor's immediate relationship to the deceased.[7] Second, in the absence of action by a third party, the profile remains active: Friends can continue to post messages on the Timeline, the profile appears in the site's search function, and the profile shows up in the program feature called, "People You May Know" (which suggests to a user that she might like to become Facebook friends with another user based on friends in common).

Third and controversially, when the site instituted a program called "Reconnect" in the fall of 2009, it started encouraging users to get in touch with people with whom they had not had recent Facebook contact—including the deceased. The site intended to increase activity among dormant users, and Facebook inadvertently began suggesting, for instance, that a user reconnect with a deceased person by writing a message on his profile. So numerous were dead users' profiles that current users who received these suggestions quickly employed other social media, such as Twitter, to bemoan Facebook's reminder that their friends were no longer active on the site. One woman lamented, "ironic that facebook is suggesting i 'reconnect' with a friend who was murdered this year," concluding her tweet with a sad face emoticon; another criticized the new program, tweeting, "facebook just told me to reconnect with justin. i would if he hadn't died seven months ago. facebook, you fail."[8]

The controversy around the appearance of the dead in the "People You May Know" and "Reconnect" features promoted awareness of the third option, that of "Memorializing" a profile. Memorializing means that no one else can log into the account, that only confirmed Facebook friends can see the profile or locate it in a search of the site, and that they can continue to post on the deceased user's Timeline (or the older design feature, the "Wall"). In other words, no one can access the deceased user's account in order to engage new friend requests or to send and respond to messages. Such responses, were they possible, might give the appearance of communication from the dead.

After the immediate outcry about the "Reconnect" feature, Max Kelly, then Head of Security at Facebook, encouraged users to promote the memorialization of deceased users' profiles:

> We understand how difficult it can be for people to be reminded of those who are no longer with them, which is why it's important when someone passes away that their friends or family contact Facebook to request that a profile be memorialized [. . .]. By memorializing the account of someone who has passed away, people will no longer see that person appear in their Suggestions [. . .]. As time passes, the sting of losing someone you care about also fades but it never goes away. I still visit my [deceased] friend's memorialized profile to remember the good times we had and share them with our mutual friends.[9]

It is Facebook's policy to memorialize accounts of all deceased users, which requires a third party filling out a form and providing a link to an obituary or news article confirming the death.[10] Since the memorialization request is simple and can be completed by any friend, presumably most profiles of deceased users are transitioned to this state rather than erroneously remaining active.

In addition to these three possible outcomes for the account of a dead user, living users devote online spaces to the deceased through Facebook "Pages" or "Groups," which any user can create. A user might create a memorial Page or Group to remember a dead friend who was not a Facebook user or to exist simultaneously with a dead user's profile.[11] Any user can create a Page or Group to serve as a memorial through the same process she or he would use to create a Page or Group promoting a business, hobby, or celebrity. In the case of a memorial Page or Group, the creator might employ it to raise money for the family of the deceased or a relevant organization, such as American Childhood Cancer Organization, or to draw attention to a cause, such as antibullying.[12] When other users wish to interact with a Page, they "like" it rather than becoming "friends" with its creator, since it is not a user profile; similarly, they join a Group rather than becoming "friends" with its creator. While users who "like" memorial Pages or join memorial Groups sometimes post comments addressed to the deceased, users' overall interactions with memorial pages may differ from their interactions with a decedent's actual profile. The practices addressed in the subsequent section of this chapter concern user profiles rather than memorial Pages or Groups; further research is necessary both to compare posting trends on memorialized profiles to posting on memorial Pages and Groups and to consider similarities with other memorial media, such as online funeral home guestbooks.[13]

Etiquette for Messaging the Dead

An emerging body of literature on death and social network sites is situated at the intersections of computer sciences and social sciences. Some of this research notes the often religiously inflected language of communication sent to deceased users.[14] The following analysis draws, in particular, on Jed Brubaker and Janet Vertesi's 2010 "Death and the Social Network," its data coming largely from Christian Facebook and MySpace users in the mainland United States, as well as on supplementary observations of Christian users among my network of friends.[15] My aim is to draw out the theological imagination that both the *practice* of posting messages to deceased users and the *content* of messages convey.

Many practices of posting on a live user's profile, by and large, continue to apply to posting on a dead user's profile. Brubaker and Gillian Hayes's study of comments on the MySpace profiles of 1,369 deceased users finds that messages addressed to the broader viewing public of the profile rather than the profile owner generally are posted shortly after the death and concern logistics about funerals and other related events.[16] Brubaker and Hayes write, "Outside of these logistical and funerary related comments, community-addressed comments are extremely rare (less than 0.1%). Users may feel it is inappropriate to address the community directly and even enforce that position by reprimanding those who do so."[17] Concerns about propriety may account for the "lack of details about the death and logistical information in post-mortem comments," and it may be that users are communicating such details through private messages or other avenues that are less easily detected by researchers.[18]

Posts frequently relate to birthdays, anniversaries of deaths, holidays, and other special occasions and express that the writer misses the deceased user and is thinking of her or him. Brubaker and Hayes note that direct messages usually are directed to the deceased, not, as one might expect, to co-mourners.[19] A typical user who engages a social network site to express general thoughts about a deceased user might post on her own page or on a fellow mourner's. She is less likely, though, to post "aloud" to the deceased's page; if she does, it likely is addressed directly to the deceased individual (e.g., "Hey sis, I'm missing you"). This mode of direct address to the deceased user dominates the death- and afterlife-related communication on social network profiles.[20]

The *form* of death-related posting practices suggests an important dimension of how users imagine the afterlife, namely that the deceased may be able to receive electronic communications from the living. Examining the content of such messages clarifies that, on the whole, users who post messages to the deceased are not uninformed or in denial about the fact that the intended recipients of their messages are dead. Brubaker and Vertesi observe that many friends return repeatedly to their deceased friend's social network profile for several years: "Such posts often clustered around calendar events, wherein posters expressed sadness that users are not present to celebrate birthdays, graduations, or holidays together with their living friends. For example, following their high school class's graduation, one friend wrote: '*I really wish you were here to go through graduation with us.*'"[21] Moreover, they observe that posts expressing "sadness that users are not present to celebrate [...] commonly end with an assertion that the user was, in fact, there, participating, or watching. As many friends comment, 'Wish you were here, but I know you're in heaven watching'"[22] References to the deceased user as "in heaven," "up there," and "with us in spirit" are common, indicating hope that not only may the dead person observe the activities of the living, she or he also may view digital messages about those events.

Among the theological implications of these trends in message content are belief in heaven and expectation that the deceased is in heaven, which suggest a strong theological confidence that God is favorably disposed toward the deceased. How far this conviction corresponds to belief in universal salvation and/or belief in hell is not readily apparent from existing research but merits further investigation. In general, posters suggest the belief that the deceased is happy with comments such as, "I kno ur livin it up up there!!!"[23] Even so, their communication practices also imply that the dead person's happiness is incomplete or at least that she or he can receive surplus happiness from expressions of love and jokes shared electronically. Put differently, the deceased is imagined as continuing to care about the living. Comments suggest the expectation that the afterlife contains many of the same features as the poster's current existence, such as the celebration of birthdays and holidays. One user acknowledges that "we're celebrating [your birthday] in different places from now on," and another inquires, "How was your Christmas? Mine was ok . . . got clothes and stuff what about you??"[24]

From this possibility of enhancing the happiness of the deceased comes the implication that the message sender and intended recipient will be reunited eventually. Users express renewed conviction about staying in touch with the deceased through electronic posts, saying, for example, "I promise not to let another year go by before I get in touch again."[25] In addition to planning to continue the relationship through future electronic communication, writers sometimes express explicitly theological expectations, such as "I'LL SEE YOU WHEN CHRIST DECIDES FOR US TO MEET AGAIN" or "See you when I get to heven [sic]."[26] Following Genevieve Bell, Brubaker and Vertesi characterize the frequent online expression of religious convictions, such as that friends will be reunited in the afterlife, as "techno-spiritual."[27] Bell investigates how people use computing technologies for religious and spiritual practices, noting that such experiences can become embedded in daily life rather than existing at the margins of technological or religious practices.[28] Similarly, Heidi A. Campbell uses the conceptual frame "digital religion" to characterize the integration of offline and online religious practices.[29] Indeed, it appears that a social network user may integrate her offline and online religious views about death, as well as blend death-related social network activity into her typical computing practices.

The form and content of posting messages to deceased users on social network sites seem to suggest three beliefs about afterlife: (1) that the deceased can receive electronic communication, (2) that the deceased is in heaven, and (3) that the living user someday will be reunited with the dead. Significantly, there does not appear to be a corresponding expectation that the deceased can send messages in return. The implication is that, though the deceased's earthly body is lifeless, she retains some kind of body that can see and hear earthly events, including computerized messages. While she is envisioned as powerful in her ability to see and hear earthly goings-on and receive digital communications, however, she is understood as unable to respond. A poster is likely to anticipate a future response from the deceased with a comment such as "I'm confident I'll see your beautiful smile again" but not to protest the absence of a response from the deceased in the present.[30] Sending electronic messages to a dead person appears to be a widespread practice, and it does not typically generate controversy (e.g., a post to a deceased person's profile likely is surrounded by similar posts from other users, not by posts reacting negatively to the practice of messaging the dead). Trends in the content of messages to the dead do not indicate that senders expect to receive replies, and it seems likely that publicly communicating such an expectation would generate surprise among other living users.

In fact, responses to another social network application indicate at least some discomfort with the possibility of receiving communication from the dead. A Facebook application called *If I Die* was launched in 2011, billing itself as "the digital afterlife Facebook application" and allowing users to create a video or text message that will be published after they die (and verification of the death). Replies to coverage of the application range from "not sure how I feel about this . . ." to "creepy," though presumably users who create messages on *If I Die* are comfortable with rather than anxious at the prospect of receiving such messages from others.[31] It remains to be seen how actual recipients of these messages from people who have died will feel. While the company's press information indicates that the application has over 200,000 users, it is not clear whether or how many of those users have died and how message recipients, if any, have reacted.[32] As use of the application grows, it may become easier to examine people's interest in not only messaging the dead but also receiving digital communication from the dead.

Additionally, *If I Die* also has run a contest called "If I Die 1st,"[33] allowing entrants to record a message of their choosing that, should they be the first entrant to die, will be posted on the website *Mashable,* with over 20 million unique users. Hence, the application bills this contest as "A chance of a death time to world fame." There are nearly 240,000 submissions for "If I Die 1st," and the application estimates—by a countdown ticker on images of headstones—that the contest winner will die in July 2014. Only in time, then, will it be possible to evaluate how the winning message is received publicly, as well as how recipients of personal messages stored by the application react to receiving them.

Interpreting the Theological Imagination

In summary, it seems that users find it comforting or at least comfortable for a deceased user's electronic identity to persist, provided that the living maintain control over when to encounter that persistent identity.[34] For social network sites to intervene and force an encounter—as with Facebook's "Reconnect" program—is unwelcome; at least some responses to the notion of receiving a final message through the *If I Die* application suggest that this, too, may be unwelcome.

So, how do we evaluate the theological imagination surrounding death and social networking for its newness and continuity with Christian traditions? First, the persistence of digital identities on social network sites—the phenomenon of profiles "outliving" their owners—amounts to a sort of immortality, a matter of potential but not necessary discontinuity with Christian traditions.[35] It is, in many ways, an enticing notion, and it is one that others have begun to address. In their analysis of Facebook memorial pages, Rebecca Kern, Abbe E. Forman, and Gisela Gil-Egui write, "If the dead are virtually memorialized, they never really die. The more in-depth the memorial and the greater its permanence, the more the deceased remain with the living."[36] Similarly, Brubaker and Vertesi contend that deceased user "Ashley is very much alive" due to "how the system continues to persist her identity in tandem with the friends who shape it with fond memories and loving remarks."[37] Both sets of authors are suggesting that living users of social network sites may realize that they are keeping their loved ones' memories alive and even that they are shaping the identities of the deceased by continuing to post on their profiles. Theologically, however, it seems clear that using new media to keep memories alive and shape how the deceased are remembered is an innovation that exists alongside of, rather than replacing or radically modifying, conventional Christian views of mortality and afterlife. The absence of expectation and perhaps of interest in receiving communication from the dead warns against conflating posters' belief in afterlife with posters' belief that the dead are still living.

The content and form of posters' practices suggest an orientation to the dead as distant and future rather than a this-worldly belief in return to life. For example, the dead are imagined as observing but from "up there," not in close proximity. Moreover, the digital communication is in service of people being reunited in the future, not in the short term, as in the commonly posted refrain, "I know we'll meet again someday." In short, social network sites are a new medium in which many users express conventional Christian ideas of eschatology as future and other-worldly.

This contention that the theological implications of sending messages to the dead represents reasonably significant continuity with dominant Christian views of death and afterlife is in keeping with the idea that what happens online often is integrated with what happens offline. Despite the supposition, which marked much of the first wave of scholarship on digital religion, that new technologies radically would reshape religious beliefs and practices, scholars increasingly argue that new media practices develop alongside, rather than in radical opposition to, offline practices.[38] In the case of religious identity, for example, the second wave of research on digital media addressed the social forces that shape both online and offline identity expression, and the third wave of research builds on this approach to explore the blending of new media into daily life and identity.[39] According to Mia Lövheim, studying online engagement as part of—not separate from—daily life helps illuminate changes to religious identity in contemporary society, a context that demands "constant revision and continuous performance."[40] Thus, to say that religion online "develops alongside" religion offline does not mean the online simply replicates the offline.[41] Rather, experimentation occurs in both spheres, and each sphere can influence the other.[42]

While new media do not necessarily remake religions, they can provide opportunities for religious innovation. In the matter of posting messages to the dead, social network sites could facilitate an unconventional eschatological sensibility. Some eschatologies that are less mainstream, meaning less common in popular Christian belief and in academic theology, include those that prioritize matters of life in the here and now over questions about what happens to human beings after death. These sorts of theologies make concerns about changing this world for the better primary and tend to exclude attention to the ethereal. For instance, queer theologian Marcella Althaus-Reid offers an unconventional theology of resurrection, reinterpreting resurrection as a *resurrection of justice,* which is a communal event.[43] The critical perspective that such a theology offers to the discussion about death and social network sites is the possibility that users might shift their focus from the deceased to the world left behind by the deceased and from the individual dead to the living community. To be clear, in a theology like Althaus-Reid's, these shifts represent not an act of forgetting the dead but precisely an act of remembering him or her.

In its present instantiation, the practice of posting messages to the dead is not radically different from other forms of memorialization, such as speaking to the deceased at a grave. However, this new medium has the potential over time to facilitate community among the living in a way that many other rituals surrounding death do not.[44] For instance, funerals may create temporary communities, but practices such as periodic graveside communications are less likely—and not necessarily intended—to be overheard by others who miss the deceased. In contrast, social network sites may connect those who remember the dead, while grieving and beyond. As noted earlier, the undeclared social standards for posting on profiles of the deceased include addressing one's comments to the profile owner, so this logic suggests that people who connect because they both have relationships with the deceased would need to communicate with one another directly—whether through social network sites or otherwise—rather than via the dead person's profile. The same undeclared standards governing memorial posting do not seem to prohibit posters from communicating with one another, as building online connections is a central purpose of social network sites.

This generation of community would not constitute resurrection in the unconventional theological sense just mentioned, though. If shared memories of the deceased—the example of her life, the way she died—help inspire a communal commitment to justice and social change, *then* this medium may contribute to a unique mode of resurrection. Presumably, the deaths likeliest to generate such commitments are those related to violence or other discernibly oppressive forces, and still the resurrection of justice is not guaranteed. A matter for the continuing study of death and social network sites, then, will be whether posting practices and content, along with less visible forms of communication such as private messages, indicate, to borrow a phrase from Althaus-Reid, hope for a communal resurrection of "dead dreams and plans for a better future."[45]

Notes

1. Name withheld, "Timeline post," Facebook, April 9, 2012. Accessed September 29, 2013.

2. The term "online friend or acquaintance" is meant to refer to a person with whom one shares a social network site connection, not to suggest that such relationships lack an offline component.

3. As of June 2013, Facebook has over 1.15 billion monthly active users. "Key Facts," Facebook, http://newsroom.fb.com/Key-Facts. Accessed September 29, 2013.

4. See Jed R. Brubaker and Janet Vertesi, "Death and the Social Network" (Position paper for CHI 2010 workshop, "Death and the Digital"), http://www.dgp.toronto.edu/~mikem/

hcieol/subs/brubaker.pdf. Accessed April 18, 2014; Jed R. Brubaker and Gillian R. Hayes, "We Will Never Forget You [Online]: An Empirical Investigation of Post-mortem MySpace Comments" (Conference publication for Proc CSCW 2011), http://www.jedbrubaker.com/wp-content/uploads/2011/01/pr464-brubaker.pdf. Accessed September 29, 2013.

5. Nathan Lustig, "2.89m Facebook Users Will Die in 2012, 580,000 in the USA," *Nathan Lustig* (blog), http://www.nathanlustig.com/tag/facebook-death-rate/. Accessed September 29, 2013.

6. For broader questions surrounding digital existence and digital estate planning, see Evan Carroll and John Romano, *Your Digital Afterlife* (Berkeley: New Riders, 2010) and Carroll and Romano, *The Digital Beyond* (blog), http://www.thedigitalbeyond.com/. Accessed September 29, 2013.

7. "Special Request for Deceased Person's Account," Facebook, https://www.facebook.com/help/contact/228813257197480. Accessed September 29, 2013.

8. Pete Cashmore, "Facebook Recommends Reconnecting with Ex-Lovers, Dead Friends," *Mashable,* October 25, 2009, http://mashable.com/2009/10/25/facebook-reconnect/. Accessed September 29, 2013.

9. Max Kelly, "Memories of Friends Departed Endure on Facebook," *The Facebook Blog,* October 29, 2009, http://blog.facebook.com/blog.php?post=163091042130. Accessed September 29, 2013.

10. "Memorialization Request," Facebook, http://www.facebook.com/help/contact/305593649477238. Accessed September 29, 2013.

11. For an analysis of 550 Facebook memorial pages, see Rebecca Kern, Abbe E. Forman, and Gisela Gil-Egui, "R.I.P.: Remain in Perpetuity. Facebook Memorial Pages," *Telematics and Informatics* 30, no. 1 (2013): 2–10.

12. See, for example, "Angels for Talia," Facebook, https://www.facebook.com/angelsfortalia. Accessed February 16, 2014; "RIP Felicia Garcia- Stop Bullying," Facebook, https://www.facebook.com/RipFeliciaGarciaStopBullying. Accessed February 16, 2014.

13. While Facebook is not the first or only social network site, it is, by far, the most popular today. In recent years, though, MySpace also had a large number of users. Though its format and tools differed somewhat from Facebook's, it shared the central function of communicating by posting messages to others' profiles, and it also shared the possibility of posting messages to the profiles of users after their deaths. Some studies of the latter practice draw on MySpace as well as Facebook posts, so it must be noted that not all data and messages discussed in this chapter occurred within the parameters of Facebook. In late 2012, MySpace was rebranded as Myspace, which promotes music and artist discovery and does not include blogs, private messages, comments, or posts, so the practice of posting to deceased users' profiles is no longer applicable to that site.

When MySpace relaunched as Myspace, many users of the original site complained online about the messages, blogs, and photos they lost. One wrote, "I just lost what amounts to 7 years of a diary, travel stories, reflections, memories of my (now dead) father, 7 years of my 20s just vanished, gone. It's not upsetting, it's devastating. I'm grief stricken." Presumably other users shared this sense of loss related to both overall content and content tied to deceased users. Commenter name withheld, "My Space Deletes Your Stuff," *Marketing Pilgrim,* June 13, 2013, http://www.marketingpilgrim.com/2013/06/myspace-deletes-your-stuff.html#comment-930206787. Accessed April 18, 2014.

14. See, for example, Brubaker and Vertesi, "Death."

15. Ibid.

16. Brubaker and Hayes, "We Will Never Forget You [Online]," 4.

17. Ibid.

18. Ibid., 9.

19. Ibid.

20. Kern, Forman, and Gil-Egui's analysis of Facebook memorial pages found that "the majority of pages returned showed that people posting to the RIP pages are writing in the second person (e.g., "watch over us from heaven"). Pages written in the second person outnumber first- and third-person pages by a margin of nearly 2:1, comprising 42.46% of pages returned. Pages in first (e.g., "I miss you so much") and third person (e.g., "she was a bright and kind person") totaled 24.78% and 26.72%, respectively. This finding seems to underscore a preferential use of memorial pages within Facebook as a way to converse with the dead" (8).

21. Brubaker and Vertesi, "Death," 2.

22. Ibid., 2–3.

23. Ibid., 3.

24. Ibid.

25. Ibid.

26. Ibid.

27. Ibid., 3.

28. Genevieve Bell, "No More SMS from Jesus: Ubicomp, Religion and Techno-spiritual Practices," in *UbiComp 2006: Ubiquitous Computing,* eds. Paul Dourish and Adrian Friday (Irvine: Springer, 2006).

29. Heidi A. Campbell, "Introduction: The Rise of the Study of Digital Religion," in *Digital Religion: Understanding Religious Practice in New Media Worlds,* ed. Heidi A. Campbell (New York: Routledge, 2013), 3–4.

30. Name withheld, "Timeline post," Facebook, May 22, 2012, http://www.facebook.com. Accessed February 17, 2014.

31. Emma Hutchings, "New Facebook App Lets You Say Goodbye after Your Death," PSFK, January 10, 2012, http://www.psfk.com/2012/01/facebook-death-app.html. Accessed September 29, 2013.

32. "Press Kit," ifidie, http://ifidie.net/. Accessed September 29, 2013.

33. http://ifidie1st.com/. Accessed September 29, 2013.

34. Jed R. Brubaker develops the concept of "persistent identity." See Brubaker and Vertesi, "Death." See also Tracey Ratcliffe, "Death and the Persistent Identity: Implications for Managing Deceased Online Identities and Digital Estates" (Conference Presentation for Community Online Conference on Networks and Communities, 2012).

35. For a discussion of the ways in which online media create a "perpetual present," see Brenda Brasher, *Give Me That Online Religion* (San Francisco: Jossey-Bass, 2001).

36. Kern, Forman, and Gil-Egui, "R.I.P.," 10.

37. Brubaker and Vertesi, "Death," 4.

38. See, for example, Stewart M. Hoover's Foreword in *Digital Religion, Social Media and Culture,* eds. Pauline Hope Cheong, Peter Fischer-Nielsen, Stefan Gelfgren, and Charles Ess (New York: Peter Lang, 2012).

39. Mia Lövheim, "Identity," in *Digital Religion: Understanding Religious Practice in New Media Worlds,* ed. Heidi A. Campbell (New York: Routledge, 2013), 46–49.

40. Ibid., 52.

41. Ibid., 50.

42. While scholars of digital religion first explored how uses of new media affected religious practices, Heidi Campbell also has considered the impact of religions on new media, proposing a theory of "religious-social shaping of technology." See Heidi A. Campbell, *When Religion Meets New Media* (New York: Routledge, 2010), especially Ch. 2.

43. Marcella Althaus-Reid, *Indecent Theology: Theological Perversions in Sex, Gender and Politics* (New York: Routledge, 2000), 121.

44. For a thorough treatment of how online media can facilitate community and an analysis of the concepts of online and offline community, see Heidi Campbell, *Exploring Religious Community Online: We Are One in the Network* (New York: Peter Lang, 2005).

45. Marcella Althaus-Reid, *From Feminist Theology to Indecent Theology: Readings on Poverty, Sexual Identity and God* (London: SCM Press, 2004), 114.

Chapter 2

Profiles of the Dead: Mourning and Memorial on Facebook

Heidi Ebert

The two key existential facts about modern media are these: the ease with which the living may mingle with the communicable traces of the dead, and the difficulty of distinguishing communication at a distance from communication with the dead.

—John Durham Peters[1]

Introduction

In 2005, Max Kelly's best friend died in a cycling accident. Four years later, he posted a blog entry describing the grief he still felt and the decisions he had faced shortly after this loss.[2] Foremost among his questions was: "What do we do with his Facebook profile?" This question was both personal and professional for Kelly; at the time, he was Facebook's chief security officer. His post sparked a burst of popular articles all asking the same question: what do we do with a Facebook profile after the person who created it has died?

In 2008, I learned, via Facebook, that a classmate of mine named Betsy had recently died. I was struck by the highly emotional posts left on her profile; people who had known Betsy in various stages of her life contributed to a large collection of condolence messages. In Betsy's absence, her profile seemed to be taking on a new purpose as a space for visitors to mourn and remember her.

In this chapter, I argue that a deceased person's Facebook profile is transformed from a tool for communication and autobiography to one for mourning and memorializing, and back again. Such a profile can be used as a space to express and share grief, and as a memorial object that preserves memories of the deceased. However, Facebook is not, as some scholars have argued, revolutionizing the way we mourn.[3] Instead, social network sites (SNSs) add another option to an existing pool of memorial resources. Rather than fundamentally altering mourning practice, then, Facebook is one of many "new electronic spaces for the communication of grief."[4] It exists as part of a continuum of practice both that has become increasingly flexible since the Victorian period and whose evolution is tied to the accelerating development of communication technologies.

A Facebook profile can function as a space for mourning, which is broadly defined as any outward expression of grief.[5] It can also become a memorial object created, whether purposefully or accidentally, as an act of memory preservation. Like death practice in general, the definition of memorial objects is becoming more flexible as the borders of death-specific spaces become more permeable and accessible; they offer a focus for mourning that can be accessed anywhere and at any time. This is precisely why I refer to a Facebook profile as a memorial object: positioning the term "memorial" as an adjective rather than a noun allows for a clearer distinction between a traditional, public memorial and an object or space used by individuals or small groups for memory-making. A memorial object is built and maintained by an audience composed of mourners rather than by an institution. One of the differentiating factors between a deceased person's Facebook page and a dedicated memorial is the contributing role of mourners and visitors. Unlike traditional memorials, which are often static and passively viewed, a Facebook profile is dynamic and the identity of its creator is modified by anyone who posts a message or tags a photograph. A Facebook user's Friends are not necessarily passive; they can also be makers of meaning. Because they are producers as well as consumers of a profile's content, they can be as essential to the functionality of the space as its creator. While a profile can always be a memorial object, however, its applications for mourning can be short lived: on Betsy's profile, visitors quickly returned to engaging with the space as though she were still alive; expressions of grief posted for her family were soon supplanted by messages that addressed her directly, much like those posted before she died. Although Facebook can be used for mourning and memorializing, Betsy's profile suggests that these uses do not replace the original autobiographical and communicative functions of the space. Instead, a profile's value in mourning may be rooted in the fact that it does not change when its creator dies. The profile's content, coupled with the fact that posted messages do not necessarily require a response, supports the illusion of an afterlife.[6] The notion of continued metaphysical presence after death facilitates the belief that the dead can receive messages from the living and that the relationships between Facebook Friends endure after death.

A Facebook profile that remains active—and interactive—after a user's death affords him or her a kind of social immortality as visitors continue to build and reshape the space. This reshaping, however, causes visitors to begin to replace the profile's creator as its subject. Because Betsy is now divorced from a space that supposedly represents her, the identity she built for herself there is covered by the material left by the living, her mourners, whose offerings eventually bury her. The space thus once again becomes primarily autobiographical, this time for the visitors, snippets of whose life narratives continuously displace older material. Although such a profile nevertheless continues to represent its deceased creator's identity, it becomes autobiographically diffuse as visitors contribute content documenting their own lives, which may in turn temper its value as a memorial object.

"Memories of Friends Departed"

Not every Facebook profile whose creator dies is memorialized, perhaps because their loved ones choose not to inform the company or are unaware of the option, and in these cases Friends continue to receive notifications about him or her. Betsy's profile is one of these; I am still reminded of her birthday every year. Friends can continue to engage with a dead person's profile whether or not it is memorialized. It does not move to a separate website, nor does it change drastically in appearance; visitors therefore do not necessarily change their behavior in the space in any substantive way. A Facebook profile's communicative and representative functions, then, do not fall away when the person who created it dies. Indeed, these profiles often continue to operate almost exactly as they did before.

Although a Facebook profile's applications for mourning are still emerging, situating the site on a continuum of death practice and interrogating exactly how and why people engage with digital autobiographical objects after their creators have died has provided a systematic way to analyze how Facebook users mourn their deceased Friends. I intentionally use a capital letter *F* to emphasize that a Facebook connection, while labeled Friendship within the context of the site itself, encompasses a wide range of relationships. As danah boyd explains, a user's Friends list is not necessarily, and is indeed unlikely to be, made up entirely of close ties or true friends. On SNSs,

Friends "are rarely only one's closest and dearest friends."[7] The Friends list may include intimate friends and family as well as acquaintances, or weak ties. I would not consider my relationship with Betsy a close tie. She was my classmate in a German course, as her older sister, Roxanne, had been several years before. Roxanne died by suicide the year before Betsy entered university, and Betsy was determined to become a counselor and to help other young people considering suicide. Betsy had an active online life and was very involved in several suicide support groups. While my offline friendship with Betsy developed slowly as we described our hometowns and hobbies in broken German, I got to know her better when we became Friends on Facebook. Like many others, I learned of Betsy's death, also by suicide, when a family member posted the news on her profile. Many Friends posted messages, and while some resembled formal condolences to her family, most addressed Betsy directly, which is a response that the authors of several recent studies of mourning on Facebook have also observed.[8]

A Continuum of Practice

Contemporary Western mourning encompasses a range of practices that evolves as technologies emerge and cultural boundaries stretch. Because a deceased person's Facebook profile can be used for both mourning and memorializing, placing it on a continuum makes explicit its relationships to other death practices and the exigencies behind them. Facebook profiles represent new "vernacular forms of commemoration" in an expanding "memorial landscape,"[9] signaling the migration of death practice farther into the mundane. Contextualizing Facebook as death practice underscores how technology and shifting social values alter mourning, but it also calls attention to certain attitudes and rituals that have remained consistent over time.

Although elements of Victorian death practices, which were especially formalized and engrained in cultural life, have not entirely disappeared, contemporary mourning is characterized more by its variation and personalization[10] than by any shared ritual: there is no longer a single cultural script governing mourners. Indeed, death practice operates "outside any collective wisdom or set of practices" and is instead "characterized by a diversity of shared rituals at the time of death."[11] The absence of a standard, overarching set of rules governing how we should mourn does not mean that mourning is a necessarily solitary project. Mourners are unified not by a codified set of practices but by the loss itself and the rituals they choose to perform: although approaches to grief may be similar or shared, there are fewer requirements or expectations for how mourning is enacted. The internet offers more space for these self-directed mourners to come together irrespective of geography. Today, mourning is less likely to follow a societal narrative or to be externalized through markers like clothing, which means the actual work of grieving is relegated to the privacy of domestic spaces. Death can instead be addressed directly on platforms like Facebook, which, for many, play an important role in daily life.

SNSs have created new public and semipublic spaces for mourning. They also highlight a blurring of boundaries between public and private life. Web-enabled death practice is nascent and its development is sometimes fraught; the Victorians, who pioneered many mourning traditions, paid great attention to the borders between public and private life. They employed many material signifiers to communicate grief, yet much of their death practice was also extremely private. For them, mourning was made visible primarily through clothing, which served "to identify the mourner, show respect for the dead, elicit the sympathy of the community, and match the mourner's sombre mood."[12] Although public markers of mourning were essential to Victorian death practice, mourning itself largely took place inside the home. Women in mourning were expected to be hidden completely from public view, identifying themselves more through their isolation than their dress. Women "could not accept formal invitations in the first year, except from close relatives, and had to avoid public places."[13] Although the social rules of mourning demanded more of women, both sexes marked themselves according to a strict set of rules.

Victorian mourners were easy to identify, then, and the social codes enforcing public appearances, dress, and other symbols of bereavement meant death was part of a shared script for everyday Victorian life. After the immense death toll of World War I, however, death once again became a much more private matter, even a taboo subject.[14] In many Western cultures, it has remained that way, and death has only moved back into the everyday relatively recently, with the help of SNSs. As Tim Hutchings puts it:

> The social media platforms used to communicate between friends can become, after the death of a participant, spaces for direct "communication" to the deceased through the same channels that individual had used while alive—moving the memorial site from a distant graveyard into the midst of life.[15]

SNSs like Facebook allow mourning and memorializing to take place more easily within the mundane. For Hutchings, SNSs have helped make memorial spaces accessible, to remove them from a specific, enclosed domain and into the day-to-day. Because a user's death does not change the functionality of his or her profile, the acts of mourning and memorializing that can take place there are not secluded or site specific, but instead exist alongside unrelated content. Such profiles are "dispersed or located within secular 'non-death' settings where their significance remains vital only for the bereaved."[16] Mourning is just one use of a multipurpose, non-death-specific space, which is not necessarily meaningful or accessible to others.

The act of engaging with a profile as a memorial space that can be visited may be commonplace, but it cannot be accidental as a visit to a traditional public memorial can be. If a page is memorialized, users who were not Friends with the deceased before he or she died cannot find the deceased person in a search, and unless a friend or family member continues to operate a nonmemorialized profile, any request Friendship would be ignored. Unlike "[d]ifferentiated 'death' spaces" such as cemeteries, public memorials, and funeral homes, which "are generally avoided unless specific visits are necessary,"[17] a Facebook user may visit a deceased person's profile for any number of reasons, but is unlikely to do so unintentionally. Such a visit usually requires a conscious choice, although it may be motivated by a link on another profile, for example. Whether memorialized or not, a profile whose privacy settings restrict access to Friends will not be visited by strangers.

Nevertheless, current death and mourning practices in general, both offline and online, are in some ways becoming "more public."[18] Yet although there are links to be made between, for example, the black armband and the Facebook post as mechanisms for broadcasting grief, this recent movement of death into the so-called public sphere is not a reversion to Victorian modes of practice but rather the product of a more generalized shift "in the boundary between public and private space."[19] Facebook has called attention to this change and, as a memorial tool, is both affecting and affected by the increasingly "permeable"[20] barrier between the public and the private. While Facebook is certainly helping to bring death and mourning into public discourse, it is not in itself making death practice more public.

Although the internet may be blurring the line between public and private life, most Facebook pages are not public spaces. By compiling his or her Friends list, a profile's creator dictates its audience; it is a controlled and curated semipublic. I can see the Wall posts on Betsy's Facebook page although they have nothing to do with me. Facebook is semipublic, but it can give the impression of being a more intimate space than it is, in part because it is often used in private: a Facebook user usually logs on alone.[21] Indeed, online writing often "feels private" to writers whether it is private, public, or somewhere between.[22] For many writers, text entered into Facebook's status bar is hardly different from an offline note to themselves. The experience of posting on a profile is simultaneously public and private because often the poster is alone, but by logging on, she places herself within a community and a network. Contributing publicly rather than sending a private message or passively observing magnifies this merging effect. While many aspects of highly structured societies like Victorian England were governed by overarching codes of behavior, then, recent social practice in general is more flexible, personal, and diffuse in part because communication technologies and social norms have developed in tandem with those norms.

Recording against Death

Communication and recording technologies have influenced the practices and attitudes surrounding death in Western culture: obituaries, for example, became common only after printing equipment allowed for wide distribution of newspapers,[23] and widespread access to photography has allowed mourners to create visual memorial objects. Critics can be quick to point out how technological changes can endanger or revolutionize social norms, at times taking an extreme view of this relationship. Angela Riechers argues that digital media are "forcing an evolution of the expected social norms for mourning behaviors and customs."[24] Riechers does not acknowledge that death practice has been bound up with recording technologies since long before the internet existed. Similarly, Brian Carroll and Katie Landry argue that Facebook is "altering the process of mourning" but temper their statement by adding that "[w]hat is happening on the profile pages of the deceased is nothing revolutionary but rather a new and in some ways logical platform for people to memorialize and grieve."[25]

Tony Walter and his colleagues also suggest that SNSs may be inducing fundamental changes in Western approaches to death and mourning. In their review of current scholarship on death and the internet, however, they also acknowledge digital objects' potential to alter attitudes toward and practices surrounding death in broader ways. In particular, the authors point to recording technologies' capacity to help integrate death and its rituals more smoothly into everyday life. They argue that in digital memorial spaces, "pictures of the dead, conversations with the dead, and mourners' feelings can and do become part of the everyday online world. [. . .] The dead and their mourners are no longer secluded from the rest of society."[26] Images of the dead, and indeed conversations with them, are becoming increasingly commonplace online, which underscores not only the power of sites like Facebook to bring the idea of death into social life but also the internet's perceived affordance of direct communication with the dead.

Because many Facebook users post on their Friends' Walls with no expectation of a reply,[27] a public message sent on Facebook to a deceased person can be indistinguishable from one sent to a living person. Many Wall posts resemble "direct communication with the deceased,"[28] which expands on the self-narratives shaped by other parts of the profile. Although Wall posts reach an audience beyond a profile's creator, most of the messages on deceased people's Facebook Walls are in the second person.[29] Even messages of condolence tend to be written in the second person and address the deceased directly.[30] A deceased person's profile therefore offers visitors a venue for "continued conversation" with the deceased as they "integrat[e] their mourning practices directly into their ongoing social relationships."[31] A profile provides a seemingly dynamic connection with its subject. The text-based, publicly posted messages on Facebook and similar web spaces "seem to reach the dead" in ways other communication media do not afford, because "a reply is not necessarily expected; communicating to a deceased person online is thus no different from communicating to a living addressee."[32] It is thus part of normal—and indeed expected—SNS behavior to write a message that is not intended as part of an immediate conversation or even of a dialogue; many Wall posts are intentionally one sided. SNSs reinforce the "fantasy of being able to transmit a personal message to the deceased."[33] Facebook allows the impulse to communicate with the dead to be externalized in the same way that speaking at a gravesite or writing a letter to the deceased might do, but on Facebook, those messages can be made visible to others.

By creating mediated presence that does not depend on the body, communication technologies from written language to portraiture to webcams have "effectively created history."[34] SNSs are just one link in the long chain of media that have helped memory to become history and the living to memorialize the dead. Recording an experience as text or image allows traces of the dead to be retained, which grants them a sustained presence among the living. Elizabeth Hallam and Jenny Hockey point out, for example, that deceased academics are positioned "within the company of living scholars" by virtue of readers' continued access to their work.[35] Any recorded text, whether inscribed in a diary, saved to a hard drive, or posted on Facebook, has the potential to create a sustained social presence for a deceased writer. With so many available means of documenting our lives, we contribute in many ways to a collection of objects that may eventually be used to memorialize ourselves. Inscription and documentation of any kind, then, allows us to remain present after death, an effect that is only increasing as new technologies quickly become available and more widespread.

Like written texts, photography allows for a kind of pseudopresence.[36] The cover and profile photographs are the largest visual components of a Facebook profile. Although the cover photo, which was introduced in 2011 as part of the Timeline redesign, is larger than the profile photo and always public, the profile image is nevertheless "one of the most telling pieces of self-disclosure" on Facebook.[37] The profile photo is designed as a single representative image of the page's subject. It is also one of the ways Facebook users preemptively construct their own profiles as memorial spaces because, as Roland Barthes suggests, "death is the *eidos* of the photograph";[38] the essence of a photograph is death. Because a photograph does not change whether its subject is living or dead, it is in a way an inherently posthumous object. A photograph turns a living person into a static mediated subject, anticipating his or her death. But a photograph, according to Barthes, does not always depict a dead subject or something that "is no longer" but rather something that "has been."[39] It represents the past without distinguishing between a living subject and a dead one.

Viewed out of context, a photograph does not reveal whether or not its subject is alive or dead. A Facebook page, of course, operates in a similar way: it represents a self as it was at the moment of its most recent update. With every new update, its subject already exists in the past just as "[t]he camera renders the moment dead"[40] because its subject is static from the moment an image is produced. As the sociologists Shanyang Zhao, Sherri Grasmuck, and Jason Martin observe in their paper "Identity Construction on Facebook: Digital Empowerment in Anchored Relationships," on Facebook, "the most implicit identity claims are visual."[41] They point out that, through photographs, Facebook users show, rather than tell, visitors about themselves. This information, they argue, is implicit; the message is embedded in the image rather than the explicit descriptions found in the text portions of the profile. Indeed, cameras are "important instruments for the shaping of self-identity."[42] Although Facebook users can construct identities using the profile and cover photos and by posting videos, these remain fixed after a user dies. Although Friends may still tag or post their own photographs that include the deceased, the profile's primary visual markers of identity are locked in. Although visitors can continue to add visual content, it is secondary to, and vastly less identity-supporting than, the profile and cover images.

Like Barthes's photograph, a Facebook page can be read as positioning its subject as already dead. Because "[p]hotographs are always taken precisely in order to remember people and events," there may always be "a degree of intentional memorialisation in photographic web material."[43] Jeremy Tambling touches on a similar idea in *Becoming Posthumous:* because a photograph's subject is static, suspended in the moment the shutter opens, the image itself is inherently posthumous and preemptively memorializes its subject. The ubiquity of photographic images has made us accustomed to processing visual information this way. "Since the photograph creates everything as posthumous," he writes, "posthumous images become the mode of perception of modern culture, making a dream of immediacy cease, and giving to perception the sense that everything exists in a posthumous state."[44] In Tambling's view, photography has influenced cultural norms in such a way that we imagine death not only in mediated representations of self, but everywhere. Recording technologies allow us, mostly unintentionally, to create and preserve objects that will be used to memorialize ourselves.

Digital communication technologies, and recording methods in general, "capture moments and make them persistent"[45] which means recorded moments are, as Tambling suggests, always already in the past. Although a post on a Facebook profile is persistent, it remains flexible: the creator of a profile always has the ability to add, edit, and delete content posted there. When he or she dies, however, the space can continue to evolve precisely because the behavior of visitors does not; many of Betsy's friends continue to post details of their daily lives as though their relationship is the same as it was before her death.

As danah boyd points out, the "social structure" of an SNS "is defined by a narrow set of rules that do little to map the complexities and nuances of relationships."[46] Facebook behavior is perhaps more forcefully influenced by social norms than in-person interaction because posted material is displayed to all Friends; because material on the site is shared, it is also is persistent[47] and is therefore always available as a reminder of users' shared social scripts. Facebook's homogenous blue-and-white color scheme literalizes this social rigidity; unlike other SNSs such as Twitter or

Myspace, the overall aesthetics of a profile is not modifiable. In December 2011, Facebook introduced Timeline, a profile structure that includes a cover photo feature that provides users some control over the appearance of their pages. Facebook claims this photo is "as unique and individualized" as each user.[48] However, there is little else a user can customize in terms of visual appearance. Although "each user's page content is unique in as far as the visual and textual memories and archives are specific to their life,"[49] it does not allow for customization, which visibly constrains identity-building outside of a prescribed architecture. Facebook's structural constraints are de-emphasized in favor of uploaded content, which supports the myth that a profile is a complete representation of identity and a truly personal, customizable object. This aesthetic fixity limits a user's authority over the appearance of a profile; he or she is therefore fully in control of neither its form nor its content, which is partially in the hands of his or her Friends.

Memory Tools: The "Real" and the "Virtual"

Digital and nondigital objects alike can function as memorial tools and as loci for the protraction of bonds between the living and the dead. Digital representations of nondigital objects are often positioned as inferior copies of or stand-ins for the real thing; they are read as surrogate or replacement objects. The anthropologist and curator Jenny Newell contrasts the digital with the *actual* or the *real*; this is really a matter of semantic convenience, but I prefer the term *nondigital* to *real* because digital and virtual objects are real, in that they exist in physical space, and engaging with them is a material experience. Newell herself later suggests that "digital objects have their own materiality" and speaks directly to interactivity, which is dependent on the body.[50] Some scholars of death studies, including Tim Hutchings and Kate Woodthorpe, upon whose work I rely here, emphasize a distinction between "real" or "actual" objects and digital ones. This is, I think, a false binary, or at least one that deserves more nuanced attention.

The cognitive scientist Donald A. Norman writes that emotional connection to objects depends on touch, arguing that "virtual" objects without "physical substance" rely only on cognitive function, whereas "physical objects involve the world of emotion."[51] For a human to connect emotionally with an object, he seems to suggest, the object cannot be digital. Norman fully separates the body from what he calls "the virtual," which runs counter to more phenomenological approaches to the digital world. This argument discounts the fact that our experience with digital objects, although less tactile because we depend on peripheral devices in order to engage with them, is nevertheless an embodied experience. Nor does it acknowledge that digital objects can evoke affect through discourse; the importance of narrative to memory and mourning cannot be overlooked.

Although a Facebook profile itself is not entirely physical, the experience of engaging with it is dependent on a physical user and is therefore a material act. Interactions on Facebook are distantly physical because the body is required to engage with the interface. The internet is not, at least not yet, the disembodied otherworld described in science fiction. As the affordance theorist Ian Hutchby notes, materiality "need not be thought of only in physical terms;"[52] he cites the telephone as "having a materiality affecting the distribution of interactional space,"[53] which arguably all communication technologies are able to do. Because communication technologies affect interactional if not physical space, and because embodiment is necessary for these interactions, the experience of mediated communication is material even if the medium is a digital one.

Facebook invites a kind of systematic memory-making that contributes to SNSs' influence on offline death practice. As digital spaces such as Facebook profiles become more valuable as memorial objects, they become more emotionally evocative. Newell writes that a nondigital object "is a *part* of the past," while "digital historical objects are usually conceived as *tools* for understanding the past."[54] Digital objects, however, can be even more visibly part of the past than nondigital ones, because they are usually time stamped. A Facebook post is always dated and is therefore never separate from the moment it was created. The text and images posted on a Facebook profile are not analogous to nondigital keepsakes and memorial objects, but nor are they necessarily atemporal, immaterial, or empty of emotion.

A digital photograph or object can indeed serve as a powerful memorial object by supporting memory and evoking affect.[55] Keepsakes are often used to support the mourning process, and in the 1990s, an entire therapeutic approach to grieving was extrapolated from the impulse to sustain connections with the dead by saving objects connected to them.[56] This approach encourages continued mediated presence in the lives of loved ones, whereas earlier approaches to bereavement favored a complete removal of any reminders of the dead and cutting all ties with the memory of loss in order to move on.[57] Memorial objects allow survivors to build a "narrative-memory" that creates "a space for spirits in the ongoing life of kith and kin."[58] If the value of a memorial object comes from its ability to support memory through narrative, an autobiographical object like a Facebook profile is especially suited to the preservation of bonds between the living and the dead, despite the fact that it is digital.

A Facebook profile's potential as a memorial object is in some ways hidden while its creator is alive: SNSs are used primarily to display social networks, to socialize, and to share information[59] and are not necessarily recognized as tools for archiving or mourning. As Joanne Garde-Hansen argues in "My Memories? Personal Digital Archive Fever and Facebook," the internet is allowing us to produce and archive our memories more easily than ever, often without being conscious that we are doing so. SNSs like Facebook are still understood as tools for communication rather than storage. SNSs, according to the sociologist Timothy Recuber, "produce digital archives almost as a by product. Threaded posts, profiles, photos, and avatars create a history of online exchanges and allow for the past to be reconstructed."[60] This is an especially germane observation in light of Facebook's 2011 redesign. The Timeline is a more overt archival tool than earlier iterations of the profile. Facebook is beginning to recast the profile as a complete record of a user's life.

The Plurality of *I*

An individual's Facebook archive is, of course, collectively built. By adding content to the space, visitors to a profile contribute to the formation of its creator's life narrative as well as their own; the identities represented there depend on others in part because identity "requires others."[61] It is always relational. Whether online or offline, autobiographical texts assume the existence of a reader and therefore depend on that reader for meaning-making.[62] The autobiographical aspects of Facebook are largely dependent on others, and this relational practice is embedded in the site's structure: a user's Friends and their interactions are among SNSs' defining features.[63] In his book *How Our Lives Become Stories,* the scholar of autobiography studies Paul John Eakin argues that "the first person of autobiography," and indeed of an autobiographical object like Facebook, "is truly plural in its origins and subsequent formation."[64] In both form and content, then, Facebook makes explicit Eakin's observations about multiplicity of the self. A public post on a Friend's Wall can help develop the identities of both the poster and the profile's subject; deceased users, however, are inactive in the formation of their own identities and the autobiographical balance skews toward the visitors. The second autobiographical stage that a dead person's Facebook profile enters after acts of mourning taper off, then, serves to represent the lives of visitors rather than the person who originally designed the site for his or her own self-representation.

The multiple authorship of autobiographical texts, whether offline or online, means physical death and social death—that is, the "withering and eventual extinction of social identity and social interaction"[65]—are even unlikelier than before to occur simultaneously. The notion of continued social life after death is a common one among death studies scholars, particularly those whose work addresses communicative technologies and media. For instance, Elizabeth Hallam, Jenny Hockey, and Glennys Howarth argue that the dead can remain socially alive because of their sustained presence in memory and the objects that support it.[66] Because visitors can still access a Facebook profile, add content to it, and engage in public discussion with each other, its biologically deceased creator is still socially alive by virtue of his or her continuing presence as "an active agent in the lives of others."[67] As long as interaction with the deceased person's Facebook page continues, he or she remains, in Hallam, Hockey, and Howarth's terms, "socially alive."[68] Put more generally, and I think more precisely, the internet "provides considerable potential for keeping social interaction and identity alive,"[69] because it continues to offer opportunities for the construction of autobiography. Although it is convenient to suggest that if the dead are memorialized online, "they never really die,"[70] it is a mediated and diffuse self that is sustained online after death. SNSs offer new mechanisms for preserving these selves and literalize the idea of a posthumous social presence.

Douglas J. Davies also addresses the notion of social death in his discussion of continuing bonds. Like Hallam, Hockey, and Howarth, Davies positions identity as being sustained for the dead in the same way it was built during their lives: collectively. The selves of the dead persist in memory but can also be perceived as actors in the lives of those who remember them and engage with their memories. Facebook and other communication technologies have "given us more convincing ways to see the dead as agentic, still present and able to be consulted for advice or asked to do things even from beyond the grave."[71] The "spirits" of the dead persist "in the ongoing life of surviving kith and kin, especially when intensified through anniversaries, photographic images of the dead and other vibrant moments of recall."[72] The internet invites more of these moments of recall not only because it is used so extensively but also because it presents a vast selection of digital objects with which memories can be associated.

Because a Facebook profile is built by visitors as well as its subject, it is both autobiographical and biographical. By leaving their own autobiographical information on a Facebook profile, visitors work to construct their own biographies in tandem with that of the page's creator. In some ways, then, autobiographical objects such as Facebook profiles are always, or are always primed to become, memorial objects. (Auto)biographical writing always positions the author as posthumous, because the narrative is only complete when its subject dies. Furthermore, a profile is never written by, nor does it represent, a singular subject. Very little changes when the creator of the profile dies because the autobiographical *I* represented on Facebook is "an illusion."[73] Facebook exploits our cultural myth of self-determination while simultaneously making explicit an individual's absolute dependence on others for identity formation. The "retrospective reproduction" in which visitors to Betsy's page participate "is precisely self-serving . . . [it] serves to construct the self."[74]

Conclusion

Mourners were online long before Facebook, at digital cemeteries and web memorials; these "specialist memorial sites" have quickly become "greatly outnumbered" by SNSs.[75] Sites like Facebook now seem to be the preferred venue for online mourning and function effectively for mourning and memorial precisely because they were not designed to be used that way. A dead person's Facebook profile, whether or not it is memorialized, is not purpose-built for death practice; it only becomes a memorial space and object when it is used as such. Facebook profiles therefore become "unintentional memorials"[76] after the death of their creators, which allows such coopted autobiographical objects to pull death into everyday life in ways that intentional, nondigital memorial tools do not. Facebook profiles like Betsy's are used for both memory-making and mourning, and therefore function as shared spaces for the living and the dead.

As a memorial object, a Facebook page "facilitates relationships between the living and the dead," but it also "encompasses the power and vulnerability of the dead who are both revered and protected. This power not only demands responses from the living but can also be appropriated by them."[77] On Facebook, the mediated selves of the dead persist, but those selves are newly mutable as authorship of the life narrative is passed from the deceased individual to his or her community of Facebook Friends. A page that was originally designed as an online representation of self, and that was used primarily to receive and display public messages, thus becomes first a "linking object" between the living and the dead[78] and finally a patchwork of personal information supplied and viewed only by visiting Friends. Although visitors to a deceased person's profile can and do use the space for memorialization, the memory of the deceased eventually becomes secondary to the needs and interactions of living visitors as the narratives of shared grief are buried by newer autobiographical posts.

A deceased person's Facebook Friends continue to use his or her profile to write their own autobiographies, representing themselves while simultaneously sustaining a connection with, and managing the identity of, the dead. The profile is always an autobiographical and biographical object, whether or not it is also a memorial object. That is, a profile's narrative and self-representative functions do not disappear when it is used as a memorial space and object. Our tendency to sequester death since the Victorian period[79] has meant that "objects of remembrance" such as photo albums and other keepsakes have been "kept in private spaces occasionally opened for momentary reflection."[80] Mourning on Facebook is similar to any other Facebook behavior, however, in that it is neither private nor specialized. Instead, the new spaces for mourning offered by the internet are making way for more public and commonplace modes of mourning and memorial. Carroll and Landry found that the most common types of posts on web memorials are "cursory comments that could be thought of as virtual black armbands, veils, or flowers left at a gravesite—symbolic and public expressions of loss and solidarity."[81] They also observed different behaviors on Facebook, pointing to the multiple authorship of a profile as well as its ability to support continuing bonds, emphasizing the fact that users' "online selves can persist long after a person's physical body has gone." Recorded texts of any technological era sustain an illusion of continued presence after death. Inscription has allowed the dead to be present among the living in ways they are otherwise unable to be; recording technologies allow users to "materialize memory,"[82] moving it into the lived world as media practice and death practice have continued to influence each other.

I was surprised by the increase in activity on Betsy's profile immediately after her death. This reaction, however, was based on my prejudices about what mourning should look like. The fact that people visit a deceased person's page and engage with it as though that person is still alive is not unusual. Even now, visitors continue to treat the space in many of the same ways they had done previously. Many more posts—holiday greetings, birth announcements, and photographs—have been added over the years, but little else has changed. The fact that the page's creator is no longer alive and can no longer respond has no great effect on the space. After a certain point, as the visitors have become more and more embedded in the subjectivity of the space, Betsy's absence from her own profile becomes less and less visible. Because a Facebook profile's deceased creator is not adding anything new to the space or editing others' posts, key elements such as the profile photo remain static while the semipublic Wall space continues to evolve. While a Facebook profile can be both a memory tool and a space for mourning, its publicness and persistence mean its original self-representative functions can be, post by post, overwritten. While it is still a biographical and an autobiographical object, the visitors replace the profile's creator as its autobiographical subject. Like Barthes's photograph, then, a Facebook page represents a living or dead subject in the same essential ways. When a Facebook user dies, her profile can become a space for mourning, but her persistent identity is managed piecemeal by visitors in ways that can sustain the space's original self-representative affordances but also, eventually, overwrite them.

Notes

1. John Durham Peters, *Speaking into the Air: A History of the Idea of Communication* (University of Chicago Press, 2000), 149.

2. Max Kelly, October 26, 2009, "Memories of Friends Departed Endure on Facebook," *Facebook Blog,* May 11, 2011.

3. See Brian Carroll and Katie Landry, "Logging On and Letting Out: Using Online Social Networks to Grieve and Mourn," *Bulletin of Science, Technology and Society* 30, no. 5 (2010); and Tony Walter, Rachid Hourizi, Wendy Moncur, and Stacey Pitsillides, "Does the Internet Change How We Die and Mourn? Overview and Analysis," *Omega* 64, no. 4 (2011).

4. Tim Hutchings, "Wiring Death: Dying, Grieving and Remembering on the Internet," in *Emotion, Identity and Death: Mortality across Disciplines,* ed. Douglas J. Davies and Chang-Won Park (Burlington, VT: Ashgate, 2012), 43.

5. Katz Hockey and Neil Small, *Grief, Mourning, and Death Ritual* (Philadelphia: Open University Press, 2001).

6. Everett Yuehong Zang, "Mourning," in *A Companion to Moral Anthropology,* ed. Didier Fassin (Chichester, UK: Wiley-Blackwell, 2012), 272.

7. danah boyd, "Social Network Sites as Networked Publics: Affordances, Dynamics, and Implications," in *A Networked Self: Identity, Community, and Culture on Social Network Sites,* ed. Zizi Papacharissi (New York: Routledge, 2011), 44.

8. See Rebecca Kern, Abbe E. Forman, and Gisela Gil-Egui, "R.I.P.: Remain in Perpetuity: Facebook Memorial Pages," *Telematics and Informatics* 30, no. 1 (2013): 2–10; and Carroll and Landry, "Logging On."

9. Timothy Recuber, "The Prosumption of Commemoration: Disasters, Digital Memory Banks, and Online Collective Memory," *American Behavioral Scientist* 56, no. 4 (2012): 536.

10. Elizabeth Hallam and Jenny Hockey, *Death, Memory and Material Culture* (New York: Berg, 2001), 92; James W. Green, *Beyond the Good Death: The Anthropology of Modern Dying* (Philadelphia: University of Pennsylvania Press, 2008), 172.

11. Jenny Hockey, "Changing Death Rituals," *Grief, Mourning, and Death Ritual* (Philadelphia: Open University Press, 2001), 186.

12. Patricia Jalland, *Death in the Victorian Family* (New York: Oxford University Press, 1996), 3.

13. Ibid., 301.

14. Ibid., 380.

15. Hutchings, "Wiring Death," 43.

16. Hallam and Hockey, *Death*, 92.

17. Ibid., 91.

18. Walter et al., "Change," 288.

19. Hallam and Hockey, *Death*, 99.

20. Ibid.

21. Kern, Forman, and Gil-Egui, "R.I.P.," 9.

22. Walter et al., "Change," 292.

23. Carroll and Landry, "Logging On," 341.

24. Angela Riechers, "The Persistence of Memory Online: Digital Memorials, Fantasy, and Grief as Entertainment," in *Digital Legacy and Interaction: Post-Mortem Issues*, ed. Cristiano Maciel and Vinicius Carvalho Pereira (Berlin: Springer, 2013), 51.

25. Carroll and Landry, "Logging On," 341.

26. Walter et al., "Change," 285.

27. Ibid., 292.

28. Kern, Forman, and Gil-Egui, "R.I.P.," 3.

29. Ibid., 9.

30. Ibid.

31. Hutchings, "Wiring Death," 51.

32. Walter et al., "Change," 292.

33. Riechers, "Persistence," 52.

34. Walter et al., "Change," 293.

35. Hallam and Hockey, *Death*, 91.

36. Riechers, "Persistence," 51.

37. Noelle J. Hum, Perrin E. Chamberlin, Brittany L. Hambright, Anne C. Portwood, Amanda C. Schat, and Jennifer L. Bevan, "A Picture Is Worth a Thousand Words: A Content Analysis of Facebook Profile Photographs," *Computers in Human Behavior* 27, no. 5 (2011): 1828.

38. Roland Barthes, *Camera Lucida: Reflections on Photography,* trans. Richard Howard (New York: Farrar, Strauss and Giroux, 1981), 15.

39. Ibid., 85.

40. Tambling, "Posthumous," 130.

41. Shanyang Zhao, Sherri Grasmuck, and Jason Martin, "Identity Construction on Facebook: Digital Empowerment in Anchored Relationships," *Computers in Human Behavior* 24 (2008): 1824.

42. José Van Dijk, "Digital Photography: Communication, Identity, Memory," *Visual Communication* 7, no. 1 (2008): 63.

43. Walter et al., "Change," 293.

44. Jeremy Tambling, *Becoming Posthumous: Life and Death in Literary and Cultural Studies* (Edinburgh: Edinburgh University Press, 2001), 131.

45. boyd, "Networked Publics," 47.

46. danah boyd, "None of This Is real," in *Structures of Participation in Digital Culture,* ed. Joe Karaganis (New York: Social Science Research Council, 2008), 145.

47. boyd, "Networked Publics," 47.

48. Facebook, "What Is a Cover Photo?" no page.

49. Joanne Garde-Hansen, "My Memories?: Personal Digital Archive Fever and Facebook," in *Save As . . . Digital Memories,* ed. Joanne Garde-Hansen, Andrew Hoskins, and Anna Reading (New York: Palgrave Macmillan, 2009), 147.

50. Ibid., 292.

51. Donald A. Norman, *Emotional Design: Why We Love (or Hate) Everyday Things* (New York: Basic Books, 2005), 80.

52. Ian Hutchby, "Technologies, Texts and Affordances," *Sociology* 35, no. 2 (2001): 445.

53. Ibid.

54. Newell, "Old," 291.

55. Ibid., 294.

56. See Dennis Klass, Phyllis R. Silverman, and Steven L. Nickman, eds., *Continuing Bonds: New Understandings of Grief* (Washington, DC: Taylor & Francis, 1996).

57. Kate Woodthorpe, "Private Grief in Public Spaces: Interpreting Memorialisation in the Contemporary Cemetery," in *The Matter of Death: Space, Place and Materiality,* ed. Jenny Hockey, Carol Komaromy, and Kate Woodthorpe (London: Palgrave Macmillan, 2010), 128.

58. Douglas J. Davies, "Geographies of the Spirit World," in *The Matter of Death: Space, Place and Materiality,* ed. Jenny Hockey, Carol Komaromy, and Kate Woodthorpe (London: Palgrave Macmillan, 2010), 213.

59. boyd, "Networked Publics."

60. Recuber, "Prosumption," 538.

61. Nancy K. Miller, "Representing Others: Gender and the Subjects of Autobiography," *differences* 6, no. 1 (1994): 8.

62. Paul John Eakin, *How Our Lives Become Stories: Making Selves* (Ithaca, NY: Cornell University Press, 1999), 63.

63. boyd, "Networked Publics," 43.

64. Eakin, *Stories,* 43.

65. Walter et al., "Change," 291.

66. Elizabeth Hallam, Jenny Hockey, and Glennys Howarth, *Beyond the Body: Death and Social Identity* (New York: Routledge, 1999), 125.

67. Ibid.

68. Ibid., 128.

69. Walter et al., "Change," 294.

70. Kern, Forman, and Gil-Egui, "R.I.P.," 10.

71. Riechers, "Persistence," 52.

72. Davies, "Geographies," 213.

73. Eakin, *Stories,* 43.

74. Miller, "Representing," 11.

75. Walter et al., "Change," 285.

76. Ibid., 281.
77. Hallam and Hockey, *Death*, 90.
78. Hallam, Hockey, and Howarth, *Beyond*.
79. Walter et al., "Change."
80. Kern, Forman, and Gil-Egui, "R.I.P.," 4.
81. Carroll and Landry, "Logging On," 345.
82. Kern, Forman, and Gil-Egui, "R.I.P.," 9.

Chapter 3

Virtual Graveyard: Facebook, Death, and Existentialist Critique

Ari Stillman

Introduction

My friend Marie calls.[1] I don't know how it comes up, but she tells me that a friend of her ex-boyfriend hung himself. She isn't friends with the deceased, but it popped up on her ex's Facebook newsfeed. She tells me that she's keenly following the posts of mourners as they stream in, piecing together who this person was and what he meant to his friends. She finds herself captivated—not striving to remember, as his friends might, but to learn for the first time. Facebook, it seems, doesn't just connect people; it immortalizes those connections. Whereas memories fade and keepsakes tarnish, the images, videos, and words of the deceased remain intact and accessible to all who were friends with the deceased in the postmodern Elysium of Facebook.

This chapter explores how Facebook has permanently, though perhaps indirectly, altered religiocultural constructs of grieving by transcending their conventional temporal, spatial, and social boundaries. It examines the medium's affordances as revealed through its use and the symbolic interactions therein, as well as the implications of both for how users relate to each other and themselves. After establishing the stakes, the chapter fleshes out how users can safeguard against falling victim to the mirage of essentializing identities on Facebook.

I begin with a brief overview situating the contemporary culture of death and grieving that paved the way for its emergent discourse on Facebook. Next, I delve into the therapeutic culture that has emerged on Facebook as evidenced by the medium's mediation of the grieving processes of its users. Following this, I then engage in a Sartrian critique of the culture of mourning on Facebook. Although other phenomenological accounts of how Facebook mediates the grieving process have tended to focus on what Heidegger terms "being-toward-death,"[2] Sartre's existentialism is more suitable to the present ontological discourse in problematizing the nature of essentialism. Finally, I consider the implications that the paradigm shift of mourning on Facebook suggest about its emergent culture and how its deleterious effects could be attenuated.

To complement my theoretical analysis, I conducted a small pilot virtual ethnography during December 2013 of Facebook users within my personal friendship network who I knew to have recently experienced a loss. Their perspectives serve to enrich and reify the theoretical understanding of the role Facebook plays in mediating the grieving process. Though the paucity of the sample size precludes generalization to a larger population, the responses from these Facebook users indicate avenues for further research.

The Emergence of Postmodern Grieving

In an age in which we are several "generations removed from knowing how to be at the bedside of the dying," it's little wonder that "death is a stranger in our culture."[3] We find ourselves akin to the prince Siddhartha Gautama, shielded by his father from witnessing suffering; yet, upon leaving the palace, he discovered sickness, old age, and death. Just as the myth of witnessing the Four Sights provoked Siddhartha's attempts to reconcile what he saw, so too do we in our day strive to find meaning in the deaths of friends and family. Yet just as it was advancements in technology that moved the dying from the home to hospitals and hospices, so are we reclaiming death with technology by reintroducing new degrees of intimacy and community for the bereaved.

Though death is largely a stranger, treated suspiciously or avoided altogether, universal apprehension and fear of it with limited exception have served as an explanatory principle across cultural histories. The world's religions offer various precepts on eschatology, or metaphysical beliefs concerning death, that have allowed their adherents to bracket out their fear of death. According to anthropologist Ernest Becker,[4] if individuals are constantly conscious of their looming deaths, they would be oppressed by existential angst and would not be able to live normal lives of comfort; such fear must be attenuated or repressed altogether in order to remedy its effects. Becker contends that, with the onset of the Enlightenment, many individuals were no longer convinced by their edified traditions and began to challenge the frameworks through which they negotiate meaning, thereby subjecting themselves to marginalization and possible anomie.[5] Becker declares that we need a new illusion to reintegrate ourselves into a moral order by which we can again bracket out thanatophobia, the fear of death, and live normal lives.[6] Even Frankfurt School philosopher Jürgen Habermas, ever a proponent of Enlightenment rationality, upon reflecting on the memorial of an agnostic friend concedes that "the enlightened modern age has failed to find a suitable replacement for a religious way of coping with the final *rite de passage* which brings life to a close."[7] In many ways, the network culture of Facebook affords individuals the opportunity to subscribe to a new nomos, or meaningful order, by which they can assuage their anxiety.

But postmodern grieving through Facebook isn't just a symptom of technological innovation, but rather—especially in the United States—it grew organically out of the multicultural, multireligious pluralism that comprises much of America. Postmodernism in this sense evokes not just the challenging of modern conventions symptomatic of cosmopolitanism, pluralism, and globalization, but also sociologist Tony Walter's typology differentiating traditional, modern, and postmodern death. While Walter refers to traditional death as being experienced in public with little premonition and modern death as experienced privately in the home or hospital, he combines the two into postmodern death in which "private experience invades and fragments public discourse."[8]

The affordances of Facebook, as will be discussed, epitomize this iteration of death. It caters especially to inhabitants of cosmopolitan cities who, growing up around myriad traditions, are seldom presented a clear and conventional modality that shows them how to mourn.[9] And if the deceased belongs to a different tradition than the bereaved, how can the latter meaningfully participate in the former's final religious rites? Because most American children do not grow up with death in their houses and thus do not learn from how their relatives respond to it, they likewise fail to develop conventional ancestral sensibilities to it. In this context of ignorance, the conflation of the public and private spheres such that "the private feelings of the dying and bereaved become the concern" takes precedence as opposed to demands of the family or church.[10] Lacking known tradition and needing an outlet, the internet generation turns to its shared culture of Facebook and the learned behavior of voicing their sentiments online. As one subject in a recent study of the role of social networking sites in memorialization shared, "it was just what you do because everyone else also seemed to be doing it."[11] This seeming conformity stems from the destabilization of institutional practices accompanying the transition to postmodernity that deprive the bereaved of an inherited toolkit for mourning. To this effect, one could argue that postmodernism—more than any other factor—created the demand for virtual memorials. Facebook merely filled the niche.

The Medium Makes the Message

Just 50 years ago, Marshall McLuhan first coined the aphorism "the medium is the message."[12] Individuals' ideas about a medium's *affordances*, or the latent possibilities for usage a medium is perceived to have, will shape what and how they choose to communicate.[13] For instance, synchronous physical interaction demands immediate responses, whereas the asynchronous nature of letter writing or e-mail allows more time to craft a response deliberately. It follows that an individual's perceptions of the affordances of one medium will inform his or her perceptions of the affordances of another medium in a process called *remediation*. This entails an individual choosing through which medium to send a message based on which would better suit his or her purposes.[14] An individual's ideas about how to use different media, or *media ideologies*, become refined through *idioms of practice* that emerge as users concertedly engage with media and intersubjectively arrive at conventional usage.[15]

However, Facebook is complicated since it is a public space often experienced by its users as private.[16] By public, I mean both Habermas's understanding of the public sphere as "a domain of our social life in which such a thing as public opinion can be formed"[17] as well as Michael Warner's more encompassing definition as dually a "social totality" and "concrete audience, a crowd witnessing itself in a visible space."[18] This is to say that Facebook categorizes and determines the type of usage that takes place within its medium as social and, therefore, public—however much individuals may experience it as private. It may be helpful to describe the public of Facebook as constituting a "social imaginary"—a term Chris Kelty, through Warner, employs to describe how people imagine their social relations with others.[19] The Online Disinhibition Effect, a phenomenon whereby users of online media tend to behave in ways that may deviate from the self they tend to present in person,[20] often informs the social imaginary of Facebook. Such deviance likely stems from the perception that interactions online are not as real as in-person interactions and the ability to dissociate from or terminate the interaction at any time by logging out or closing the browser window. *Ipso facto*, the Online Disinhibition Effect, combined with Facebook's affordance enabling users to curate individuated profiles and the ability to tailor their experience to their normative specifications through selective engagement,[21] illudes users into thinking they can privatize public space.[22]

This development reflects what Robert Bellah calls "ontological individualism," a worldview in which the individual assumes primary reality and society is treated as second-order as a means to maximize self-interest.[23] It denies the social realism of Facebook—that interactions in a virtual realm are real and can have real-world consequences[24]—and thereby encourages solipsistic behavior.[25] Whereas Bellah believes that an individual's public and private lives should dialectically nurture one another and "that the impoverishment of one entails the impoverishment of the other,"[26] conflation of the two endangers one's ability to successfully delimit reality and process life events. In this vein, grief can be differentiated from mourning as the private, intrapsychic response to loss, whereas mourning can be understood as the more public process of integrating loss into one's ongoing life.[27] Conflation of these public and private realms, especially in broadcasting traditionally spiritual processes for public exposure, can subvert social norms and complicate, if not exacerbate, the mourning process.[28] This social fact of postmodern grieving primes Facebook as a fertile space in which new forms of meaningful interaction can occur.

Such a latent affordance manifests from concerted recognition and consecration of cyberspace as sacred space.[29] As Stephen O'Leary posits in his chapter, "Cyberspace as Sacred Space," in *Religion Online,* this potency represents a pursuit of fulfillment of "authentic spiritual needs now unmet by the major institutions of religious tradition."[30] Drawing from Jonathan Z. Smith's observation that "There is nothing that is sacred in itself, only things sacred in relation,"[31] we can infer that while Facebook is not inherently sacred, users can make it so—or at least sanctify an individual's page—simply by treating it or relating to it as such.

It follows that an individual can consecrate his or her own page as sacred just as one can believe one's bedroom or apartment is sacred apart from the profane outside world. The only difference is the circumstances that lead to others sharing in that sense of sacred space apart from its curator. As Mircea Eliade prescribes, an object can become sacred simply by being recognized as such, while it retains its profane nature to other perceivers who don't share that recognition.[32] The event of death can catalyze such a circumstance whereby individuals jointly begin to treat the deceased user's page as sacred space as presently described.

Facebook Is the Answer

A confluence of factors contributes to Facebook becoming the default destination for many to express grief and remember the deceased. First, it delocalizes the deceased's final resting place so relatives and friends unable to travel for whatever reason are not precluded from having a place to direct their grief. In an age when families can span the globe, it may not be clear where the deceased, if they desired to be interred, should be buried. While that decision falls to the next of kin or whoever has power of attorney, a virtual memorial can help alleviate the potential sense of guilt at being unable to attend the final rites of the deceased. In this vein, Facebook could serve as a kind of substitute for not being able to do so. While it's unclear how this might change depending on varying degrees of intimacy to the deceased, Facebook potentially allows the bereaved to say goodbye, to fill a void, to search for answers, and to feel connected to the community with which they process the loss.

This delocalization further allows those emotionally close to the deceased to learn of personal relationships they may not otherwise have known about. Because we live in a world in which we have many connections, some of which likely aren't known by family members and so will be overlooked in making the funeral announcement—or connections who are hard to reach and so wouldn't learn of the death until sometime after the fact—posting on the deceased's Facebook Wall allows for knowledge of the deceased's passing to spread far and instantaneously by popping up on friends' newsfeeds.[33] This means that, unless friends of the deceased are part of the 29 percent of Americans who lack a Facebook account (10% for those between 18 and 29),[34] all pertinent connections will be notified of the death.

Likewise, unlike a cemetery, a virtual memorial is accessible via online connectivity at all hours of the day and night.[35] Because individuals may not be emotionally ready to go public with their grief or may live in a community that favorably views mourning for an extended period of time, the accessible nature of online memorials means that individuals can grieve at a time befitting them and in a manner that grants them ample opportunity to formulate their words from the privacy of their computer, tablet, or smartphone. Or as Denise Carson, author of *Parting Ways*, observed, it grants the bereaved a "platform to organize our reflections" in a manner for which raw grief might not allow.[36] In this sense, Facebook memorials create a culture of virtual sitting *shiva*—the traditional Jewish period of mourning—during which grievers can come and go as they please, for access to the shrine is universally accessible, and mourning can become a largely, if not wholly, individualized process.

Most important of all, perhaps, is the voice it affords the bereaved to commune with and privately spend time with the deceased. Users can look through photos and posts—some sending private messages to the deceased akin to a prayer. As one Facebook user who grieved in this way said, "Some part of me felt like he might've heard." Commenting and browsing through pictures and old posts may provide a way to relive memories with the deceased that might generate nostalgia. Such practices may find their pre-Facebook counterparts in reviewing old photo albums or relics associated with the deceased, but not everyone has such physical keepsakes. In a manner of speaking, then, Facebook democratizes this phenomenon by making such virtual mementos publicly accessible to experience privately.

Facebook memorials also encourage a tremendous social component whereby individuals can publicly declare their sentiments on the Wall of the deceased or in their own status updates. As I write this, checking Facebook sporadically as I'm wont to do, I notice a post from an old college friend, TJ, with whom I haven't talked to in so long that I forget what his initials stand for.[37] He posted about his grandfather's funeral and meeting old military friends who flew in from across the world; hearing stories about his grandfather airdropping into Germany, with whiskey in hand; stories about philandering in liberated countries; stories about his grandfather's first wife and the love they shared. He concluded with saying:

> So in the end, I feel, the story goes on [. . .] and it has within it more laughter than tears. More cause for pride than sorrow. Immortality is relative [. . .] So as long as he exists within our collective minds, the Idea of my grandfather goes on. To the extent humanly possible, I think that is as close to immortality as anyone can hope to get.

This is quintessentially what Facebook does: it allows the story to be told and live on in the memories of those who knew the deceased while sharing those memories with others, thereby enriching them. In such a manner, it fosters communities of memory—individuals bound together through the common denominator of the deceased.[38] As Kimberly Hieftje notes, "It is therefore important to appreciate the significance of not only writing messages to the deceased but also [. . .] reading [them as well]."[39] This process speaks not only to the catharsis Facebook affords individuals but also to the possibility of eliciting or soliciting other mourners in *telecopresence*—that is, electronically linked together space[40]—into meaningful discourse and "share in the sorrow," as one Facebook user said, toward that catharsis.

Broadcasting such sentiments through a status update to one's digital network or posting on the Wall of the deceased to their digital network could make others aware of one's melancholia, potentially inviting sympathizers into discourse. The outpouring of statuses and posts demonstrating shared concern constitute a "focused gathering"—a term sociologist Erving Goffman uses to describe a set of individuals immersed in and relating to each other through a common activity.[41] Such a focused gathering,—even though it's often experienced remotely on Facebook through a screen as a "synthetic situation"[42]—encourages grievers to share their sentiments by seeing that others are voicing their condolences and grief, thereby suggesting that similar postings will find a sympathetic audience.[43] When individuals "Like" or comment on such a post, as one Facebook user confessed, "It makes you feel as if your feelings are important and not insignificant." Responses to such posts in the form of comments or personal messages can then lead to deepening old friendships or forming new ones—made possible through the "context collapse" in which individuals comprising multiple social contexts are brought together[44]—as the bereaved reach out to comfort one another.

In this way, Facebook helps to connect those who are left behind, which is part of the grieving process. It can help the bereaved relive memories with other grievers while also allowing them to learn more about the deceased through others who may have known him or her on a different personal level. This ability to connect indicates three important points:

- First, seeing how other people's experience with the deceased are similar to one's own by reliving those memories authenticates who the deceased was to the bereaved. The bereaved may find comfort in noting such similarities, perhaps because they affirm that the capacity in which the bereaved knew the deceased was demonstrative of the latter's character.
- Second, mourning on Facebook facilitates the bridging of social networks through the creation of a community of memory from a similar response to a shared event.[45]
- Third, it signifies the fractal nature of individuals such that few if any of their connections can claim to know them holistically.[46] As such, by seeking out more information on the deceased, the bereaved hope to piece together who the deceased was based on what others say about him or her just as Marie did at the onset of this exposition.

By bonding with others over the deceased, friends and family can hallow their connection to the dearly departed who lives on through the lives he or she brings together.

But just as individuals may be apprehensive about how to respond to death, so too might they have different media ideologies about how one should use Facebook to mediate the mourning process. Rather demonstrably, one Facebook user differentiated a funeral from the deceased's Facebook Wall by sharing:

> A funeral is for saying goodbye and doing it as a community of the people who made up the deceased's life. Interacting with the Facebook Wall of the deceased may be a shallow way to do that, but in my opinion it's more of a self-centered thing to do, unlike a funeral.

Here it appears that such a community of memory assembles in person at a funeral, whereas the user regards one that manifests on Facebook not only as inferior but also oriented more toward individual grievers. While it is unclear from that user's words what exactly is self-centered about interacting with a deceased user's Facebook Wall as compared to attending a funeral, another Facebook user's perspective may clarify:

> The funeral is less about you or even the person who has died, and more about the family of the deceased person. It's a somber affair–people are crying, everyone's dressed in black, etc. On Facebook, you're not exposed to those raw emotions or the somber attitude.

Of course, funerals are not held only for the deceased but for those who knew him or her—especially family and close friends. The primary difference in these accounts seems to lie with the vocative object—either loved ones or the deceased. At a funeral, as one Facebook user said, "usually the people who were the closest get to speak. But on Facebook, even if you knew the person just a little bit you can share a memory."

Although many grievers engage with others on Facebook, its affordance as a public space experienced privately allows for the bereaved to focus on themselves and not communally attend to those who might need the most support. Thus, while some users may believe that the same concerns and rules apply to interacting at funerary events as posting on the deceased's Wall, others may find expressing grief on Facebook to be more of an egocentric indulgence. Indeed, the two serve different functions, so a Facebook memorial cannot adequately be compared to the ceremony of a funeral.

Yet for what they do—whether honoring the family of the deceased or providing the extended network of the deceased with a platform to organize their reflections—each serves its function. In this way, Facebook becomes a technospiritual system capable of mediating communication about and to the deceased.[47]

Through investigating the affordances of Facebook for mediating the grieving process, I have discussed how Facebook extends the sanctioned grieving time often confined to formal funerary events, affords additional space in which grievers can mourn, and allows grievers to more intentionally decide "how to participate (or not) within a broadly public setting."[48] Because the Facebook profiles of the deceased present more than what Brubaker et al. differentiates as "static content" such as an obituary but also "dynamic content" by which users interact with the deceased's Wall,[49] a Facebook memorial constitutes a sacred living text. *Ipso facto*, a memorial's content, can grow as users who maintain access interact with it. In this way, the community of memory becomes a recursive public, "a social imaginary concerned with the conditions of possibility for its own association."[50] Yet these underlying conditions of possibility, as I will discuss in the next section, challenge the authenticity of the interactions within the discourse itself.

A Phenomenological Ontology of Facebook

Few people would say they joined Facebook just to be on Facebook, but rather they did so because their friends use Facebook.[51] This social gravity that drives individuals toward conforming to the social norm of being on Facebook[52] suggests a lack of individual autonomy.[53] But doing something because one's friends are doing it is not a denial of freedom in the Sartrian sense if one is aware that one's actions are motivated by their doing so. While participation in the public realm guarantees the reality of our existence through social discourse[54] and may function "to make self-esteem possible" through internalization of affirmation from others,[55] it also subjects the psyche to arresting circumstances that—especially on Facebook—obfuscate one's consciousness of his or her freedom to "be" differently. While one's relations to others contribute to the facticity of our existence, such relations on Facebook can cause misapprehension of the possible—understood as concrete actions in a concrete world from which the for-itself chooses how to project itself.[56] Sartre employs the term "being for-itself" to mean the subjective part of existence in which one has the ability to transcend or negate any part of its objective being through the project of action in the world. The term "being in-itself," in contrast, refers to the objective parts of existence.

One mediates interactions through what Sartre calls "The Look"—a phenomenological interaction that informs ontological roles. In his being-as-subject, one initially encounters another being as an object—part of his surroundings. However, he subsequently realizes that The Look he gives the other in his encounter is an objectifying one and consequently recognizes the other as a temporarily objectified subject with similar capacity. Correspondingly, he is made aware of his own potential to be objectified: the realization that his being can be stripped naked to its facticity in the eyes of another who cannot see his freedom to transcend it. The only way he can then reaffirm his freedom and escape the shame of his contingency made obvious is to once again look upon the other as an object—vulnerable to the same shame before his eyes. In this way, Sartre views all concrete relations with others as a battle for transcendent subjectivity: a lifelong experience of alternately objectifying the other with The Look and being objectified by receiving it in turn. The individuated, privatized experience of Facebook serves to exacerbate this constant struggle.

The affordances of Facebook demand that users decide what parts of their identity to make public and what parts to maintain as private. Yet with the collapsing of the public and private modes in which Facebook is experienced and information is shared, consequences emerge for how others perceive us and how we perceive others.[57] As Sartre outlines, the idealized *Other*—that is, other users—

> can be considered neither as a constitutive concept nor as a regular concept of my knowledge. He is conceived as *real,* and yet I cannot conceive of his real relation to me. I construct him as object, and yet he is never released by intuition. I posit him as *subject,* and yet it is as the object of my thoughts that I consider him.[58]

Sartre problematizes the obtuseness of mediating the role of the Other and the impossibility of true intersubjectivity in informing one's consciousness. The nature of Facebook makes us assume a constant subjective other whereby we begin to actively and intentionally participate in our own objectification rather than simply feel it as a consequence of positing the other as a subject in an encounter. Being for-itself reconstitutes as being in-itself—constructing and curating a profile intended as being for-others.[59]

Effectively, following Goffman, we put the "face" in Facebook—projecting a social value intended for others to internalize as characteristic of ourselves.[60]

Taking the existence of Others as a constitutive element of our existence, as Sartre does, their anonymization due to Facebook's lack of certain affordances for interaction presents unique challenges.[61] Unless sharing the screen with others, Facebook is experienced privately. As users interact with its interface without the knowledge of nonpresent others, one can never tell when he or she is being "looked at." This could engender a neurotic, constant apprehension—"a permanent possibility of being seen"—thereby enthralling being in-itself as being-seen-by-another to an imagined plurality of cyber-based generalized others.[62] This phenomenon of Others looking at one's profile without one's knowledge—colloquially known as "Facebook stalking"[63]—precludes normal face-work by which one appraises an encounter and decides whether and how to prevaricate or take any number of lines of action.[64] "To be looked at is to apprehend oneself as the unknown object of unknowable appraisals—in particular, of value judgments."[65] With Facebook, the anxiety of not knowing what people really know about you that has always been a possible insecurity becomes precipitated to visceral reality.[66]

Yet while one "can discover [oneself] in the process of becoming a probable object for only a certain subject,"[67] doing so with respect to Facebook profiles[68] risks conflating our presented "face" with some essential characteristic that we come to believe we have—what Sartre calls "bad faith." Likewise, the assumption of a constant subjective other as exemplified by the previous "neurotic" example risks essentializing others' profiles—conflating them with the people they are projected to represent and engendering a "precession of simulacra"[69]—one begins to indulge a "holographic" conception of the other (and even the self) not based in reality—alternatively called the *hyperreal* or *hypersigil*.[70] In the feedback loop of putting on a "face" or projecting a persona, others receiving that persona and then treating the persona's being in-itself accordingly, and the being-as-subject internalizing and reifying how one as being-as-object is treated, one tries to assume the reinforced persona without basis in reality.[71] While some social scientists such as Tom Boellstorff and Joohan Kim embrace the idea of ontological extension in virtual worlds and reflexive identity formation symptomatic of "telepresence" or the "experience of 'being there' in a virtual world,"[72] Sartre would condemn it as demonstrating bad faith unless one's virtual self had the same phenomenological characteristics.

Alternatively, one might argue that performativity is a natural facet of human interaction by which individuals outwardly assume a role oriented toward receptivity by a given audience that in turn confers identity and affirms fulfillment of the ascribed social role.[73] Because of the potency for identity construction and formation of self-esteem as discussed, "every individual is seen to be strongly actuated by a desire to be seen, heard, talked of, approved and respected by the people about him, and within his knowledge."[74]

With funerals, this often takes the form of demeanor images, symbolic interactions in which individuals find themselves in a social position to display their qualities as being for-itself-for-others.[75] Some people find symbolic importance in attending a funeral to show the family of the deceased that they cared. Some family members and friends send flowers or make donations while others just wait in line to offer their condolences to the immediate family. Each such action—sincerity notwithstanding—reflects a performative social role on behalf of the funeral attendee that affirms the individual's adherence to his social responsibility and exonerates him from feelings of guilt or speculation as to why he did not attend.

While interacting with the Facebook Walls of the deceased may very well be genuine expressions of grief, the acutely performative nature of Facebook interaction suggests latent motivations. Because each person in a subject's network is linked through that person, there emerges a heightened desire to affirm one's connection to the deceased by validating the relationship in the eyes of others. And, given the cognizance of Facebook being a public sphere in which interactions can be seen by others, individuals tend to post in a manner for which their being-for-others extends to the public sphere and not just the deceased's immediate family—what might be called being-for-strangers or being-for-the-public. The conscientiousness of funeral attendees of their performativity—which could be informed by or contingent upon the relative immediacy of the death and level of grief—constitutes Facebook users' interactions as falling in the realm of semiotics over that of phenomenology. This is not to say that Facebook interactions do not foreclose the constant battle for subjectivity, but rather that their performative element often demands they be viewed in terms of the symbolic interaction by which self-conception is mediated.[76]

With this understanding, the "Like" function on Facebook takes on an interesting valence. Individuals often Like a post by another user to perform an approbation of the user's sentiments or other content shared in the manner of orientation previously adduced to Habermas. Similarly, if other users don't demonstrate that they like what an individual posts by

Liking the post, the individual can simply remove the post lest he find his subjectivity passively rejected. With these functions, the Like button takes on a multivocal significance—or rather reveals its latent multivocality—when its primary object, the original "owner" of the Facebook page, has died. Users will instead Like posts that confirm the sentiments they share with other users who have voiced them, effectively confirming the accuracy of the pronounced perception of the deceased's being. As one user shared, "When someone liked a photo of me and the deceased [sic], it showed how [the deceased] had a similar impact on other people . . . [and] help[ed] in the grieving process." The difference between Liking a post by an individual user on that user's Wall and a post by others on that user's Wall is that the former seeks to demonstrate approval of the one user, whereas the latter subconsciously serves to affirm one's own relation with the deceased even if it epiphenomenally affirms that of the user who posted it. In other words, the performativity involved in Liking another's post, while by its nature implicates being seen by others, becomes less a "metric for the deceased's significance" as some have argued[77] and more so a metric for conveying approval of the contained message and consequently the relationship of the poster to the deceased. The more that a post is Liked, the more that post is affirmed, and the more it validates the content of the post.

As for the posts themselves, while they similarly serve to communicate primarily with an individual user (unless others are "tagged" in the post), after the death of a user, postings become reoriented largely toward demonstrating one's connection to the deceased's extended network. Facebook users said they wrote on the Walls of deceased users to "offer my own condolences [. . .] to their family who might be reading their wall" or "want[ing] his parents to know his friends cared about him a lot." This conscious performativity is tantamount to attending a funeral for the same reason as discussed earlier. The principal difference is that in the public sphere of Facebook, such posts are often oriented to many imagined others besides the family. This idiom of practice in which individuals seek to prove they maintained close connections to the deceased—exacerbated with democratization of speech on Facebook as compared to funerals—has pejoratively-though-fittingly been termed "social necrophilia."[78] Since other users will notice generic, perfunctory posts (RIP, you will be missed, etc.), many of them share unique tidbits—often reflecting a recent interaction or the context in which they knew the deceased[79]—to demonstrate how connected they were to the deceased. But if postings were just about social responsibility or duty to post, there would be less variation in the messages. Being recognized by a target audience such as the deceased's family is not enough when everyone in the deceased's network can recognize the poster. It could be said the equivalent might be walking up to the podium and performing an unsolicited eulogy during a memorial service so everyone present can observe one's intimacy to the deceased.

This nebulous nature of authentic performativity calls into question whether posting on the deceased's Facebook Wall automatically constitutes memorializing the deceased, or if, in fact, such a post cannot vulgarize or even vandalize the sacred space. If the latter, such a view could stem from Facebook's algorithm that can result in a user's post on the deceased's Wall appearing in his newsfeed if the profile has not been memorialized. It could also stem from wanting to avoid seeing potentially unsavory posts that might challenge or otherwise alter the view one has of the deceased—a subtopic I will touch on shortly. To do so, however, one is faced with the finality of defriending the deceased—forever foreclosing one's access to the deceased's profile-turned-shrine.[80] This permanence affords the possibility of closure characteristic of traditional pre-Facebook times, yet its option likewise affirms Facebook's individualized affordance for allowing the bereaved to close the door when they are ready and not sooner.[81]

Regardless of what the bereaved choose to Like, post, or not act upon at all, each has a function that contributes to individual mourning. Liking a post is a supportive act that cumulatively conveys approval, whereas posting itself is a creative act that contributes content. Liking, additionally, is less visible and oriented toward affirming the designated sentiment as well as one's own connection with the deceased based on resonance with what is Liked, whereas posting is more oriented toward being seen and affirmed. It is not surprising, then, that users post similar terse sentiments on the deceased's Wall or bracket out "speech" altogether by Liking the posts of others instead—allowing "marginalized grievers" to still express something.[82]

What is important to understand is that the grieving process is not the same for everyone and that Facebook affords numerous ways to interact with the deceased's Wall. Some use it "to reminisce," "leave a comment to honor or remember [the deceased]," or "read other tributes to the individual" in order to get "a sense of what the deceased person meant to [others]." As one user phrased it, "visiting a page of a deceased friend and writing on their wall is like journaling or revisiting a yearbook." The imagery of each of these speaks to Facebook's affordance as a public space experienced privately—allowing multiple individuals to occupy the same space yet mourn alone at their convenience. Other users referred to the dynamic content of Facebook by which they could "document a memory I had of the person." More than a living text to which users can contribute and modify, the desire to document reflects both the cultural desire to be the "unofficial biographers of ourselves" reflective of expressive individualism[83] as well as consideration of a "theoretical future audience" in formulating the content of posts.[84]

A Portrait of an Artist as a Dead Man

Beyond documentation, however, at stake in the living text of the deceased's Facebook Wall is an ongoing process of collaborative identity construction. As the "fragile" facts and events of the deceased's life become eclipsed by the recency of "factual evidence" in the form of the memories shared on his or her Wall, it becomes all the more important to manage the impression that they compositely form.[85] While some users keenly noted the social norm characteristic of "the American grieving process, which is to talk about only the good things and pretend [the deceased] never did anything wrong," it's important to acknowledge the subtle dynamic of postmortem impression management. Strife can ensue when "the cultural values of the commenters conflict with others' understandings of the deceased."[86] If someone posts something seedy about the deceased, it falls to anyone perturbed by the message to counter the comment or otherwise defend the deceased with another post. Should there be any doubt, however, a "hierarchy of legitimacy" emerges in which users defer to family members and sometimes close friends who, whether by tacit consensus through common knowledge of their relationship to the deceased or outright legitimizing their closeness to the deceased, perform the role of undertaker in preserving their desired impression of the dearly departed.[87] In this way, "differences in opinion are negotiated through a complex process of legitimacy, status, and validation."[88] Moreover, the family or whoever Facebook granted deputized "ownership" of the deceased's profile to after reporting it for memorialization is charged with curating the account—whether that involves pruning flagrant posts or disabling it altogether. As such, the final authority on managing the impressions about the deceased on Facebook, despite the democratization of memory through its co-construction, lies with its designated stakeholder empowered as the deceased once was in life.[89]

The ontological significance of this becomes clear when considering, as Sartre does, how the past becomes solidified when identity is no longer reflexively constructed. Individuals are part of our past—or, rather, we share a past with them—thereby informing our identity-in-process since our existence is relationally informed.[90] Yet individuals have many particular pasts that they share with their concrete relations. The task of memorializing on Facebook, then, can be said to mediate the many particular pasts into one united, definitive past—a collective memory.[91] Whereas concrete relations constitute the for-itself-for-others, death ontologically reduces the for-itself-for-others to the concrete object of being for-others.[92] Put simply, the identity of the deceased belongs to those who construct it. In this sense, by constructing the fixed identity of the deceased, we are effectively reconstructing and renegotiating how our concrete relation informs our actuality in the present. Since constructed memory is the myth we tell ourselves about ourselves,[93] we're ontologically invested in crafting it to our liking.

With the reduction of being for-itself-for-others to being for-others, the question arises: to whom does the identity of the deceased belong? Survivors of the deceased must incorporate the past of the deceased into their own beings lest the deceased and their pasts become annihilated.[94] In other words, their memorials preserve them—they become how they are remembered: they become their constructed past.[95] As Sartre notes, "In so far as I am the object of values which come to qualify me without my being able to act on this qualification or even to know it, I am enslaved."[96] One is looked at without being able to look back. Ontologically, therefore, death negates freedom. The identity of the deceased, then, belongs to whoever will preserve its "being for-itself which is for-itself only through another."[97] Facebook affords this master-slave relation to as many connections as the deceased had up to the moment of death, thereby amplifying the number of survivors who might preserve his or her past through memory. Inversely, Facebook also allows for parents to create profiles for their unborn child—effectively enslaving it—so that it comes into the world with "friends" who are for it-self before it can be for-itself.[98] Without freedom, we are nothing but objects.

Recently, however, a new application, aptly called "If I Die," allows users to craft a final "status update" in the form of text or video that will be published to the user's profile once one's three designated trustees report the death to Facebook for verification. What would it mean then, asks Chris Colcord, for someone to Like such a status?[99] Would the phenomenology reflect the user-as-user, or would it reflect the previous discussion on performance—or perhaps a combination of both? But contrary to Colcord, who dismisses worrying about how one's final status update should read as indicative of a meaningless existence, such an existential concern more likely reflects being for-itself desiring to transcend the ontological circumstances that condemn it to eventually being only for-others just as much as being for-itself is condemned to freedom. It is that freedom to make oneself—to manage the impressions others might form—that inspired the application and has contributed to its success. The idea of seeking to shape one's digital memory, Viktor Mayer-Schönberger says, "offers us a strategy of continuity to transcend our individual mortality."[100] Practically speaking, it is seldom different than composing a will that dictates how one can be for-itself-for-others after losing the freedom to do so. As Sartre is keen to note, death renders us "defenseless before the judgments of others" as the for-itself forever becomes in-itself, fixing one's identity in the past.[101]

Being-Toward-Death: "His Name Is Robert Paulson."

More than a public sphere experienced as private, Facebook's affordance might better be understood as potentially rendering its users into public figures through the publication, circulation, and discussion of private information. As social theorist Anthony Giddens observes, modern society contributes to our egoism through the superimposition of individual freedoms upon the traditional moral order.[102] Effectively, instead of being elevated to celebrity status through "natural" social processes and enjoying the cult of mourners—as much as the dead can be said to enjoy anything—that publicly pronounces their grief, everyone now can attain celebrity status through the internet and Facebook especially. Similar to the "If I Die" app, a related app, "If I Die 1st: a once in a death time chance to world fame," offers users the opportunity to "leave a message to be heard by the world" often reserved for those who achieved worldly acclaim in life. Yet being-toward-death in this way, while perhaps nobly intended, betrays a false consciousness of inauthentic living. It remains to be seen what tools Facebook will implement that attend to the growing desire to manage the postmortem content of one's Facebook page.

Such "immortality projects" falsely or perhaps prematurely essentialize existence in an effort to edify meaning or purpose in one's life.[103] Hackneyed condolences on the deceased's Wall that "you will not be forgotten" may signify the poster's thanatophobia and own fear of being forgotten that motivates him or her to co-construct virtual memorials in symbolic avoidance of becoming a tombstone with an illegible, weathered name. Yet Facebook democratizes fame by allowing anyone to be immortalized. It reinforces what psychologists Jean Twenge and Keith Campbell call the culture of narcissism already propagated by social media in conveying that everyone is special and worthy of remembering.[104] As author Chuck Palahniuk quips, affirming Sartre's ontology of identity, "Only in death will we have our own names since only in death are we no longer part of the effort. In death we become heroes."[105] In effect, we all become Robert Paulson—Palahniuk's character in *Fight Club* who, after dying as an anonymous "space monkey," is given back his name as his comrades attribute fixed meaning to his life. Since memorialized pages theoretically will never be taken down, everyone effectively can sip from the elixir of life.

But this sense of immortality on Facebook is shortsighted and delusional. Since the profiles of the deceased are only accessible to the latter's Facebook friends at the time of death, when those friends all die, the memorialized page will exist remotely in cyberspace as an inaccessible, vestigial memorial to someone long deceased and forgotten—the precession of simulacra that Jean Baudrillard calls the "desert of the real."[106] Realizing this, we come closer to the truth of what it forebodes as the internet generation ages: for many people, Facebook already is a virtual graveyard—dead friendships full of memories, nothing more.

In this vein, the social network becomes exposed for what it is: "Facebook doesn't connect me to anyone, it connects me to Facebook . . . [as] an accomplice to my own isolation."[107] As much as mourners can use it as a crutch, taking their time to process and acclimate to the death, it can also "prevent them from moving on with their lives," as one user shared—fixating on what was or could have been in the insulation of their privatized experience.[108] As Facebook exposes more people to death and with greater frequency, the social networking site–turned-virtual-graveyard may, in fact, reintroduce death back into our living rooms, which were "renamed [from parlors] in the twentieth century to clear [their] reputation as the place reserved to honor and lay out the dead."[109] For a generation that has reinvented the famous imperative *carpe diem* with the acronym YOLO, for You Only Live Once, it would do us well to reconsider being-toward-death that we may better inform being-toward-life.

While phenomenologist Martin Heidegger believed dying well to mean facing "death-as-death"[110]—awareness of its encroaching inevitability and corresponding existential orientation—could facing Facebook-death be different? Would living well with respect to Facebook-death mean constructing our digital identities such that, should we suddenly die, we would not wish to change how our being for-itself-for-others would be frozen as being-for-others? If so, in the Digital Age, we can extend the maxim "live today like you'll die tomorrow" to "post always like you could die at any moment." Living deliberately, then, the dead bury the dead—for they live authentically before their past becomes them.

With the proliferation of social media that shows no signs of abating, who is to say what is authentic in the real world, anyway—or that the real world even exists as more than a construct—and does the medium of inter-action make a difference? Aside from sensory details, can placing a digital rose *on* a virtual memorial truly be said to be different than placing a real one on a gravesite when both are symbolic gestures?[111]

Despite the severely problematized nature of mourning on Facebook that I have discussed, a remedy does exist: authenticity. We must strive to experience Facebook, like life, authentically and not essentialize ourselves on it. A person is not reducible to his or her profile, nor can a person's par-ticular past be said to be his or her past—total and indelible. Our identities are constantly in flux through our choices, actions, and relations with oth-ers until they all cease through death. Further, as beings-toward-death, we must realize the existential role death plays as a motivator in our lives to dispel the illusion of it as a nonfactor. Such bracketing through "character armor" precludes genuine self-knowledge.[112] Finally, we must emancipate ourselves through awareness of what Charles Taylor has called the "dark side of individualism" that discredits the order of things and brings about disenchantment of the world.[113] This means that we need to critically re-consider the cultural hermeneutic of Clifford Geertz's relativism in which "societies, like lives, contain their own interpretations."[114] It is not that every era and society has a characteristic framework through which it sees itself as with neomodernization, and that of postmodernism is to deconstruct pre-vious frameworks anachronistically or postcolonially, but rather the seem-ingly condescending, Marxian notion that the masses cannot be trusted to see things the way they really are or help themselves.[115] Individualism, for all its empowerment, is the opiate of our age. Our greatest threat to authen-ticity is ourselves, who willingly subscribe to the ideology of ontological individualism that locates moral authority within our individual selves. In the mirror of society, until we can see past ourselves, we will never actually see ourselves, for we are foregrounded by the background. Now that we know what we do—that we lay at the center of our own problem—we can actively conduct ourselves more authentically.

While many of the social media offshoots of Facebook that particularize certain aspects of it (such as Instagram for sharing pictures) function solely through the sharing of new content, other peer social networks such as LinkedIn afford similar access to user profiles. Yet with very different niche markets and platform affordances, users likely will not treat the profiles of deceased users the same as they might on Facebook. And, if Daniel Miller is right in predicting the downfall of Facebook given its fall in popularity among younger users,[116] then members of that demographic will need to create or appropriate another venue to organize their reflections and mediate their grief. Its difference in affordances will be telling of what we can expect from its content and information exchanged.

Notes

1. All names referenced from personal experience are pseudonyms to protect the individuals' identity.

2. See, for instance: Elaine Kasket, "Being-Towards-Death in the Digital Age," in *Society for Exisential Analysis Annual Conference*, London, 2011, 393.

3. Denise Carson, *Parting Ways: New Rituals and Celebrations of Life's Passing* (Berkeley: University of California Press, 2011), 5.

4. Ernest Becker, *The Denial of Death* (New York: Free Press, 1973), 17.

5. Peter L. Berger, *The Sacred Canopy: Elements of a Sociological Theory of Religion*, 1st ed. (Garden City, NY: Doubleday, 1967).

6. Becker, *The Denial of Death*, 189.

7. Jürgen Habermas, Michael Reder, Joseph Schmidt, and Ciaran Cronin, *An Awareness of What Is Missing: Faith and Reason in a Post-Secular Age*, English ed. (Cambridge, UK, and Malden, MA: Polity, 2010), 15.

8. Tony Walter, *The Revival of Death* (London and New York: Routledge, 1994), 39.

9. Shanyang Zhao, "The Digital Self: Through the Looking Glass of Telecopresent Others," *Symbolic Interactionism* 28, no. 3 (2005): 399.

10. Walter, *The Revival of Death*, 41.

11. Kimberly Hieftje, "The Role of Social Networking Sites in Memorialization of College Students," in *Dying, Death, and Grief in an Online Universe: For Counselors and Educators*, ed. Carla Sofka, Illene Noppe Cupit, and Kathleen R. Gilbert (New York: Springer Publishing, 2012), 43.

12. Marshall McLuhan, *Understanding Media: The Extensions of Man* (New York: McGraw-Hill, 1964), 25.

13. Ilana Gershon, *The Breakup 2.0: Disconnecting over New Media* (Ithaca, NY: Cornell University Press, 2010), 3.

14. Ibid., 5.

15. Ibid., 3, 6.

16. Charlotte Aull Davies, *Reflexive Ethnography: A Guide to Researching Selves and Others*, 2nd ed. (London and New York: Routledge, 2008), 167.

17. Jürgen Habermas, *Jürgen Habermas on Society and Politics: A Reader*, ed. Steven Seidman (Boston: Beacon Press, 1989), 231.

18. Michael Warner, *Publics and Counterpublics* (New York and Cambridge, MA: Zone Books; Distributed by MIT Press, 2002), 49–50.

19. Christopher Kelty, "Geeks, Social Imaginaries, and Recursive Publics," *Cultural Anthropology* 20, no. 2 (2005): 186.

20. John Suler, "The Online Disinhibition Effect," *CyberPsychology & Behavior* 7, no. 3 (2004): 321–26.

21. Zhao, "The Digital Self," 399.

22. Ari Stillman, *Mapping MAPSS: Intertextuality across Territories* (Chicago: University of Chicago, 2013), 18.

23. Robert N. Bellah, *Habits of the Heart: Individualism and Commitment in American Life* (Berkeley: University of California Press, 2008), 143.

24. Stillman, *Mapping MAPSS*, 19.

25. Bellah, *Habits of the Heart*, 244.

26. Ibid., 163.

27. Lynne Ann DeSpelder and Albert Lee Strickland, *The Last Dance: Encountering Death and Dying*, 9th ed. (New York: McGraw-Hill Higher Education, 2011), 313.

28. Renée Gavitt, *Discerning Paradoxical Binaries within Digital Memorials: Youth's Struggle for Transitory Permanence on Facebook* (Bennington, VT: Bennington College, 2011), 37.

29. Mircea Eliade, *The Sacred and the Profane: The Nature of Religion*, Harvest Book (New York: Harcourt, 1959), 65, 45.

30. Stephen D. O'Leary, "Cyberspace as Sacred Space," in *Religion Online: Finding Faith on the Internet*, ed. Lorne L. Dawson and Douglas E. Cowan (New York: Routledge, 2004), 55.

31. Jonathan Z. Smith, *Imagining Religion: From Babylon to Jonestown*, Chicago Studies in the History of Judaism (Chicago: University of Chicago Press, 1982), 55.

32. Eliade, *The Sacred and the Profane*, 12.

33. Alice Marwick and Nicole B. Ellison, "'There Isn't Wifi in Heaven!': Negotiating Visibility on Facebook Memorial Pages," *Journal of Broadcasting & Electronic Media* 56, no. 3 (2012): 379.

34. "Social Networking Fact Sheet," Pew Research Internet Project, http://www.pewinternet.org/fact-sheets/social-networking-fact-sheet/. Accessed April 19, 2004.

35. Kathleen R. Gilbert and Michael Massimi, "From Digital Divide to Digital Immortality: Thanatechnology at the Turn of the 21st Century," in *Dying, Death, and Grief in an Online Universe: For Counselors and Educators*, ed. Carla Sofka, Illene Noppe Cupit, and Kathleen R. Gilbert (New York: Springer Publishing, 2012), 21.

36. Carson, *Parting Ways*, 272.

37. All names of personal connections have been changed out of respect for privacy. In the case of TJ, I substituted one acronym for another.

38. Pamela Roberts, "The Living and the Dead: Community in the Virtual Cemetery," *OMEGA-Journal of Death and Dying* 49, no. 1 (2004): 71.

39. Hieftje, "The Role of Social Networking Sites in Memorialization of College Students," 44.

40. Zhao, "The Digital Self," 390.

41. Erving Goffman, *Encounters; Two Studies in the Sociology of Interaction* (Indianapolis: Bobbs-Merrill, 1961).

42. Karen Knorr Cetina, "The Synthetic Situation: Interactionism for a Global World," *Symbolic Interactionism* 32, no. 1 (2009): 61–87.

43. Malcolm R. Parks and Lynne D. Roberts, "'Making Moosic: The Development of Personal Relationships On-Line and a Comparison to Their Off-Line Counterparts," *Journal of Social and Personal Relationships* 15, no. 4 (1998): 532; Carla K. Sofka, Illene Noppe Cupit,

and Kathleen R. Gilbert, "Thanatechnology as a Conduit for Living, Dying, and Grieving in Contemporary Society," in *Dying, Death, and Grief in an Online Universe: For Counselors and Educators,* ed. Carla Sofka, Illene Noppe Cupit, and Kathleen R. Gilbert (New York: Springer Publishing, 2012), 4.

44. Marwick and Ellison, "'There Isn't Wifi in Heaven!,'" 379.

45. Clifford Geertz, *The Interpretation of Cultures: Selected Essays* (New York: Basic Books, 1973), 416.

46. Mark Lipton, "Forgetting the Body: Cybersex and Identity," in *Communication and Cyberspace: Social Interaction in an Electronic Environment,* ed. L. Strate, R. Jacobson, and S. B. Gibson (Cresskill, NJ: Hampton, 1996), 343.

47. Jed R. Brubaker, Gillian R. Hayes, and Paul Dourish, "Beyond the Grave: Facebook as a Site for the Expansion of Death and Mourning," *The Information Society: An International Journal* 29, no. 3 (2013): 158.

48. Ibid., 160–161.

49. Ibid., 154.

50. Kelty, "Geeks, Social Imaginaries, and Recursive Publics," 185.

51. Paul McClean, "An Existentialist Critique of Facebook," in *Young Freethought* (blog), November 18, 2010 (3:57 PM), http://www.youngfreethought.net/2010/11/existentialism-facebook_18.html.

52. David Brooks, *The Social Animal: The Hidden Sources of Love, Character, and Achievement,* 1st ed. (New York: Random House, 2011), 34.

53. Jean-Paul Sartre, *Being and Nothingness; An Essay on Phenomenological Ontology* (New York: Washington Square Press, 1966), 803.

54. Hannah Arendt, *On Revolution* (New York: Penguin Books, 1965).

55. Becker, *The Denial of Death,* 81.

56. Sartre, *Being and Nothingness; An Essay on Phenomenological Ontology,* 805.

57. Dominic Basulto, "The Existential Angst of the Facebook Timeline," in *Big Think* (blog), October 18, 2011 (9:54 PM), http://bigthink.com/endless-innovation/the-existential-angst-of-the-facebook-timeline.

58. Sartre, *Being and Nothingness; An Essay on Phenomenological Ontology,* 310.

59. Zhao, "The Digital Self," 397.

60. Erving Goffman, *Interaction Ritual; Essays on Face-to-Face Behavior,* 1st ed. (Garden City, NY: Anchor Books, 1967), 5.

61. Zhao, "The Digital Self," 310.

62. Sartre, *Being and Nothingness; An Essay on Phenomenological Ontology,* 345; David L. Altheide, "Identity and the Definition of the Situation in a Mass-Mediated Context," *Symbolic Interactionism* 23, no. 1 (2000): 9.

63. McClean, "An Existentialist Critique of Facebook."

64. Goffman, *Interaction Ritual; Essays on Face-to-Face Behavior,* 12.

65. Sartre, *Being and Nothingness; An Essay on Phenomenological Ontology,* 358.

66. Basulto, "The Existential Angst of the Facebook Timeline"; Zhao, "The Digital Self," 388.

67. Sartre, *Being and Nothingness; An Essay on Phenomenological Ontology,* 345.

68. Daniel Miller, *Tales from Facebook* (Cambridge, UK and Malden, MA: Polity Press, 2011), 179.

69. Jean Baudrillard, *Simulacra and Simulation* (Ann Arbor: University of Michigan Press, 1995), 1.

70. Michael Talbot, *The Holographic Universe*, 1st ed. (New York: HarperCollins Publishers, 1991).

71. Klint Finley, "Hypersigils Reconsidered," in *Technoccult* (blog), February 18, 2010, http://technoccult.net/archives/2010/02/18/hypersigils-reconsidered/.

72. Tom Boellstorff, *Coming of Age in Second Life: An Anthropologist Explores the Virtually Human* (Princeton, NJ: Princeton University Press, 2008); Joohan Kim, "Phenomenology of Digital-Being," *Human Studies* 24 (2001); Parks and Roberts, "'Making Moosic,'" 532–33.

73. Habermas, *Jürgen Habermas on Society and Politics*, 49, 54.

74. Arendt, *On Revolution*, 110.

75. Goffman, *Interaction Ritual; Essays on Face-to-Face Behavior*, 82.

76. Zhao, "The Digital Self," 401.

77. Marwick and Ellison, "'There Isn't Wifi in Heaven!,'" 396.

78. Stephanie Buck, "How 1 Billion People Are Coping with Death and Facebook," Mashable, http://mashable.com/2013/02/13/facebook-after-death/. Accessed November 17, 2013.

79. Marwick and Ellison, "'There Isn't Wifi in Heaven!,'" 392.

80. Brubaker, Hayes, and Dourish, "Beyond the Grave," 160.

81. Heather Schröering, "Posthumous Posting: On Death, Dying and Facebook," *Echo Magazine*, 2013, 58.

82. Brian Caroll and Katie Landry, "Logging On and Letting Out: Using Online Social Networks to Grieve and to Mourn," *Bulletin of Science, Science & Technology* 30, no. 5 (2010): 341.

83. John B. Thompson, *The Media and Modernity: A Social Theory of the Media* (Stanford, CA: Stanford University Press, 1995), 210.

84. Marwick and Ellison, "'There Isn't Wifi in Heaven!.'"

85. Arendt, *On Revolution*, 227, 239.

86. Marwick and Ellison, "'There Isn't Wifi in Heaven!,'" 393.

87. Ibid.

88. Ibid., 394.

89. Ibid., 396.

90. Sartre, *Being and Nothingness; An Essay on Phenomenological Ontology*, 165.

91. Daniel D. Martin, "Identity Management of the Dead: Contests in the Construction of Murdered Children," *Symbolic Interactionism* 33, no. 1 (2010): 37.

92. Sartre, *Being and Nothingness; An Essay on Phenomenological Ontology*, 166.

93. Marshall Sahlins, *Historical Metaphors and Mythical Realities: Structure in the Early History of the Sandwich Islands Kingdom*, Asao Special Publications (Ann Arbor: University of Michigan Press, 1981), 14.

94. Sartre, *Being and Nothingness; An Essay on Phenomenological Ontology*, 166.

95. Ibid., 167.

96. Ibid., 358.

97. Ibid., 321.

98. Basulto, "The Existential Angst of the Facebook Timeline."

99. Chris Colcord, "Facebook and Existentialism," in *Fort Wayne Reader* (2012).

100. Viktor Mayer-Schönberger, *Delete: The Virtue of Forgetting in the Digital Age* (Princeton, NJ: Princeton University Press, 2009), 91.

101. Sartre, *Being and Nothingness; An Essay on Phenomenological Ontology*, 169.

102. Anthony Giddens, *Capitalism and Modern Social Theory: An Analysis of the Writings of Marx, Durkheim and Max Weber* (Cambridge, England: Cambridge University Press, 1971), 115, 99.

103. Becker, *The Denial of Death*, 121.

104. Jean M. Twenge and W. Keith Campbell, *The Narcissism Epidemic: Living in the Age of Entitlement*, 1st Free Press hardcover ed. (New York: Free Press, 2009).

105. Chuck Palahniuk, *Fight Club*, 1st ed. (New York: W. W. Norton & Company, 1996), 178.

106. Baudrillard, *Simulacra and Simulation*, 1.

107. Colcord, "Facebook and Existentialism."

108. Zhao, "The Digital Self," 400.

109. Carson, *Parting Ways*, xiv.

110. Martin Heidegger, "Building Dwelling Thinking," in *Poetry, Language, Thought* (New York: Harper & Row, 1971).

111. See Slavoj Žižek, *The Sublime Object of Ideology*, Phronesis (London and New York: Verso, 1989), 30; Baudrillard, *Simulacra and Simulation*, 2.

112. Becker, *The Denial of Death*, xii.

113. Charles Taylor, *The Ethics of Authenticity* (Cambridge, MA: Harvard University Press, 1992), 4, 3.

114. Geertz, *The Interpretation of Cultures*, 453.

115. Karl Marx and Friedrich Engels, *The Marx-Engels Reader*, ed. Robert C. Tucker, 2nd ed. (New York: Norton, 1978), 54.

116. Daniel Miller, "What Will We Learn from the Fall of Facebook?," in *UCL Social Networking Sites & Social Science Research Project* (Global Social Media Impact Study blog, 2013).

Chapter 4

Tweeting Death, Posting Photos, and Pinning Memorials: Remembering the Dead in Bits and Pieces

Candi K. Cann

Introduction

As real-life communities have been either replaced or accompanied by virtual online communities, grief and mourning online have also found a place in the bereavement process. Chat rooms and grief support groups began this trend, followed closely by the emergence of social networking platforms. Observance of grief and mourning on social network platforms reveals a common syntax of grief. Standard practices include the posting of a picture of the deceased—either alone or with the person posting— as one's status update or profile picture. This identifies the social media user, to those aware of the individual passing, as one who is in mourning. Also, written messages and pictures are frequently posted to the deceased person's Facebook page (if they were a Facebook friend), Twitter feed, or Instagram account on birthdays and anniversaries of the day of death. The language utilized is usually deeply private and personal but written to the deceased and replicating the language that previously one might have used in speaking to the deceased at the tombstone itself.[1] These three online mourning practices seem to have spontaneously emerged within social network platforms, are framed by end-user constraints within the social network program itself, and are now transferring to other newer forms of social media. In this chapter, I survey some of the more recent practices emerging on the newest social media platforms—Twitter, Instagram, and Pinterest—examining how these newer forms of social media are contributing to the changes in expression of grief online.

Tweeting Death: #rememberingthedead

Of the three social network platforms discussed here, Twitter (founded in 2006) is the oldest and the most popular. Twitter is essentially a microblogging social network platform that allows its users to "tweet" (i.e., send and read) messages of a maximum of 140 characters. Tweets are public and available online, but only those registered with Twitter can post tweets regularly. It was not until 2011 that Twitter allowed photos and videos to be posted along with messages, and it did so to compete with third-party photo platforms—such as Facebook and Instagram—which incorporated both photos and photo sharing as part of its software. Twitter's two main features are its short message format and the hashtag. All tweets (i.e., messages on Twitter) must be 140 characters or less, including spaces and any punctuation. This means that typical tweets tend to be short pithy statements, emotionally packed exclamations, clichéd comments (and therefore instantly recognizable), or intentionally shortened and punctuated phrases.

Tweets originated as a way to make a quick commentary on one's thoughts or day, but in bereavement, one often finds stock mourning phrases, like "R.I.P. Paul Walker—we will miss you!" or "Can't believe you're gone, Paul Walker! R.I.P.!" Acronyms and recognizable statements are often tweeted so that the person tweeting can relay an involved thought in a brief way. While these phrases are dictated by Twitter's end-user constraints, one cannot help but wonder about the impact on the reduction of one's mourning into a phrase that can be packed into 140 characters. In contrast to obituaries, which generally charge by the word or by the inch, Twitter packs the mourning experience into a short phrase, abbreviated acronyms, and emotions expressed through emoticons. Tweets cannot be, for function's sake, heavily nuanced, and thus tend to be easily recognizable and obvious.

Twitter might be most known for its #hashtag feature which has several more notable functions: organizing miniblurbs into recognizable categories as a way to connect one's tweet with other tweets on the same topic (e.g., #remembering Madiba, #Obamaselfie, #Missu Mandela!); providing the function of secondary commentary or explanation to a miniblog (e.g., "I'm so sad today #RIP Grandma"); and, most subtlety, as a counterpoint to the original tweet in a sarcastic tone (e.g., "Love going to a funeral #saidnooneever"). Though there might be other functions, these three seem to be the most commonly used function of the twitter hashtag. The hashtag, however, also provides a search function, allowing users to track the number of tweets that reference a particular hashtag. In this way, hashtags are said to be "trending" when a particular topic is utilized or referred to in hashtags included in the tweets of a large majority of people.

Examining some of the more popular hashtags in 2013 reveals communal remembrance and memorialization of both individuals and larger catastrophes, illustrated in three of the more popular ones: #Madiba and #RIPMandela (6.5 million tweets alone in the first 12 hours following the announcement of Mandela's death);[2] #Boston Strong (27 million tweets); and #Thatcherdeath (over a million tweets in four hours following her death). This communal remembrance, and the tracking of hashtags, provide a recognizable discourse on mourning regarding events, revealing the extent to which certain phrases represent social grief. Just like Facebook pages, "likes," and hits on various websites, one can track the social impact of certain deaths and community catastrophes through tweets. Bereavement tweets reveal the need not only to share mourning as a group and on a public platform, but also to identify oneself as a griever. Beyond the scope of this chapter, but needing further examination, is a deeper exploration of what those tweets reveal about communal grief—and whether bereavement tweets are part of a "tweet trend" of grievers seeking to identify with a group, or stem from genuine individual grief, which is then relayed on a public platform. Regardless of the answer, bereavement tweets reveal a deep need to grieve on a communal level, as a group. In this way, bereavement tweets resemble the black armbands of 50 years ago, concurrently symbolizing both bereavement and solidarity.

Mourning Mom: A Death on Twitter

The other form of bereavement tweets are more individual and pertain to individual loss, and, yet, are shared on a public level. The most recent and well-known example is that of Scott Simon, the NPR reporter who live-tweeted his mother's death during her last days and hours. Simon has 1.3 million followers, so his network is fairly extensive, and he first started tweeting the experience when his mother entered the ICU, not realizing his mother would not live through the next week. Simon writes:

When I first went to my mother in the ICU here in Chicago, more than a week ago at this point, I didn't know it was going to be her death bed and I, of course, was hoping and praying that it wouldn't be her death bed. But she was so interesting. And of course I was there all day, and it was the most interesting thing I was hearing all day. She was funny and perceptive and bright and sparkling and this is just something that I wanted to share. I don't think it's any less sacred because it was shared with a lot of people and it must be said, you know, there was a lot of stuff that I didn't share. There was a lot of stuff that I will tell only my wife and maybe someday my children. I certainly had a sense of proportion and delicacy. I don't think my mother knew much about Twitter or social media platforms but I would read her an occasional message from someone in Australia, someone in Great Britain or Singapore and she was very touched. She was an old showgirl and I wouldn't—I didn't tweet anything and wouldn't have that I didn't think she would be totally comfortable with.[3]

Simon's tweeting of his mother's death, and then his grief after she died, were not new, but his large following made this act far more visible. Simon received some backlash for tweeting about this subject, but Simon gave the impression that his mother was aware and appreciated her broad audience to this life event. He wrote, "I am not sure my mother understands Twitter or why I tell her millions of people love her—but she says she's ver[y] touched."[4] Other tweets write of how deeply appreciative his mother was that well-wishers hailed from all parts of the world. As his mother became sicker, Simon continued to tweet as his mother died, announcing the death, and the devastation he felt after in a poignant series of tweets that seem both heart wrenching and intimate:

July 29, 7:27 P.M.: "Heart rate dropping. Heart dropping."[5]

July 29, 8:17 P.M.: "The heavens over Chicago have opened and Patricia Lyons Simon Newman has stepped onstage."[6]

July 30, 8:14 A.M.: "You wake up and realize: you weren't dreaming. It happened. Cry like you couldn't last night."[7]

July 31, 11:27 P.M.: "So much important flotsam in the wake of a life. USPS says fill out change-of-address for deceased. Wish I knew to where . . ."[8]

August 1, 11:14 A.M.: "Day of my mother's interment. Left hand quavered so much, daughter had to help w/ buttons. Glimpse of my future."[9]

August 4, 6:47 A.M.: "Our children want to know if you're dead forever. I tell them yes. But I wonder about that too."[10]

August 5, 6:10 P.M.: "Between last minute flights, fees, lawyers, forms, cemeteries etc. how do families afford deaths?"[11]

Simon's use of Twitter to mark the last days and death of his mother, and then to mourn her death, marked three cultural shifts in the use and attitudes surrounding social media—(1) it offered a sense of sanction to the usage of social media as a form of documenting difficult events (a sort of personal diary both public and accessible), (2) it revealed the extent to which social media has become a verification (or not) of the importance of an event (the social currency generated by the number of followers one has was given by Simon to his mother in a way that lent more importance to her own life), and (3) it provided updates in real time to the death in a way that was both illuminating and terrifying. Death in this case truly became a spectacle—one that could not be avoided or turned away from. In other words, death interrupted life through Twitter. This last event is the one that I think actually undergirds much of the criticism that Simon experienced by tweeting his mother's death.

The response, to this new way of documenting, and then mourning, a death, was mixed, and one caregiver of aging parents writes on the AARP website that she asked her parents how they'd feel about her tweeting at their deathbeds. "If it's going to make you more comfortable and help you get through as a form of venting, I say, 'Go for it,'" answers her mother. (Her savvy mother dismisses Simon's critics, saying, "He just needs an internet hug.")[12] Comments on other websites were not so gentle, and were critical of both the underlying spectacle involved in using technology to publicize one's personal experiences, to criticizing the use of technology at all during this critical life moment. Commenter Bartleby wrote, "What's with the tweet when he said he was holding his mother's hand? I imagined him by his mother's bedside doing just that . . . and typing in his tweet with his other hand. It's his way of dealing, but in my experience, sometimes you're more in the moment if you just put your mobile device away."[13] The critique here is not just of Simon, but a greater question regarding technology. When the user of technology—whether it be snapping a photograph, or tweeting a moment—is so busy trying to *capture* the moment that she forgets to be present *in* the moment, is there something lost? Time is indeed ephemeral, but "capturing" it through tweets and photos does not make it any more permanent.

Social Media and Social Hierarchies: The Case of Philip Seymour Hoffman

As people rely more heavily on social media to express themselves in daily life and access daily news,[14] and as news outlets increasingly utilize social media platforms to report first on events, death also interrupts life more frequently, and the traditional hierarchy of life is being challenged, if not ignored, in death and bereavement. Before social media platforms were so prevalent, a hierarchical protocol was observed in notifying the family and friends of the deceased about the death before news agencies and the broader public were informed. Now, however, as this incident reveals, the family and friends of the deceased often find out about the death from the broader public, an inversion of traditional social hierarchies. The recent death of Philip Seymour Hoffman is one such example, as the Twitter account of the *Wall Street Journal* broke the story by tweeting that the actor had died in his apartment of a heroin overdose. Since the *Wall Street Journal* has over 4 million followers on Twitter, it was only a matter of minutes before news of Hoffman's death spread on the internet, and the tweet disclosing his death was "retweeted more than nine thousand times and favorited more than eleven-hundred times."[15] While this reveals the extent to which Twitter is used as a platform for breaking news, Hoffman's family had not even been alerted yet to his death, while news of it was already spreading on Twitter, again revealing the extent to which social media platforms, and Twitter, in particular, are changing the hierarchical nature of who should find out about the death first. Additionally, details about Hoffman's death, including the fact that he died with needles still in his arm, and bags of heroin littering his apartment, publicized Hoffman's drug overdose and heroin addiction, publicly and permanently recording Hoffman's private problems before his family had been notified. While authors of *The New Yorker* write that "his death was something else: an opportunity to create, participate in, take solace in, and share a narrative of grief in a new kind of media economy where currency is measured in links, favorites, and retweets,"[16] his death also revealed that traditional hierarchies (the family and close friends of the deceased) can be usurped by social media platforms. Twitter may allow for quick and instant access to news, but it also does not discriminate in its audience.

Technology, Social Capital, and the Transformation of Class

The overturning of traditional hierarchies through social media and technology is contributing to a new definition of class and power. Where class has more traditionally been defined as a group of people who share social and economic status, the use of technology and, more specifically, social media platforms inverts and challenges traditional power structures. The notion of "class" as it relates to spheres of influence remains in place, but *who* has access to these spheres of influence is changing as a direct result of new forms of social media. Our digital selves, as expressed through these new forms of social media, feel as important and can sometimes even eclipse our real personas. One can craft and shape one's digital avatar so that the influence of social media comes to reflect and even outweigh our "real" social capital. Thus while the notion of "class" is not new, technology, and particularly social media platforms such as Twitter or Facebook, allow us to access audiences that earlier would have been limited by our own strata in society. Now a middle-class suburban corporate worker can influence a much broader spectrum of people across income levels, race, geography, and so on, than ever before. The criteria used to access those strata has shifted; technology makes possible, champions, and ultimately reinforces, digital "capital" that one earns and spends in elevating oneself to that class. Facebook, Twitter, Pinterest, and Instagram all reflect this changing notion of a mobile class identity—how one gets there, how it is used and related to, and then is expressed through and reinforced by technology. Where earlier, in death and in grief, the immediate family occupied the primary position in bereavement—and this role was mirrored in most grief rituals and rhetoric (from funerals and wakes to obituaries and memorials)—now one's "followers" and "fans" are likely to usurp this hierarchy in a variety of ways (e.g., finding out first about the death, revealing details that would before have been private, mourning online on a platform that neither recognizes nor distinguishes those who were closest to the dead, etc.). The democratizing effects of technology may be disturbing to those accustomed to more traditional hierarchies in grieving, as the social currency generated by those in bereavement are no longer the exclusive capital of close family members and friends. For someone with a close relationship to the dead, finding out about the death through social media can certainly be expected to be upsetting and disturbing. Another aspect of this transformation of "class" as spheres of influence is the measuring of meaning or importance based on one's likes, Twitter tweets and retweets, Pinterest pins, and Instagram posts, and reposts. Statistical tracking of social media platforms reinforces this as top stories are discussed as evidence of importance.

No event is merely local in the presence of social media. The problem with this, however, is that, like Baudrillard's theory on the saturation of simulacra,[17] we have begun to see this alternative online universe as a replication of the real. For Baudrillard, the saturation of simulacra was the idea that people are so inundated with media images, and constantly barraged with pictures, ideas, and concepts from media, that these things begin to take on a larger reality than our own everyday realities. In this way, the virtual becomes the real so that the real begins to imitate the virtual; in other words, rather than art imitating life, life imitates art. One's social currency begins to feel *real* and the importance of presence becomes neglected. Perhaps more importantly, one fails to see that our spheres of influence are often tightly tied to systemic stratification of class, race, gender, and technology. The poor, with limited resources to newer forms of technology, will not have the same spheres of influence as the wealthy. Though Twitter, Facebook, Pinterest, and Instagram platforms are themselves free, the poor will have less access to both the hardware (smartphones, laptops, and computers) and the education necessary to learn how to use them. In this way, though social media in some ways democratizes grief, it also reinforces more traditional structures of power already in place. You would have to have a Twitter account and either a computer or a smartphone to be able to tweet and receive tweets to be an important person in the online world.

Everyone's a Photographer: The Shift from Memento Mori to Death as a Public Consumable: Instagram, Twitter, and Pinterest[18]

Photos of the dead—pictures of corpses in hospitals or in caskets at funeral ceremonies—are often displayed today in public social media—on Pinterest boards, in tweets, and in Instagram feeds—in ways that are disruptive and much more public than before, when photographs might have been taken, but only shared with one's private social circle. Where death masks[19] and photography of the dead were visual memorializations most often limited to the immediate family and friends of the dead, these new forms of death photography are public, accessible, and sometimes unavoidable, making them seem shocking or even distasteful to those not accustomed to death as a public consumable. Additionally, once an image is posted online, it is difficult if not impossible to take it down,[20] leaving the dead in a virtual liminal state online. Aceti writes in his recent work that these representations of the dead online make it difficult for us to die, both literally and figuratively. Drawing on Baudrillard's theories of the saturation of simulacra, Aceti makes the argument that "the data uploaded also acts as a constant reminder of the absence that is re-played." As Jacques Derrida writes: "I believe that ghosts are part of the future and that the modern technology of images [...] like cinematography and telecommunication [...] enhances the power of ghosts and their ability to haunt us."[21] For Derrida, the dead haunt the living in their absence, and photos of the dead remain forever present, a spectral ghost in a virtual web, both here and not here.

Pinning Photos and Remembering the Dead: Pinterest

Pinterest is advertised as an online "scrapbooking" site,[22] and it largely became popular with those interested in a virtual way of cataloguing arts and crafts and recipes. Since its inception in 2010, it has expanded its functionality but continues to mainly appeal to young, well-educated and higher-income women.[23] Likewise, a 2012 Pew Center survey found that women are five times more likely to use Pinterest than men, representing the largest gender difference in usage on any social networking website.[24] Pinterest has shown phenomenal growth in its popularity as a social network platform. With 4000 percent growth in its first year alone, Pinterest now accounts for 15 percent of all social network usage.

Because of its end-user constraints, Pinterest groups postings in categories known to Pinterest users as "boards." In this way, at least, memorialization of the dead is constrained and confined to categorical groupings. All "pins" (photos, comments, links, and content shared) are public, so anything pinned to the Pinterest board is automatically available for public consumption.[25] Additionally, Pinterest users "follow" one another, subscribing to their friend's new posts, and, in this way, have no control over the content or timing of images posted. In this way, Pinterest is like Twitter, in that one has one's own pins, but then follows another's pins. Instagram functions similarly to both Pinterest and Twitter, only is more exclusively limited to visual rhetoric.

Remembering the Dead through Their Photographs: Instagram

Instagram is also a fairly new social network. Established in October 2010, and recently purchased by Facebook, Instagram claims 90 million monthly users.[26] Instagram is an online photo- and video-sharing social network that allows users to snap photos, apply instant filters to the photos (e.g., black and white, sepia, and even Polaroid-like filters that make a photo look aged) along with short sayings and quotes, and upload them to an internet site. It is similar to Facebook and Twitter in that it allows its users to regularly update one's status, follow other users, and comment on postings, but it differs from these social network platforms in that it is largely centered on photos and videos—visual rhetoric—to relay its message. The main difference in Instagram from Pinterest is its end-user audience: while the users of Pinterest are mostly white, middle-class, and female, the users of Instagram are largely between the ages of 18 and 29, and of both genders.[27] Like Pinterest or Twitter, users of Instagram follow each other and sign up to receive automatic updates of other users' photographs. Additionally, now that Facebook has purchased Instagram, one's Facebook friends can automatically see the Instagram photos one is posting in their Instagram feed, as well. In this way, the social networks truly are connected, and the audience of postings intersect and are frequently interrelated. These applications and their accessibility resulting from widespread smartphone use guarantee the continuing increase in photo-sharing social network platforms. The growing popularity of these social network platforms reveals that their usage is increasing the most with the youngest generation, and demonstrates that grief online is fast becoming a permanent—and pervasive—phenomenon. Online grieving customs are emerging from the end-user constraints of social media platforms, affecting and changing real-life bereavement practices in everyday life, with the fuzzy line between what is deemed to be personal and private, and that which is public shifting dramatically.

Like Pinterest and Twitter, Instagram has a default privacy setting set for public consumption (though, in Instagram, one can change these settings to private or a select audience), meaning that often the photos posted are immediately available not only on the Pinterest board and Instagram feed but also on the World Wide Web. The ramifications of this are that postings by users (including photos of the dead) are often widely available and immediately public, with the bereaved sometimes upset over the spectacle of their dead ones as permanent public visual rhetoric. This fuzzy line between private and public is what is perhaps most difficult about this new form of visual remembrance: while some find comfort in remembrance through posting pictures of the dead, others are disturbed and haunted by it.[28] In both Pinterest and Instagram, the user or audience has no control over what other users choose to post to their accounts, and if someone chooses to post pictures of themselves with the dead, or of the dead solely, then, like Twitter followers, one might be surprised by the dead being resurrected online. Susan Sontag writes in her book *On Photography,* that, "All photographs are memento mori. To take a photograph is to participate in another person's (or thing's) mortality, vulnerability, mutability. Precisely by slicing out this moment and freezing it, all photographs testify to time's relentless melt."[29] The online photo then becomes at once both the living and the dead—a reminder of our mortality—and even more so when it is a photo of us *with* the dead.

Rest in Peace: Digital Memorialization

Memorialization takes various forms on these social media sites. Along with pictures of the dead themselves, pictures of visual rhetoric are also posted in remembrance of the dead, such as *memento mori* boards, poems about death, or even pictures of tattoos inked in honor of the deceased. Pinterest boards reflect the visual rhetoric of death on several levels—from an attempt to broaden the conversation on death and dying, and celebrating this through the reposting of mourning objects such as Victorian mourning jewelry, and so on, to the "collecting" of poems and literary snippets recording experiences with death and bereavement. All of these boards function to make death a somewhat more acceptable topic, though still being relegated to the fringes of the usual Pinterest boards, which are most often recipes, decorating ideas, and arts and crafts.[30]

Memorialization on Pinterest and Instagram includes the reposting of pictures of the living with the deceased while they were still alive (much like Facebook), which allows the bereaved to quickly identify themselves as mourners having a connection with the dead, and claiming a social status as such through their social media.[31] Posters will usually claim their status as grieved by using stock phrases ("R.I.P. Dad!") or announcing the intent of the photo as a testament to one's right to claim bereavement status (e.g., "Here is a picture of my brother two years before he died. I miss you and still wish you were here!"). Others will remember the dead at regular intervals (e.g., death anniversaries, birthdays of the deceased, etc.) by posting old pictures of the dead on their sites. Some will choose to memorialize through postings of pictures of places that the deceased liked or things they cherished, but almost always a picture of the deceased is the preferred method of memorialization.[32] Less common is the trend of posting photos of the tombstone, the burial ground of the deceased, the deceased themselves (in their viewing or in their coffin), and sometimes pictures of the poster with the deceased in a last self-portrait (not unlike the previously popular death portraits), usually taken at a viewing or a funeral. Occasionally, posters upload selfies (digital self-portraits—often close-ups of one's face or upper torso) taken of themselves at the funeral, alone and not actually with the dead body, identifying themselves as bereaved to their followers and friends and capturing the bereavement moment itself.

Selfies: Remembering Last Good-Byes

This practice of taking snapshots with the dead or at the funeral itself, like postmortem photography[33] of 150 years ago, seems to be a reemerging practice, as highlighted by the recent trend in news posts and articles on the subject. This practice was most recently highlighted with a collection of selfies posted on the website of *The Atlantic* and underscored by news media catching President Obama taking a self-portrait with other attendees at the funeral of Nelson Mandela in South Africa.

James Hamblin's recent piece in *The Atlantic* on "Selfies at Funerals,"[34] a compilation taken from Tumblr of self-portraits snapped on smartphones at funerals, interspersed with more traditional snippets of poetry and literature grieving both death and the passing of time, received an incredible amount of attention in the media. Responses range from the bewildered and critical ("kids today are so vain"[35]) to the mundane ("I can't believe they dress like that to a funeral"[36]) to thoughtful and insightful (one comment on the blog, wrote that "the selfies—are a testament to our transience, our mortality, since the photo captures a moment that will never return"[37]). *The Atlantic* also received some heavy criticism for running such an insipid piece on its site, while simultaneously noting that "Selfies at Funerals" was one of the most viewed and e-mailed pieces over the course of several weeks.

The subject of the funeral selfies in the *Atlantic* piece are nearly entirely young kids and teenagers, who have grown up with the medium of the internet and smartphones present to document every key moment in their lives. Taking pictures today is a sort of pictorial diary—a visual way of documenting and recording experiences, and is not very different from the *memento mori* of the past 150 years of death photography. Popular from its inception as a way to document experiences, photography has never before been so cost-effective and accessible to such a broad audience. Visual documentation previously supplemented written archives, but it now seems to often replace or even supplant it. The key difference is that, today, these photos and thoughts are made public—whereas before, our reflections on the world and the way it was experienced was largely private and only selectively shared. Additionally, the funeral selfies show that death is still an important and relevant experience for young people—that these self-portraits are an attempt to interpret the meaning of death in their lives.

These selfies are an attempt to self-identify as mourners within their social networks in a socially recognized medium that their peers will recognize and understand. In a world that is losing socially recognized traditions of funeral attire, decorum, and rituals,[38] it should be little surprise that young people today are creating their own mourning customs through the socially recognized syntax of social networks and photography. The previous wearing of a black armband has been replaced with a funeral selfie in order to proclaim one's mourning status. One aspect of these selfies largely overlooked is the language and tone of the accompanying comments by the selfie posters. Many of them offer tributes to the deceased and speak of how sad they are. These tributes can help interpret the selfies. While the selfies may at first glance seem egocentric, the tributes that often accompany the pictures indicate that the photos are the final conversation between the person pictured and the deceased. These photos are a tangible way to say goodbye *in person*. That final conversation is not a mere mental memory but captured and frozen in time through photography, and perhaps it is an attempt to transcend the distance between the living and the dead. In this way, photographs might be seen as a liminal state of being for the photograph subject: forever "betwixt and between," the subject of the photo is caught in one moment but never uncaptured as it were.[39] Both the grief of the photographed individual and the tribute to the dead are memorialized through the selfie. Some funeral selfies are not that different from death photography two centuries ago—they reveal images of the living with the deceased in their coffin at the funeral. Other selfies, though, are not pictures of the deceased at all, but merely of the mourner, in her mourning state—dressed for the funeral, and sometimes displaying a sad face for her friends to see. What marks these selfies as different from the death photography, however, is the permeation of these photographs into every aspect of our lives—and the forced confrontation of photographs of the dead, and bereaved, into our daily lives. With the removal of the dying process into hospitals, and the dead into funeral homes,[40] Americans expect death to be separated from everyday life—we no longer want to see death in our homes, and certainly not interactions with the living in pictures accessible on the internet or on our phones. Selfies bother us because they bring death to life when we no longer expect it—in a world where cemeteries are banished to the suburbs, and bodies are embalmed, interacting with the dead makes us uncomfortable. Even when the dead are not part of the picture, the mourner is, and the viewer is confronted with the reality of death (albeit perhaps a reality that focuses more on the bereaved than the dead themselves) that forces the viewer to acknowledge death's disruptive nature.

Social Media and a New
Syntax of Grief

All three of these newer forms of social media studied here in the chapter—Twitter, Pinterest, and Instagram—have, like other older forms of social media such as Facebook and Myspace, helped to bring the conversation of death to the fore, and they have been instrumental in contributing to newly emerging rituals of bereavement and mourning online. They continue to allow broader access to the bereavement experience but sometimes at the expense of immediate friends and family, whose close relationships to the dead were more traditionally privileged in the past. These newer forms of technology have also contributed to a redefining of the notion of class—as one of spheres of influence. This new understanding is in some ways closer to the more traditional notion of class as status and place in society, farther away from the more capitalist notion of class as something that can be purchased or acquired through monetary influence. The difference, of course, is that the spheres of influence can be reached more democratically and are not passed down through nobility or sanctioned by rulers. Structural issues of poverty, race, and gender, however, remain embedded in this new understanding of class as spheres of influence. Overall, though, this cultural and social shift is important, as it is changing the ways in which we mourn and grieve, and the communities through which we understand and process our grief.

Virtual communities are both complementing and supplanting real-world communities in which we conduct our grief work, and it is still early yet to see whether these virtual communities are helpful in processing grief or not. One thing is certain—in a world where we cannot take time to grieve and where talk of death makes people uncomfortable, the virtual world is nearly the opposite, with death a common topic. Visual rhetoric of the dead complicates these new forms of bereavement as the dead are both present and absent, haunting us with their return in both photographs and video recordings. Additionally, photos of the dead are often disruptive and disturbing, reminding us that death neither discriminates nor cares about good timing. Etiquette rules and rituals regarding bereavement on the internet are still being formulated, so traditional rituals of mourning seem out of place at times, when a new grammar of mourning online is still being formalized. As Susan Sontag wrote about photography, "In teaching us a new visual code, photographs alter and enlarge our notions of what is worth looking at and what we have a right to observe. They are a grammar and, even more importantly, an ethics of seeing."[41] Similarly, social media sites provide a constant social commentary on what is worth mourning, and how to conduct those new mourning rituals.

New Social Media: Is Online Mourning Changing?

While the landscape of online mourning can be expected to change with each new social media platform, there are a couple of notable changes occurring already. One shift is the move from semiprivate mourning to that in a completely public space. The public function of tweets, pins, and posts of mourning shifts private sentiment to public expressions of solidarity, and mourning online takes on a snowball effect, rather than occurring in separate civic spaces. Public and communal grief is returning to society through social media, as new communities formed in virtual spaces bond together over death events, and reveal a communal identity shaped over grief. Additionally, the 'value' of a person's life becomes measured in the number of posts and tweets, rather than merely in their personal milestones and contributions to society.

From an academic perspective, the new forms of social media are public and searchable, allowing for statistical metrics to be applied to mourning tweets, pins, and posts. This will allow for social scientists to track trends in mourning at a broader scale, and to examine the role of bereavement in everyday life, and across social strata. Additionally, mourning sentiments are becoming shorter, exclamatory, and often expressed in visual rhetoric. The public and social nature of newer social media will only continue to increase the "spectacle" of mourning, and the usage of stock phrases of mourning statements may cause internet mourning to become less individual and stylized, with much of the language of mourning reduced to stock acronyms (e.g., #RIP) and phrases. That being said, social media continues to be the birthplace of many new phrases (#YOLO,[42] or #TBT[43]) and there is little doubt that this will occur in bereavement as well. As the usage of social media platforms such as Twitter, Pinterest, and Instagram continues, new forms of bereavement language, visual rhetoric, and mourning rituals will continue to emerge.

Notes

1. For a deeper analysis on these practices, see my chapter, "Virtual Memorials: Bereavement and the Internet," in *Our Changing Journey to the End: Reshaping Death, Dying, and Grief in America*, ed. Christina Staudt and J. Harold Ellens, 2 vols (Santa Barbara, CA: Praeger, 2013), 193–206 (vol. 1.).

2. "Mandela through Social Media—How Twitter Is Talking about Madiba with Video," *Biznews.com*, December 13, 2013, http://www.biznews.com/keke-lekaba/. Accessed January 12, 2014. *Biznews.com* reports, "the morning after President Zuma announced the passing away of former President Nelson Mandela, we went about doing a report to just see what

mentions were out there and what people were saying. Just looking from about 8 PM on the 5/12/2013ʾ to about 8 AM, there were about 6.5 million global mentions of the word 'Mandela.' That includes all the other hash tags like RIP Mandela etcetera, so about 6.5 million. We wanted to understand where these were coming from and how South Africa features in all those tweets that are going out there. The country that had the most active users around the mentions was the United States and the celebrity that was retweeted the most around this was Lady Gaga. Some of the other things we looked at . . . we wanted to see how many of these mentions were actually coming from South Africa. Only four percent of those mentions were actually coming from South Africa, so all the others were global mentions and we tracked it from the 5th of December and the 6th of December, going into this weekend to see how the mentions would actually be sustained on social media. We saw that the 5th of December and the 6th December had the most mentions, the 5th of December having about 4.4 million mentions and the 6th of December having 4.4 million mentions and after that, it started going down. The 7th of December had 800,000 mentions, the 8th of December had 500,000 mentions, the 9th of December had 400,000 mentions, and it went up a bit on the 10th of December, which was the memorial."

3. NPR Staff, "Scott Simon on Sharing His Mother's Final Moments on Twitter," *National Public Radio,* July 30, 2013, http://www.npr.org/blogs/alltechconsidered/2013/07/30/ 206987575/Scott-Simon-On-Sharing-His-Mothers-Final-Moments-On-Twitter. Accessed December 30, 2013.

4. Monica Hesse, "NPR's Scott Simon Takes Twitter to a New Frontier: His Mother's Hospital Bed," *The Washington Post,* July 29, 2013, http://www.washingtonpost.com/ lifestyle/style/nprs-scott-simon-takes-twitter-to-a-new-frontier-his-mothers-hospital-bed/ 2013/07/29/44cc67ea-f86f-11e2-8e84-c56731a202fb_story.html. Accessed March 24, 2014.

5. Scott Simon. NPR Twitter feed; @nprscottsimon: https://twitter.com/search? q=scott%20simon%20heart%20rate%20dropping%20heart%20dropping&src=typd. Accessed March 20, 2014.

6. Scott Simon. NPR Twitter feed; @nprscottsimon: https://twitter.com/ search?q=scott%20simon%20the%20heavens%20over%20Chicago%20have%20 opened%20and%20Patricia%20Lyons%20SImon%20Newman%20has%20stepped%20 onstage&src=typd&f=realtime. Accessed March 20, 2014.

7 Ibid.

8. Ibid.

9. Ibid.

10. Ibid.

11. Ibid.

12. Quote taken from Jeanne Dennis, "Death and Dying: Living and Dying in 140 Characters," *Huffington Post,* September 6, 2013, http://www.huffingtonpost.com/jeanne-dennis/scott-simon-mother_b_3866213.html. Accessed March 18, 2014.

13. Original comments posted on article by Dan Amira, "NPR's Scott Simon Is Live-Tweeting His Mother's Death and Making Everyone Cry," *New York Magazine,* July 29, 2013, ymag.com/daily/intelligencer/2013/07/npr-scott-simon-live-tweeting-mothers-death.html. Accessed March 24, 2014.

14. As of 2013, nearly two-thirds of Americans were Facebook users, and 16 percent were Twitter users, with half of all Americans getting their news from social media platforms.

As these statistics are rapidly changing, and social media penetration of American society continues to transform both social exchanges and news acquisition, these numbers will only continue to increase. See Amy Mitchell and Emily Guskin, "Twitter News Consumers: Young, Mobile, and Educated," November 4, 2013, http://www.journalism.org/2013/11/04/twitter-news-consumers-young-mobile-and-educated/. Accessed March 21, 2014.

15. Paul Ford and Matt Buchanan, "Death in a Crowd," *The New Yorker*, February 4, 2014, http://www.newyorker.com/online/blogs/elements/2014/02/how-social-media-wrote-its-eulogy-for-philip-seymour-hoffman.html. Accessed February 6, 2014.

16. Ibid.

17. Jean Baudrillard. *Simulacra and Simulation* (Ann Arbor: University of Michigan Press, 1994).

18. For more on death on Facebook and other Internet grieving sites, please see my chapter "Virtual Memorials: Bereavement and the Internet," in *Our Changing Journey to the End: Reshaping Death, Dying, and Grief in America,* ed. Christina Staudt and J. Harold Ellens, 2 vols (Santa Barbara, CA: Praeger, 2013), 193–206 (vol. 1) or chapter five of my book *Virtual Afterlives: Grieving the Dead in the Twenty-First Century* (University Press of Kentucky, 2014).

19. For more on the role of death masks in mourning, and their later relationship to the photographic image, see André Bazin, and Hugh Gray. "The Ontology of the Photographic Image." *Film Quarterly* 13, no. 4 (1960): 4–9.

20. Once pictures are posted online, if the image has been shared, copied, or downloaded by anyone else, the photo remains, even if the original image is removed by the initial poster. This means that there is little control over visual rhetoric, and pictures can take on a greater cultural and social significance than was originally intended. For more on this, see Aceti, Lanfranco, "Eternally Present and Eternally Absent: The Cultural Politics of a Thanatophobic Internet and Its Visual Representations of Artificial Existences," *Science, Technology and Society* (forthcoming; abstract available at http://research.sabanciuniv.edu/23350/. Accessed July 14, 2014).

21. Quote by Derrida, in Ken McMullen's film *Ghost Dance* (London: Mediabox Limited, 2008).

22. See http:// www.pinterest.com for more information.

23. Raphael Ottoni, Joao Paulo Pesce, Diego Las Casas, Geraldo Franciscani Jr, Wagner Meira Jr, Ponnurangam Kumara guru, and Virgilio Almeida "Ladies First: Analyzing Gender Roles and Behaviors in Pinterest," in *Proceedings of ICWSM* (2013), 457.

24. M. Duggan and J. Brenner, *The Demographics of Social Media Users* (2012), http://bit.ly/XOWHJq. Accessed December 30, 2013.

25. Catherine Hall and Michael Zarro, "Social Curation on the Website Pinterest. com," *Proceedings of the American Society for Information Science and Technology* 49, no. 1 (2012): 1–9.

26. Christina DesMarais, "Facebook's Instagram Says It Has 90 Million Monthly Active Users." *PC World* (2013).

27. Maeve Duggan and Aaron Smith, "Social Media Update, 2013," *Pew Research Internet Project,* December 30, 2103, http://www.pewinternet.org/2013/12/30/social-media-update-2013/. Accessed March 23, 2014.

28. A good exploration of the disturbing effects of grief is found in Jennifer E. Brown's article, "News Photographs and the Pornography of Grief." *Journal of Mass Media Ethics* 2, no. 2 (1987): 75–81.

29. Susan Sontag. *On Photography* (New York: Anchor, 1990), 15.

30. For more on this, see Raphael Ottoni, Joao Paulo Pesce, Diego Las Casas, Geraldo Franciscani Jr, Wagner Meira Jr, Ponnurangam Kumara guru, and Virgilio Almeida, "Ladies First."

31. See the following for more on emerging practices of mourning online and how these practices are changing the landscape of grief and bereavement today: Tony Walter, Rachid Hourizi, Wendy Moncur, and Stacey Pitsillides. "Does the Internet Change How We Die and Mourn? Overview and Analysis," *Omega—Journal of Death and Dying* 64, no. 4 (2011): 275–302.

32. Ibid.

33. See Jay Ruby's "Post-Mortem Portraiture in America," *History of Photography* 8, no. 3 (1984): 201–22 for more on the popular role of post-mortem photography in American history.

34. James Hamblin, "Selfies at Funerals," *Atlantic Monthly,* October 29, 2013, http://www .theatlantic.com/health/archive/2013/10/selfies-at-funerals/28097. Accessed February 22, 2013.

35. Ibid.

36. Ibid.

37. Ibid. This comment recalls Barthes in *Camera Lucida,* who writes, "What the Photograph reproduces to infinity has occurred only once: the Photograph mechanically repeats what could never be repeated existentially" (p. 4). For Barthes, like Derrida, the photograph is a return of the dead to the world of the living. Barthes goes on to write that "Death is the *eidos* of the Photograph" (p. 15). For more on this subject, see Roland Barthes, *Camera lucida: Reflections on Photography* (London: Macmillan, 1981).

38. For more on the transitions in both mourning and funeral rituals and their disappearance, see Philippe Aries, *The Hour of Our Death* (New York, 1981), 166; and Douglas Davies, *Death, Ritual, and Belief: The Rhetoric of Funerary Rites* (New York: Continuum, 2002).

39. While Turner doesn't discuss the liminal aspects of photography, Kevin Jones, Todd Lewis, and Kenneth Zagacki discuss the liminal space between life and death occupied by photographs in the aftermath of 9/11. See Victor Turner's *The Ritual Process: Structure and Anti-Structure* (1969), 94–130; and Kevin T. Jones, Kenneth S. Zagacki, and Todd V. Lewis. "Communication, Liminality, and Hope: The September 11th Missing Person Posters." *Communication Studies* 58, no. 1 (2007): 105–21.

40. For more on this, see James W. Green's *Beyond the Good Death: The Anthropology of Modern Dying* (Philadelphia: University of Pennsylvania Press, 2012).

41. Sontag, *On Photography,* 3.

42. YOLO stands for "You Only Live Once," and is popularly used when identifying an event that is unusual or might represent a once in a lifetime opportunity, such as a trip to Tahiti, or bungee jumping off a cliff.

43. TBT stands for "Throw Back Thursday," and is utilized when the poster posts an old picture from their past. It is usually posted on a Thursday, though posters also post on Fridays with #FBF, or Flash Back Friday.

Part II

Online Memorialization and Digital Legacies

Chapter 5

eMemoriam: Digital Necrologies, Virtual Remembrance, and the Question of Permanence

Michael Arntfield

Every spring, the Society of Professional Obituary Writers (SPOW) holds its annual symposium where, among other awards—colloquially known as "the Grimmies"—a juried prize for best online or otherwise digital obituary is up for grabs.[1] Most of the attendees represent accredited news media from across North America, and as obituary historian Marilyn Johnson argues, this burgeoning attendance suggests that in spite of the palliative state of print journalism, newspapers' quintessential guilty pleasure—the obituary column—is flourishing in both popularity and cultural relevance.[2]

What increasing attendance at and interest in the annual SPOW Conference suggest—along with its collective recognition of the surging relevance of online obituaries—is that, as obituaries have shifted into a digital format, that shift brings with it changes with respect to form and content alike. The latest digital iterations of these funerary narratives are thus not merely electronic transcripts of their analog and hardcopy antecedents, but are, for better or worse, media artifacts with their own distinct interfaces, histories, and collective symbolism. As a cultural phenomenon that corresponds with what is likely the darkest period for city and regional dailies on record, the eleventh-hour fandom surrounding death narratives aptly represents a full-circle return to obituary columns as revenue-generating blotters in earnest—content relegated to the most valuable print space and thus the historical purview of advertisers rather than newsmen. The ability of obituary columns to once again serve as rainmakers for now struggling newspapers also reveals their transparently commercial origins and protracted struggle for credibility as genuine forms of memorialization.

The veritable explosion of digital obituaries commensurate with the increasing interactivity, customizability, and general sophistication of the World Wide Web intensifies this scrutiny while additionally exposing the historical economization of death stories in the commercial press. The digitization of traditional forms of memorial writing, funerary portraiture, and other culture-specific forms of multimedia solemnization additionally broaches timely questions about death and remembrance. Such questions include the relationship between memory and technology, as well as the sustainability of earlier memorial traditions as they now exist digitally. The architecture of this convergence between memory, technology, and tradition is comparatively tenuous in an online world defined by both instantaneity and equally instant gratification—phenomena that on their face would seem antithetical to concepts such as permanence and reverence that are customarily affiliated with the dead. Finally, the emergence and popularization of the online necrology raise the question whether digital forms of remembrance fundamentally reject traditions that have stood for centuries in the offline world, or if they instead seek to replicate them while at the same time enabling accessibility, and whether this balancing is sustainable or if there is instead an inherently preferred form of remembrance.

While newspapers and other conventional physical media still offer—and to some extent rely on—paid obituaries and death notices as extensions of classified advertisements, the narrative obituary (the so-called Siberia of journalism)[3] has traditionally been authored at the sole discretion of an experienced journalist or essayist who autonomously discerns the newsworthiness of select lives—and deaths—warranting *public* reflection. Digitization has, in turn, forever changed the selection process in terms of what lives are deemed worthy of written public commemoration, as well as who is able to author the associated content. Moreover, memorial digitization has accelerated a shift toward "space-biased" versus "time-biased" media with respect to funerary content, whereby writings that were traditionally intended to have limited access but stand the test of time (visitation and condolence books, mausoleum inscriptions, etc.) have increasingly followed the standards of industrial newspapers by now maximizing distribution and dominating space at the expense of durability or sustainability.[4] While this democratization and mass diffusion of obituary and memorial content have their merits, there are inarguably corresponding problems that ensue, including how to preserve authenticity while also mitigating ephemerality. In other words, while time-biased and space-biased media historically tended to be mutually exclusive and at odds, conceptually speaking,[5] the digitization of what is essentially *all* media has enmeshed these two phenomena into an awkward alloy of both.

This convergence and the ensuing economization of information have led to an obsession with present-mindedness and planned obsolescence whereby one finds the "systematic, ruthless destruction of the elements of permanence essential to cultural activity" in all forms of literary and artistic expression.[6] Since the term was first coined, planned obsolescence has gone on to describe a host of not only technological, but also intellectual and creative products and processes. This includes the end of conventional authorship and a shift toward writing and publishing as purely economic processes with preplanned lifecycles.[7] Thus, the role that permanence— and perhaps more importantly, the expectation of permanence—plays in the socially complex processes of mourning and remembrance as closely guarded cultural rites is additionally complicated by digitization. The digitization and multimediation of obituary content therefore broach questions about who the intended audience is for these narratives as they shift from being literary to graphic texts, and from memorials in earnest to multimedia spectacles. Because the modalities of obituary writing and prevailing trends in memorialization have historically reflected as much about the living as they do the dead, resigning oneself to the concept of a planned obsolescence in the process of remembrance is therefore bound to be troubling.

With these questions and revelations serving as points of departure, this chapter investigates, through both a sociohistorical and technological lens, the rise of digital obituary and memorial in the online age, and how—as extensions of the obituary column's unapologetically commercial origins— the open-sourcing and digitization of content reflect wider trends in online journalism; it is a precarious but unavoidable system where opinion now drives content and technology drives distribution. As the paid obituary tradition emblematic of print capitalism now resurfaces in a digital milieu, we must confront how obituaries and other narrative modes of remembrance struggle with the concept of permanence in an asynchronous environment where access is unlimited and memorial environments unstable—and potentially unsustainable. This chapter additionally examines the role of social media and other performance-based, multimedia platforms that maximize the public spectacle of obituary content, publicizing and commodifying the processes of remembrance and mourning, with the understanding that such trends aggravate rather than mitigate existing problems of ephemerality and superficiality.

In looking back at the origins of online obituary, and the digitization of funerary writing generally, one finds something of an anomalous history when compared to other trends in digitization. Unlike the shift from analog to digital formats in other commodity-driven markets (e.g., home computing, gaming, and even musical recording and distribution), the digital obituary is something of a rarity in terms of its ability to engender newly customized circuits of consumption rather than drawing on existing ones, while at the same time creating a highly customizable and interactive "commemorative environment" that favors creative human-computer interaction and an open-source multimedia format.[8] Tracing the origin of obituaries as cultural and historical documents that are inherently *active* consequently requires a study of what historical factors have contributed to the current cultural conditions surrounding memorialization, including what now seems to be the "right" to a written death in the digital world.[9] In reality, such entitlements are not necessarily a product of the online age and its culture of instant gratification but, rather, can be traced to the early Industrial Era when obituaries were in their nascence and when precipitous changes in technology allowed memorial writing to transition from an elitist pursuit to a populist one.

In examining the genesis of obituaries and memorials in the West, the reality is that they have always been tied to capital, and it is merely the nature of the user experience that has changed. Vincent Mosco argues that as these texts have shifted into the online world, this process of digitization increasingly monetizes them;[10] thus the case could be made that obituaries have by their very nature always been socially and economically intricate products prone to monetization. They have perhaps always reflected broader trends in society, reflecting in death the same hierarchies, rivalries, and complex socioeconomic stressors that exist in life. In moderating public discourses on wealth, status, charity, nobility, intellectualism, martyrdom, and public service, obituaries have often pushed conventional narrative boundaries and cultivated debates through frequently polemical content. On the other hand, obituaries have also traditionally employed, as a matter of marketability and readability, a commercialized "invisible metronome"[11] that readers come to rely on as its own literary device. This is the dichotomy that defines the obituary as an instrument of legitimate memorialization: historically bold, contrarian, and provocative in terms of content, yet also remedial and even pandering to the masses in terms of style. This dichotomous history is not lost on the digital obituary; in fact, on the contrary, it is embraced.

Looking back even further in terms of how obituaries have served to reflect these types of "mass" interests in a digital form: obituary writing of one form or another actually dates to antiquity, including visitor graffiti and unsanctioned epigraphy in the Roman catacombs as early as AD 290, all of it "open source" by definition. Thus, in considering the naturally interactive origins of obituary writing and reading, we learn something about its digital present and future. From the humble beginnings of obituary writing as unsolicited writings, etchings, and sketches that amounted to grave vandalism during the socioeconomic and political vicissitudes of the Roman Imperial Crisis, one finds a literary tradition that suggests funerary writing and commemoration is ultimately expected to be a public affair—one that is delegated within the public sphere as a calibrator of social and political climate. It might then be argued that obituaries are both much larger than the person being eulogized or memorialized, and much too important to be left to the sole discretion of newspapermen.

In the early American experience, the Colonial Era and early Republican newspapers such as the *New York Gazette* (1725–1744), the *Massachusetts Spy* (1770–1904), and the *National Intelligencer* (1800–1867) featured frequently detailed death notices as *ad hoc* news items until the rise of the daily, professionally written obituary column that drew its design and format from the vertically formatted memorial columns of antiquity.[12] While industrialization and the transparent commercialization of print journalism (and emergence of print capitalism) were certainly a major influence on the production of newspaper necrologies, the popularity and loyal readership surrounding obituaries that followed have to some extent always functioned as a reflection of larger social realities. These are realities that have most often been directly attributable to the character and policies of the corresponding president in office, the most notable in the context of early print obituaries being President Andrew Jackson.[13] Obituary writing and trends in public commemoration during their formative years can therefore be disaggregated in terms of style into either Jacksonian or post-Jacksonian traditions, in reference to the two consecutive terms of the eponymous seventh U.S. President, from 1829 to 1837. It is also the legacy of the latter iteration, the post-Jacksonian tradition, which contours the style and structure of digital obituary content today.

As a decorated combat veteran and U.S. Army General dubbed "Old Hickory" in reference to his rugged, everyday demeanor and deportment, Jackson would ultimately have a major influence on collective perceptions of status, most notably with respect to public service. Following Jackson's time in office, and cresting around the time of his death in 1845, obituary authorship began to demonstrate a secularization of content while at the same time reflecting a wider array of lives deemed worthy of literary commemoration.[14] While earlier colonial newspapers, up to and including some Jacksonian-era publications, tended to print strictly "ecclesiastical necrologies" in the tradition of church-sanctioned funeral ceremonies,[15] and while such entries were initially limited to politicians, aristocrats, and persons of wealth and influence, by the mid-1840s funerary writing had come to include the middle classes as much as the social and political elite.

As the progenitor of the press supplanting the church as the institution primarily charged with shaping public discourses on death,[16] the post-Jacksonian obituary tradition brought changes that were shaped not only by the cultural effects of Jackson's presidency but also by technological factors. In fact, beginning in roughly 1838, the year after Jackson's second term in office had ended, improvements in the efficiency of printing and distribution helped loosen the admission criteria in terms of who was deemed worthy of public commemoration. Changes in production enabled wider distribution, and in part because of expanded readership, newspapers quickly recognized the need to court previously overlooked demographic groups.[17] Many of these readers were military veterans like Jackson, including Revolutionary War veterans who would soon begin dying off en masse and whose deaths would help galvanize obituary readers of all political stripes and across all social classes.

In the aftermath of post-Jacksonian reforms with respect to obituary content and with obituarists embracing a more populist model of remembrance, print necrologies came to take on a reputation as more of a diversion or guilty pleasure amongst readers than any sort of attempt at *real* news. Even the venerable *New York Times* obituaries were lampooned as little more than the "Irish sports page"[18] by pedantic traditionalists who felt that obituaries should have remained reserved for those occupying specific offices or boasting distinguished pedigrees. Today, in a world defined not by broadsheets but by organic, online pages that require continuous and circuitous editing and updating—and where unvetted comments can be used to overshadow, interpolate, or manipulate original reported content—the Roman practice of open-source funerary writing as well as the post-Jacksonian tradition of engaging mass audiences both seem to have foreshadowed the current zeitgeist of digital remembrance. With the analog print obituary having served as a vehicle for not only disseminating information on death but also securing an official account of one's life, the process of digitization to some extent alters the meaning of death itself. In keeping with basic McLuhanian postulates that the medium *is* the message—or that the aesthetic and experiential architecture of any media product inevitably contours how it is both interpreted and consumed[19]—the digital memorial has changed the interface between the writer and reader of its content, and by extension the relationship between the dead and the bereaved to the point where digitization and memorialization share a symbiotic online relationship.

Digitization as both a technological process and a cultural phenomenon—and to some extent an ideology—is therefore not merely the conversion of text or other media from an analog to a computational or modifiable format (HTML, XHTML, etc.) that can be read numerically or mechanically. Rather, according to Mosco, it involves the transformation of words, images, sounds, and other experiential phenomena into a common language, the long-term repercussions of which can never be fully forecasted.[20] More specifically, digitization offers enormous gains in terms of the celerity of information—less the information itself that is static, as much as the speed with which it travels—and allows for all digitally compatible technologies to engender the commodification of information; it is a process that, in the case of digital obituaries and memorials, might be described as "kitschification."

The process of kitschification, from the German meaning literally "to cheapen," transforms memorialization into a consumption practice in earnest.[21] Kitschification existed well before the rise of digital remembrance in the way of memorial trinkets, souvenirs, and even macabre keepsakes from graves and memorial services; it can generally describe the theme-parking and gift-shopping of death and remembrance. As a form of funerary "consumer therapy," kitschifcation has enabled a figurative and literal ownership of the dead—and death generally—for centuries.[22] In brief, kitschification functions as a type of surrogate remembrance through mass-produced, prepackaged forms of memorialization and sentimentality. Kitschification, and the collection of kitsch items, whether real or virtual, enables a process of "mourning through consensus" that is collective in nature.[23] Some ethical considerations that dovetail from this exploitative process becoming an accepted practice include whether kitschification, or the flagrant commercialization of online obituaries, is a necessary compromise in order to defray operating costs and ensure the permanence offered by traditional offline memorials. Alternatively, one might question whether kitschification is in fact an aggravating rather than mitigating factor with respect to ephemerality, and whether it amounts to profiteering on the backs of the dead and at the expense of the living—an issue potentially raised by traditionalists or technological late adopters who remain wary of this practice.

Whether it is a practice that will ultimately fall out of favor as the internet evolves and collective tastes and values change remains to be seen, and will ultimately help determine the future, if any, of digital memorials defined—and funded—through kitschification.

Other points to consider include how the anonymity afforded by the internet might affect memorial vandalism and virtual grave desecration through hacking, and whether the compulsory security requirements of such sites, in addition to maintenance costs, pose another threat to site stability and sustainability, let alone a more abstract concept like permanence. Further, increasing maintenance costs, security costs, and other unforeseen expenses of the digital memorial environment may make it prone to dramatically fluctuating costs in the long term, especially given its fluid and expanding nature. If users will be solely responsible for such maintenance costs, this would differ drastically from the fixed costs of acquiring a burial plot, headstone, and other prepaid funeral and memorial expenses. There are also a number of statutory regulations that require the oversight of how physical gravesites and places of remembrance are designated and administrated, measures that are in part designed to offer guarantees that people get what they pay for and can, in fact, rest in peace—and in one place. In the case of digital memorials and even virtual gravesites, no such assurances or failsafe measures currently exist.

Perhaps the best case study to examine in this context is that of the digital cemetery and memorial site known as *Cherished Lives*.[24] This site, once offering a range of digital funeral services, emerged ca. 2006 and remained in operation—accepting the upload of death data, including detailed textual and pictorial content—until an indeterminate date in 2009. *Cherished Lives* was, like many digital memorials, both lauded and defined, at least during its seminal period, by its ability to eschew many of the same issues that prevent what is for many cost-prohibitive or logistically impossible in terms of memorialization in the offline world. By circumventing the need for landscaping and restorative measures, in addition to the front-end expenses associated with acquiring burial plots, stonework, and other funerary costs, the site circumvented many of the geographic impediments of traveling to visit a similar place of mourning and remembrance in an offline context.

At the height of its development, *Cherished Lives* also boasted exceptional production values and used elaborate Flash Media vignettes to connote a specific sense of place, offering a detailed narrative and personalized experience for each visitor once they arrived. Upon loading the homepage, the visitor was, through a first-person point of view, ushered to the main

entrance of a classic Victorian-inspired mortuary, the double doors opening to reveal a maudlin female undertaker who, once provided with the
name of the deceased through the use of keyboard and confirming they
were, in fact, digitally interred there, escorted the visitor to an idling black
sedan for the final leg of the journey down the winding cemetery roads to
the specified grave. Once at the graveside and electronically signing the register, visitors would have a new window open in the web browser to reveal
a memorial photograph and biographical details of the deceased, as well as
customized musical selections. In spite of these elaborate production values and painstaking attention to decorum and detail—or perhaps as a consequence of their cost-prohibitive nature in the long term—by mid-2009
Cherished Lives and the stories, images, and memories it housed had been
summarily purged from the web. The cemetery, mortuary, and purportedly
"cherished lives" honored there had been digitally razed, having vanished
from cyberspace and replaced instead with a splash page advertisement for
the domain provider who was at that time selling the space and monthly
hosting. At the time of writing, the space is still unclaimed and remains
for sale.

Contemporary sites that remain in existence and that offer digital memorials of similar design and decorum include the European-specific *Virtual
Grave*[25] remarkably similar in appearance and interface to the American-
based *Cherished Lives*. With a register known as the "Book of the Dead,"
as well as a separate pet cemetery, *Virtual Grave* even boasts a "catacombs"
section where the visitor is, again through a first-person point of view, led
into a labyrinth of virtual underground crypts where the digital dead are
immured behind a series of hyperlinked wall markers. The home page for
Virtual Grave greets visitors with palatial gates, English gardens, and stone
reliefs in the romantic style of the traditional rural cemetery, but also features an underground network of crypts that approximates the original
Roman catacombs.

Not surprisingly, these elaborate treatments come at a cost paid not only
by those wishing to solemnize loved ones in this space but additionally by
visitors who are prompted to visit the site's boutique where memorial kitsch
is hawked and peddled through a conspicuous "shop" link atop the home
page. From there, visitors are taken to an online store where grave goods intended for use specifically within the digital graveyard are also available for
sale. These goods range from conventional, secular items of respect (e.g.,
flower arrangements) to religion and culture-specific items (e.g., stones and
pebbles for placing atop grave markers, virtual headstones). In the case of
perishable items such as "fresh" flowers and "new" candles, there are expiry

dates set for removing these items by cemetery caretakers and requiring newly purchased replacements. As in the case of offline graves, evidence of attendance by loved ones is often expressed through the presence of these purchased goods at some graves, while others appear seldom visited and neglected, and are devoid of such items. The fact that, in the case of *Virtual Grave,* the memorial provider and cemetery caretaker are also the retailer of the associated grave goods could be a conflict of interest in the offline world, but in the digital milieu this is perfectly acceptable.

Less elaborate sites, consisting largely of HTML or XTML script and some basic graphic treatments on a single scrollable page, approximate both the vertical memorial columns of antiquity and vertically oriented copy edit format of newspaper obituaries. One such example is the "online burial ground" *MyCemetery,*[26] where the comparatively retrograde format reflects the fact that the site is kitsch-free; there is no gift shop or additional goods and services for sale to defray the operating costs. In fact, like many open-source wiki sites, the curators and webmasters instead ask only for donations in order to help maintain the site to its current standards. Before users are able to upload an epitaph and accompanying memorial photograph, they must first agree to the terms of service and navigate the optional donation field; however, no monetary contribution is actually required before proceeding to the next stage where the user is able to begin populating obituary content. In spite of marked differences with respect to decorum between these sites, this dichotomy is negotiated by the fact that epitaphs, photographs, reflections, and other emotive content, regardless of format, can reach a massive, global audience. It might be the case that the universal access afforded by the internet, and the digital construction and installation of what would be prohibitively costly memorials to replicate in the offline world, make kitschification something of a necessary evil, as it were, among digital memorial caretakers endeavoring to provide a comparable aesthetic experience.

To this end, digital obituaries and memorials inevitably serve as reminders of how obituarists have always been plagued, not unlike morticians and commercial funeral providers, with trying to suppress the inherent contradictions and exploitations of their work for the sake of appearances, including their often-overlooked economic relationships with the dead. These are subtle contradictions and interconnections often described as "the cash nexus" that solders memorialization to inevitable monetization, and for which the obituary serves as the prevailing signifier.[27] Given that obituary columns in American newspapers and in much of the Western media can be traced to advertising departments and paid classifieds, this construct of a cash nexus fronted by the digital memorial should come as little surprise. Mired from the outset in questions of intent and harboring ulterior economic motives, this once "gray area" of journalism[28] now operates with unapologetic ostentation and little decorum in its brazen economic interests online. Digital memorialization thus reveals, for the first time, the obituary—until now, rather vague territory in terms of journalistic merit and ethics—as a mass marketable, nakedly commercial product.

Traditionally speaking, consumers of analog media have been able to confound the commodification of information and commercialization of death endemic to the print obituary by anonymously recycling the original text. Examples include leaving a newspaper atop a café table or on a seat on a commuter train for carrying forward by strangers, or someone lending out copies to friends or acquaintances, knowing they will never make their way back but will instead be passed on in perpetuity as each new custodian of the newspaper advocates its continued circulation during its brief lifespan; such had historically been the ellipses of early obituaries and print memorials. The internet, however, has interrupted this cycle and all but dispensed with anonymous and private readership, effectively displacing both the intimacy of grave visitation and anonymity of obituary readership. As visitors can be tracked by internet protocol (IP) address, cookies, and other data captured by a site's metrics, including length and frequency of visits, those attending virtual memorial are never really alone. By both synthesizing the obituary, the memorial, and the gravesite as discreet locations and distinct experiences unto themselves and creating a multimedia death experience that reduces these once-separate facets of mourning into a single digital product that can be actively monitored, virtual remembrance also streamlines the solemnization of the dead as a measure of efficiency.

Unlike other methods used in the multimediation of death and remembrance whereby digital technologies are used to complement or supplement traditional offline memorials rather than supplant them entirely, such as interactive digital installations (e.g., Vidstone Serenity Panels) that can be appended to or overlaid on existing memorials and sepulchra, the purely online memorial experience is one that rejects the offline experience. In this case, it is important to distinguish between obituaries, memorials, and gravesites that are *digitized*—digital versions of offline referents—versus *digital,* which exist purely in an online format.

In reference to the latter, digital memorials, they are ostensibly more accessible and enable visitation in real-time, but they also exclude those who are unable to access or acquire the necessary technologies, such as stable internet connectivity, a compatible operating system, and the required software updates. Even with the required technologies available, the lack of a physical referent or offline antecedent is by no means a guarantor of accessibility, nor—as seen in the case of *Cherished Lives* and other sites—an ameliorator of perishability.

While pilgrimages to offline, tactile places of mourning, whether personal or public, may prove onerous to some, there is a reasonable expectation of the content found there being preserved. Conversely, the digital obituary or multimedia memorial affords a certain instantaneity of access that permits intermittent, even repetitive visitation at no direct cost, but it does so with the explicit awareness that this access—like the textual, pictorial, or multimedia content therein—is ultimately perishable. The trek to Arlington National Cemetery, for instance, or even a historical family plot may be costly and labor intensive, but visitors ultimately won't find a 404 error or denial-of-service notice once they arrive.[29] The "rhetorical permanence" of the physical memorial has traditionally been predicated on the manner in which the graveside visitor experiences the materiality of loss through his or her own spatial proximity to the memorial or even the corpse.[30] The digital memorial, however, is both ethereal and ephemeral in its construction, occupying a space and yet no physical place. Unlike conventional brick, mortar, and marble memorials, the digital memorial's real estate is not so much real as it is surreal, even hyperreal: a place where, as Aaron Hess asserts in one of the seminal studies on virtual memorials, materiality is measured not in acres but in bytes[31]—units of digital information that can be decompiled when visitor attendance proves unsustainable or unprofitable.

Digital obituaries and online memorials, while offering immediate access and interaction, are also inevitably at the mercy of webmasters, domain providers, and digital curators who come and go. Most importantly, these sites are all also at the mercy of dollars and cents. Like their offline, analog forerunners, the sustainability of digital forms of mourning and remembrance is therefore dependent upon economic viability. In fact, what one might liken to digital necropolises—sequestered places reserved for the dead, far removed from day-to-day life, and that offer a combination of gravesites for those interred on site and memorials for those buried elsewhere—prove to be especially susceptible to weathering. This includes weathering not only in terms of physical exposure to the environment or vandals, but also in terms of a lack of maintenance resulting from insufficient operating capital to pay for domain space, or disinterest and disinvestment on behalf of visitors.

In some cases, disinvestment may be distinct from disinterest and simply reflect the prevailing technological culture of a given region or market group. For instance, technological differences that vary by region (e.g., access to a local area network or cultural differences stemming from collective responses to or rejections of technology) might prejudice the ability of some mourners to compose or otherwise create forms of digital memorialization, thus mimicking the same barriers to access posed by elusive offline memorials. Digital mourners may therefore still reflect, even at this juncture, early adopters or, at the very least, early majority consumers in the technological innovation adoption cycle. Either way, there would seem to be an ensuing schism between those actually dying—or those memorializing them—and those who define their sentimental events primarily through digital platforms. The fact that no firm metrics are made available or otherwise published by online obituaries, memorials, or digital necropolises may, in turn, dissuade mourners from blindly uploading content for fear that the site may not be in the best financial health and therefore offer the same degree of permanence as an offline, physical memorial. In cases where mourners choose to simply supplement existing offline content, as many funeral services providers now do through the use of secondary, online registries and condolence books, the purpose-specific digital necropolis faces an additional threat to its sustainability: social media.

The role played by social media as an outlet for remembrance proves especially probative when considering the epistemology of permanence in online memorials. It is additionally relevant in the context of recent scholarship on both how online personas are generally vulnerable to intrusion and how estate planning now often encompasses detailed instructions for executors on the management or dismantling of social media profiles upon death, the "digital afterlife."[32] In fact, the prevalence of social media sites and their ability to transform web connectivity and interactivity, as well as both user experience and expectations, cannot be overstated in the context of revolutionizing digital remembrance.

Having helped define the shift to Web 2.0 (the internet as a building platform where discernible places can be constructed) and even Web 3.0 (the current Semantic Web), social media has, during its brief history, systematically changed the complexion and cultural impact of the multimedia, online memorial. While earlier and conceptual iterations of social media endemic to the early World Wide Web (IRC, ICQ, MSN Messenger, etc.), including some that still remain in existence (Friendster, Myspace, etc.), could be used for disseminating death notices and even creating basic memorials, the ability of some of the current prevailing platforms to supplant traditional forms of remembrance is really just beginning. Facebook in particular merits specific scholarly attention in this context, if for no other reason, due to its massive digital footprint and ability to pervade widespread daily communication among a disparity of demographic and psychographic groups. As such, Facebook has a forged an identifiable and substantive relationship to the dead that merits further investigation.

Examining the intersection between Facebook as the most pervasive iteration of social media on record and the symbolic itinerary of funerary writing reveals a system where one of two recurring scenarios defines the prevailing culture of digital remembrance. The first involves new user profiles that are created from scratch to serve as memorials and solicit condolences, epitaphic reflections, and the democratic upload of multimedia content such as photographs that capture the true essence of the deceased, rather than the more formal images that typically compromise funerary portraiture. It should also be noted that, unlike specifically designed online memorial and obituary sites—what I've already described as digital versus digitized memorials—the construction and maintenance of Facebook tributes carry no associated costs, whether compulsory or voluntary; they also typically supplement some other form of memorialization or funerary narrative. The second type of recurring Facebook memorial profile involves profiles harvested from the dead by the living to serve as impromptu tributes. Notably and disturbingly, attendance at these memorial profiles is not necessarily contingent on the visitor having an existing acquaintance with the deceased or their family. Sometimes known as "lurkers" or the online versions of cemetery trespassers,[33] these types of random and often morbidly curious visitors have more recently been categorized the online equivalent of "emotional rubberneckers."[34] Given the inherently voyeuristic architecture of Facebook and of digital culture generally, curious and sometimes perversely intentioned visitors congregating around digital memorials seem to be increasingly indulging in an online version of what is now recognized as a form of pop mourning known as "dark tourism."

Describing road trips and other forms of travel, both foreign and domestic, to sites of death and tragedy that simultaneously serve as vehicles for catharsis, vicarious trauma, and simple morbid curiosity, dark tourism has been a well-established but unnamed industry for decades, and with online versions more recently exposing the practice as another facet of funeral kitsch. Distinct from pilgrimages to places of burial or sites of tragedy that serve an ideological or spiritual purpose, dark tourism shrinks space and time to configure sentimentality into something tangible and therefore marketable.[35] More importantly, dark tourism is about mourning as consumption and is expressly public, rather than intimately private.

The enmeshing of memorial sites and digital obituaries with social media is thus something of a natural pairing, with Facebook memorials thus representing a form of kitschification that has evolved simultaneously with other forms of funerary merchandising. As visitors *qua* consumers are to some extent able *consume* death through dark tourism, its digital manifestations in places like Facebook are often minimized as innocuous forms of nostalgia. In fact, the internet's ability to cultivate new nostalgia industries has been self-evident since the dawn of the web. In addition to the online auctioning of memorabilia, the dissemination of old television episodes and other media esoterica, and the ability to use social media to reconnect with persons from our past, the veritable nostalgia industry prorogated by digital culture, and social media in specific, makes the web a natural setting for digital remembrance and dark tourism as a binary nostalgia industry.[36]

Where dark tourism can be understood, whether online or offline, as amounting to a layperson's "field work" of sites of death, disaster, and atrocity,[37] dark tourism and social media serve as concomitant outlets for the irrationally nostalgic economization of death and remembrance. The marriage between death and remembrance in a digital forum thus represents the inevitable terminus of the secularization of death that occurred during the 19th century, in part through the way industrialization changed not only newspaper reportage and served as the genesis of the obituary column, but also with respect to internment practices. The shift from intramural churchyard burials to the more familiar cemetery landscape tradition—at least in America as a result of a comparative abundance of available land—made expanding the scale of funerary rites more feasible as compared to existing rituals in Europe.[38] Initially undertaken for hygienic purposes given the horrific conditions of most city churchyard cemeteries, the shift to professionally designed and maintained cemeteries marked a needed improvement in terms of attracting visitors while signaling an important shift toward the economic privatization of mourning rituals. With this privatization came the emancipation of the dead from the church and their becoming a commodity within the secular free market.

Once a private grave or site of personal tragedy is parlayed, for whatever reason, into a locale of collective interest and elevated to a dark tourism destination in the offline world, popularity is gauged through the statistics gleaned—and dollars derived—from such free-market attendance. As certain sites maintain or increase their popularity and are nominated as preferred places to visit, one is then prompted question what happens to those less popular sites attracting less traffic. Additionally, one might consider how the ensuing differences in numbers reflect what can be interpreted as the reification of a public memory, or, more accurately, the *popular* memory.

As the distillation of the post-Jacksonian obituary tradition, popular memory amounts to the "personally situated interpretations" that reflect the language communities of those most readily affected by death once assembled in an online forum. In other words, these are the death stories of "ordinary people" and their need for social texts that speak to their daily reality.[39] Popular memory is therefore publicly authored and functions in the digital milieu—like a type of funerary crowdsourcing—as the proverbial shared file of death in the online age, as well as the preferred, readily marketable, and most familiar narrative of remembrance. In this sense, *popular* denotes a vernacular version of collective memory that, as Bridget Fowler describes when discussing the evolution of the obituary from analog to digital form, is something "which emerges from the settled subordinate classes [. . .] linked to representative figures [. . .] linked to collective representations, carnival festivities, and to popular movements."[40]

Popular memory is, at its simplest, a form of collective remembrance whereby funerary metrics to some extent measure the value of lives, as well as what lives are ultimately deemed worthy of celebration and commemoration. In a purely digital context, the virtual memorial or obituary on its face appears to transmute remembrance into a commodity and equate solemnization with trendiness. Digital forms of remembrance ensure that no hypertext epitaph is ever read anonymously or privately, that no visit to a virtual graveside is ever done confidentially, as such acts now carry with them an inherent element of performance. Distilled from over two centuries of increasingly secular, economized, and multimediated forms of memorialization, the digital obituary content endemic to social media sites like Facebook represent digital modes of remembrance that, by their very design, ensure quantifiable and empirical evidence of public attendance and fandom that approximates the circuits of consumption established by dark tourism. In examining Facebook memorials as sites of dark tourism in earnest, it is popular memory that ultimately prompts users to elect certain profiles and memorials for visitation over others, thus continuing the self-perpetuating cycle of evidenced fandom and elevating specific deaths—and lives—over others. More specifically, the reflections and grave goods left by visitors at select Facebook memorials engender a funerary system controlled by a particular type of popular memory and quantifiable trendiness best described as a "sepulchral hierarchy."

Sepulchral hierarchy can be defined as the process by which online obituaries and memorials enable the development of status systems among the digital dead; it describes the manner in which the dead are, seemingly at random in many cases, digitally "celebritized" and how digital remembrance can be used to empirically measure the value, whether real or perceived, of a life through tabulated visits and published records of attendance. This hierarchy additionally influences the manner in which memory and the performance of mourning converge to quantify traditionally qualitative and anecdotal qualities, such as virtue, nobility, charity, and kindness. Now operating on a sliding scale of fandom that is measured through visitor attendance not only in the way of metrics monitored behind the scenes, but also through "likes" and other forms of electronic endorsement that are proactively disclosed and expressly public, the perceived egalitarianism of death that was the original objective of funerary writing in the Western tradition[41] has largely been purged. For instance, the Facebook memorial page created in honor of 15-year-old Amanda Todd following her well-publicized suicide in Port Coquitlam, British Columbia, in 2012 amassed hundreds of thousands of "likes" within months of its inception, and within a year had surpassed 1 million. Todd's Facebook memorial is also something of a watershed in terms of the proneness of well-publicized or popular digital necrologies to vandalism. The fact that Todd's suicide was itself highly publicized—her posting an online video prior to hanging herself in which she cited ongoing torment at the hands of bullies as pushing her to take her own life—elevated interest in the profile from the outset. With that interest came a proportionate number of visitors who sought to duplicate, satirize, desecrate, or compromise the memorial. This included vandals from as far away as New Zealand who, in lacking the technological expertise to disrupt service to the site, instead mired it in offensive images and messages—the digital equivalent of memorial graffiti.

Beyond mere "hits" or "likes" as verifiable markers of popularity and visitor traffic to a site as tracked by webmasters, site metrics can prove misleading and in themselves may not always reflect genuine visitation or reverential attendance. In some cases, attendance can actually be artificially inflated by a process known as hypertunneling, when visitors arrive at a site by chance and then leave soon after to continue browsing and delving further into the cyberspace with no real-end destination—a course of events normally reflected in a site's recorded bounce rate and exit rate. Visits to memorials or graveyards in the offline world are often similarly transient or inadvertent given that they often double as places of general public access and transit, offering nonmourners a place of solitude, reflection, or physical exercise by virtue of their utilitarian and multidimensional design. The difference is that, in the offline world, this type of secondary access is, like primary access by mourners, not something that is intentionally tracked by the custodians of the space, nor overtly advertised by visitors; this is, of course, not the case in the online world where all memorials are by default dark tourist attractions that track attendance by their very design.

With respect to social media sites such as Facebook, sepulchral hierarchy not only nominates specific names for adulation and artificially inflated popularity, but in doing so, also ascribes visitors with a certain prestige, elevating their own status through such postmortem associations, even when these visits occur by happenstance or incidentally due to some other browsing activity. As visitors, perhaps referred to improvised Facebook memorials through friends or the automated recommendations of the network itself, congregate en masse at these locations, participation in memorial forums such as discussion threads and wall postings serves to enhance the social capital of the visitors through their ingratiating themselves with memorials that offer visible evidence of being popular; consequently, the visitors themselves are vicariously popular, involved, and stakeholders in the hierarchal process.

Once again, as with many of the other defining features of digital memorials and obituaries, this phenomenon is not without its analog antecedents; Charles Dickens noted what he called the socially charged "fat atmosphere of funerals" that developed in response to their secularization and acquisition by the commercial press.[42] This yearning for inclusiveness in the memorialization process, and participation in the rituals of death and memory, also approximates a digital extension of what—during the same period back in America—has since been coined "necro citizenship."[43] In brief, necro citizenship describes the industrialized shift in the West toward the collaborative or collective authorship of public memory through death narratives, including how such narratives create psychographic and ideological groups who define themselves by death as a vehicle for solidarity, community, and freedom.

In a digital format, necro citizenship takes on exaggerated forms where, like other types of artificial or hyperinflation, it is wholly unsustainable and demands a market correction—a figurative click of the refresh button. The hyperinflation of online narrative content and its ability to ultimately be counterproductive and render feedback useless—and thus imperil digital platforms either built or otherwise dependent on such content as a matter of credibility—was first identified in context not of online memorials but of online auctions. Well before the rise of the Semantic Web where the open sourcing of sites came to define user experience, seller feedback on auction sites was ultimately found to be so disproportionately and hyperbolically positive that it actually proved detrimental to credibility and, by extension, sustainability among overly popular sellers.[44] As digital forums and digital cultures evolved under this model to become communities grounded in "cyberbole,"[45] the digital memorial and virtual forms of remembrance, from obituary authorship to grave attendance, are likely the worst offenders in terms of disingenuous content.

It is this exaggeration and reconciliation of earlier traditions, most notably the post-Jacksonian memorialization system and the manner in which dark tourism destigmatized the idea of funerary kitsch and death collectibles, that draw visitors seeking membership and looking to ingratiate themselves with the dead with no lasting investment. In this sense, popular memory—like nostalgia—is antithetical to real memory and is more accurately described as a longing for other people's memories, or for the idea of a specific time and place that may or may not have existed outside of its digital iteration. This is in part why the future of a sustainable and renewable digital afterlife is one not grounded in empirical indicators of popularity that might warrant continued kitschification, but in the modalities of new media.

While digitization and new media are frequently—and erroneously—used interchangeably, the reality is that the digital amounts to "informationalism" and the exploitation and economization of information which in turn engenders the end of the creative process.[46] Conversely, new media is "new" only in that it combines existing, physical media with a web interface, yet never liquidates the original medium during this convergence process.[47] While new media is to some extent reliant on informationalism and digitization as a means of numerical constants to standardize virtual content,[48] the spatial sense wrought by new media is rooted in the fact that we have from the outset equated the web with physical places known and intimately familiar to us. The fact that digital memorials go to such great lengths to try and replicate the experiences of the physical world as accurately as possible suggests that the offline referent prevails as the intrinsically preferred form of remembrance.

Given that the web itself is really in a natal state when looking at the speed with which it is evolving and leaving behind earlier versions, modes of digital remembrance will no doubt undergo a variety of transmutations and experimental versions before collective expectations of what exactly constitutes permanence are stabilized. In the meantime, all evidence suggests that memorial practices that espouse purely digital forms at the expense of either establishing or preserving offline analogs are overlooking one of the key tenets of the web's initial conceptualization. Specifically, the web was designed not to replace but to defy territoriality. As such, there are no *places* of remembrance in cyberspace, only *spaces*. Like the vacuum of outer space, this is a fluid domain that expands and contracts and is continuously in flux—a space that because it is infinite, can offer neither finality nor permanence as we know it.

Notes

1. "Grimmies," *Society of Professional Obituary Writers*. Society of Professional Obituary Writers.com, 2014, http://www.societyofprofessionalobituarywriters.org/the-grimmies.html. Accessed January 16, 2014.

2. Marilyn Johnson, *The Dead Beat: Lost Souls, Lucky Stiffs, and the Perverse Pleasures of Obituaries* (New York: Harper Collins, 2006), 127, 187–88.

3. Mike Nichols, dir., *Closer*, Columbia Pictures, 2004. Film.

4. Harold A. Innis, *Empire and Communications* (Toronto: University of Toronto Press, 1950), 5–7.

5. That is, insubstantial paper-based products that could be produced, transported, and circulated cheaply and quickly across massive distances on one hand, and stone or metal-based products that were static in space but built to endure the elements and remain intact for centuries on the other.

6. Harold A. Innis, *Changing Concepts of Time* (Toronto: University of Toronto Press, 1952), 15.

7. Kathleen Fitzpatrick, *Planned Obsolescence: Publishing, Technology, and the Future of the Academy* (New York: New York University Press, 2011).

8. Aaron Hess, "In Digital Remembrance: Vernacular Memory and the Rhetorical Construction of Web Memorials," *Media, Culture & Society* 29, no. 5 (2007): 812–30. Print. 812.

9. Armando Petrucci, *Writing the Dead: Death & Writing Strategies in the Western Tradition* (Stanford, CA: Stanford University Press, 1998), 98.

10. Vincent Mosco, *The Digital Sublime: Myth, Power, and Cyberspace* (Cambridge, MA: MIT Press, 2004), 155–56.

11. Johnson, *The Dead Beat*, 31.

12. Petrucci, *Writing the Dead*, 28.

13. Johnson, *The Dead Beat*, 10.

14. Janice Hume, *Obituaries in American Culture* (Jackson: University of Mississippi Press, 2000), 55–56.

15. Petrucci, *Writing the Dead*, 65.

16. Carolyn Kitsch and Janice Hume, *Journalism in a Culture of Grief* (New York: Routledge, 2008), xiv.

17. Hume, *Obituaries in American Culture*, 39.

18. Johnson, *The Dead Beat*, 46.

19. Marshall McLuhan, *Understanding Media: The Extensions of Man* (New York: McGraw-Hill, 1964), 8–9.

20. Mosco, *The Digital Sublime*, 155.

21. Marita Sturken, *Tourists of History: Memories, Kitsch, & Consumerism from Oklahoma City to Ground Zero* (Durham, NC: Duke University Press, 2007), 19.

22. Ibid., 14.

23. Ibid., 110.

24. *Cherished Lives*. Cherished Lives.com, 2009. http://www.cherishedlives.com/. Accessed March 4, 2009.

25. *Virtual Grave*. Virtual Grave.eu, 2014, http://virtualgrave.eu/. Accessed April 11, 2014.

26. *My Cemetery*. My Cemetery.com, 2014, http://www.mycemetery.com. Accessed April 12, 2014.

27. Bridget Fowler, *The Obituary as Collective Memory* (New York: Routledge, 2007), 110.

28. Ibid., 111.

29. The recent government shutdown resulted in the curtailment of some services at Arlington Cemetery, though access to the graveyard itself was unaffected and visitations to interments continued unabated. See "Arlington National Cemetery Will Be Open If the Federal Government Shuts Down," *The Official Website of Arlington National Cemetery,* September 30, 2013, http://www.arlingtoncemetery.mil/news/NewsItem .aspx?ID?376a2906-6584-4468-89e5-0c697e28f662.

30. Hess, "In Digital Remembrance," Print. 816.

31. Ibid., 820.

32. Rhiannon Williams, "Social Media Users Warned to Prepare for Digital Afterlife," *The Telegraph,* October 21, 2013, http://www.telegraph.co.uk/technology/news/10393996/ Social-media-users-warned-to-prepare-for-digital-afterlife.html. Accessed January 16, 2014.

33. Johnson, *The Dead Beat*, 184–85.

34. Jocelyn M. DeGroot, "'For Whom the Bell Tolls': Emotional Rubbernecking in Facebook Memorial Groups," *Death Studies* 38, no. 2 (2014): 79–84, 79.

35. John Lennon and Malcolm Foley, *Dark Tourism* (London: Continuum, 2000), 81–82.

36. Originally declared a mental illness in the 17th century, nostalgia-from the Greek *nostos,* meaning to return home and by extension, homesickness-was first used to describe the melancholia associated with prolonged periods away from one's primary place of residence. Industrialization and changing ideas about home and work, however, soon shifted the understanding of nostalgia from being a spatial dislocation to a temporal dislocation, with a specific time rather than a specific place being the home we long for.

37. Lennon and Foley, *Dark Tourism*, 3.

38. James Stevens Curl, *The Victorian Celebration of Death* (Detroit: Partridge Press, 1972), 169.

39. Hess, "In Digital Remembrance," 815.

40. Fowler, *The Obituary as Collective Memory*, 33–34.

41. Petrucci, *Writing the Dead*, 24.

42. Curl, *The Victorian Celebration of Death*, 179.

43. Russ Castronovo, *Necro Citizenship: Death, Eroticism, and the Public Sphere in the Nineteenth-Century United States* (Durham, NC: Duke University Press, 2001), 15.

44. David Weinberger, *Small Pieces Loosely Joined: A Unified Theory of the Web* (Cambridge, MA: Perseus, 2002), 5.

45. Mosco, *The Digital Sublime,* 43, 45–46.

46. Manuel Castells, *The Rise of the Network Society* (Cambridge, MA: Blackwell, 2000), 99.

47. Lev Manovich, *The Language of New Media* (Cambridge, MA: MIT Press, 2001), 20.

48. Ibid., 28–30.

Chapter 6

The Restless Dead in the Digital Cemetery

*Bjorn Nansen, Michael Arnold,
Martin Gibbs, and Tamara Kohn[1]*

Introduction

Following the emergence of online memorials or so-called virtual cemeteries and the growing popularity of memorialized profiles on social media platforms, researchers from a range of disciplines have become increasingly interested in how new technologies stimulate new ways of enacting and experiencing the commemoration of death. Despite the breadth of research, studies of death in the digital domain have predominantly focused upon the cultural status, meaning, and practices relating to death as they are performed *within* digital environments. However, following innovations in locative media, ubiquitous computing, and the Internet of Things,[2] digital technologies are increasingly *intertwined* with physical environments. Just as digital technologies are intertwined with the materiality of the home, the city, and the body, so they are intertwined with the materiality of the cemetery, the headstone, and the coffin.

In this chapter, we explore the emergence and growth of *the digital cemetery* by exploring some recent examples of digital applications, products, and services. Here, the rituals associated with interring the dead so that they may rest or repose within the cemetery shifts to accommodate an increasingly "restless" posthumous existence. The restless dead are both emerging through these hybrid interfaces of the digital and the physical, materialized in more lively forms of media and exhumed within a network of social and technical connections previously delimited by cemetery geography and physical inscription in stone. We argue here that the deployment of digital cemetery technologies points toward an individuation of the commemoration of death (in contrast to an institutionalized commemoration), toward an ongoing temporality (in contrast to permanence), and toward animation (in contrast to repose).

Death and the Emerging World of Digitally Enlivened Objects

Digital platforms are increasingly important for contemporary practices associated with commemorating the deceased. Just as the internet is implicated in the changing customs and rituals of everyday social life, it is implicated in changing customs and rituals associated with death and commemoration. Unsurprisingly, digital commemoration emerged as the internet became readily accessible and an integral part of people's communicative practices. Digital commemorations first took the form of online memorials in the late 1990s, when memorial websites were created and hosted by families and friends. Since then, the user-friendly tools and interfaces of Web 2.0 platforms, which allow people to more easily create, author, and publish content,[3] have enabled digital commemoration to grow in popularity and to diversify in form. Many people are now appropriating the general-purpose resources of social networking sites to connect with others and share in the digital commemoration of the dead. Platforms include: tribute pages and memorials hosted on specialist memorial websites (e.g., Legacy.com); blogs created to commemorate loved ones; videos posted on video-sharing sites such as YouTube; repurposed and memorialized pages on social networking sites (e.g., Facebook); and virtual-world commemorations and ceremonies.[4]

In tandem with the practice itself, there is a growing body of research addressing issues around the dead in online environments. Following the emergence of online memorials and their growth through social media platforms (aka virtual cemeteries[5]), studies have explored topics such as the practical management of digital assets and estates;[6] the ways new technologies effects the experience of mourning, and how social support takes shape in online networks;[7] and how the dead continue to persist and participate within the platforms and protocols of social media.[8] Among other things this research has found that posting comments on the Walls of dead Facebook users, often addressing the deceased directly, is a common and well-documented practice. For many people, interaction through social networking technologies like Facebook has become a large part of how they maintain social presence in the lives of others. Similarly, the practices of posting to and addressing the dead through social media networks, maintains the social presence of the death within the social networks of the living.

It has been noted that these new forms of social persistence are dynamic, or, in our terms, animated and temporal. They are *animated* in the sense that the dead are no longer in repose, but remain socially active. They maintain a social presence and a place in social life which is animated as it is engaged and addressed within the social networks of the living. They are *temporal* because they are worldly, secular, and mundane engagements unmediated by church or sacrament, as well as being relatively temporary, impermanent, and effervescent. These new forms of digital commemoration therefore contrast in important ways with gravestones, epitaphs, or printed obituaries, by providing more opportunities for social engagement, and for change and development over time.[9]

Tim Hutchings describes the shift accompanying Web 2.0 social media applications as one where memorials are no longer created within designated "virtual cemeteries" or as stand-alone websites, both of which have "clear parallels with the role of the physical cemetery, which relocates the deceased to a place which is accessible but separate from the spaces usually occupied by the living."[10] In contrast, in a Web 2.0 environment, it is simple to convert existing social media profiles into memorials and this "integrates their mourning practices directly into their ongoing social relationships."[11] The possibilities for maintaining the social presence of a person following her or his death afforded by social media has prompted researchers within human-computer interaction to consider how the dead may be accommodated within the design of digital networks.[12] This research has predominantly focused upon the cultural status, meaning, and practices of commemoration *within* digital environments. It has largely been concerned with new digital platforms and practices, leaving aside the implications of digital technologies for traditional physical places and materials associated with death. However, digital technologies are increasingly entwined with physical environments and everyday practices with implications for commemoration and memorialization; implications that should be addressed.

Computing technologies are increasingly moving beyond their historical desktop location and screen-based graphical user interface. They are now mobile rather than desk-bound, and they are increasingly attached to the body or embedded in all kinds of places and objects. There are a range of terms that attempt to capture this shifting paradigm of computer interaction, including locative media,[13] ubiquitous computing,[14] and the Internet of Things.[15] While these terms have different inflections or emphasis, they nevertheless share a common interest: trying to understand what the increasing entanglements of physical and digital mean for our everyday lives and relationships.

Locative media explores the intersection of digital technologies with place, while ubiquitous computing imagines augmenting everyday objects and embedding computing in everyday environments with technologies for sensing, monitoring, tracking, and actuating. GPS-enabled smartphones provide the most evident example of locative media and ubiquitous computing. The more recent Internet of Things has a vision for a world of more intimately entangled relations between digital and physical, anticipating the ways objects will be interconnected through internet protocols to create networks of smart objects sharing data.[16]

The digital augmentation of everyday artifacts means that computer interactions are increasingly embedded through both the physical and social environment. New questions are raised about designing for a world of digitally enlivened objects[17]—a world where once passive things can conceivably become more animated or responsive to human action through the interactivity enabled by computing technologies.[18] The horizon of locative, ubiquitous, and ambient computing suggests that information sensing, processing, and networking will spread into the physical world and operate at multiple scales, from the body, to the building, to the city, to the globe. While this ubiquity addresses the geographic distribution of computation everywhere/everyware,[19] it also implies possibilities for embedding computational capacities into the physical stuff of *every-thing*. This entanglement of objects and informatics—a computational materiality—does not simply apply to the explosion of new smart appliances and gadgets. It also provides a breadth of possibilities for digitally mediating or augmenting the ordinary and existing everyday material objects that populate our daily social lives as well as our deaths and rituals of commemoration.

Digitizing the Cemetery

There is of course a prehistory to the entangled phenomenon of the digital cemetery. For example, the so-called Talking Tombstone with a built-in screen emerged in the late 1970s, and it was publicized in a 1977 issue of *People* magazine. This article introduced John Dilks, a computer engineer from New Jersey, and his invention, a solar-powered headstone containing a recording device and video display screen, to play audio and visual biographical information, as well optional extras including a sensor to activate the media when someone approached the gravesite in the cemetery. The product was priced at US$39,500 for a vandal-proof headstone covered by bulletproof glass,[20] and so it remained an expensive and largely inaccessible (even if desired) option for adding media to gravestones.

Further, the digital mediation of commemoration is not limited to the cemetery, and forms of digitally mediated funeral service utilizing slide-shows, podcasts, and streaming video are now common. Shifting to more personal and individualized celebrations of life rather than formal ritu-alized religious services marking a death,[21] it is increasingly common to see a PowerPoint loop displaying biographical images of the deceased at a funeral, while the practice of streaming funeral services online is also growing—and the funeral industry is responding by facilitating these systems.[22]

In cataloging the following examples of digital applications, products, and services mediating the cemetery, we are also suggesting that, collec-tively, these forms of hybridity manifest a shift away from traditional ritual structures managed by institutions, representations of the permanence of death, and representations of the dead in repose. Rather, they manifest a shift toward highly individualized commemorative forms that maintain the social presence of the dead through time in an environment that is increas-ingly mediated and animated by digital technologies.

Living Headstones

Building on the legacy of the "Talking Tombstone" is the deployment of internet-connected, screen-embedded, and digitally tagged headstones that are able to connect to digital content (e.g., Living Headstones).[23] An example of this updated version is the "Living Headstone," which works by embedding a quick response (QR) code on a gravestone. QR and RFID (radio frequency identity) tags are machine-readable labels, like barcodes, that attach to physical objects so that these objects articulate with digital links and content. They have been most commonly used for supply-chain product tracking and logistics, but following the ubiquity of smartphones, which enables digital tags to be scanned to open a website, QR tags are now used for many purposes (e.g., marketing products, accessing informa-tion on historical sites, paying parking fees). They have become important conduits in the digital intertwining of the physical world. QR tags are often used to annotate objects to create new forms of tangible and social interac-tion;[24] and now posthumous interaction as well.

The Living Headstone, for example, attaches or engraves a QR code to a headstone, which is then readable by smartphone and connected to a unique, personalized online memorial page. This digital space is "similar to a personal Facebook page," where,

> a "Living Headstone" archive site contains information you and friends can add about your loved one, such as: an obituary, family heritage and history, photos, comments by friends and relatives and even links to share content on popular social sites such as Facebook or Twitter.[25]

Location-based information for the gravesite and a map to locate the memorial in the cemetery is also provided in this effort to create a hybrid interactive gravestone. The designers describe this as an interactive "living" memorial that is a legacy for future generations. It is clearly individualized, subject to change through time, and seeks to animate the dead.

Digitally Augmented coffins

> Introducing the CataCombo Sound System; a revolutionary customised sound system for audiophiles on the other side.[26]

While QR-enabled headstones have been reported widely and are, in many ways, quite a modest way to digitally mediate the cemetery, another recent design invention has imagined a more intimate and peculiar way to integrate new technologies with traditional artifacts: by digitally augmenting coffins with entertainment systems. For example, Pause Ljud & Bild, a Swedish audio equipment company, has released a product called the CataCombo Sound System, which integrates an audio system into a coffin to allow people to "embrace your passion for music in this life, and the next."[27] Promising to "redefine [. . .] life after death entertainment," the CataCombo comprises a two-way speaker system, Intel core processor, 8-inch subwoofer, and a music server that connects to a 7-inch LCD monitor attached to the headstone. The monitor displays the playlist and the current song that is currently playing to visitors in the cemetery. The system is managed from the Cata Play app to create a customized audio file, which sources a playlist from Spotify that can be created by the deceased prior to death and updated posthumously by the living.[28]

With this digital coffin augmentation, a visitor to the gravesite of a loved one is able to view an audio playlist on a screen embedded in a headstone, showing "what song is playing six feet under."[29] The screen may also show images of the deceased while they were alive. Whether the volume of the music playing below the ground can be adjusted and heard aboveground by visitors is unclear, as is whether their customers really believe the dead are being entertained. Still, the intention is to suggest that the dead can continue to be involved in the activities of the living, through the monitor and the shared playlist.

In addition to computer-mediated coffins and headstones, the practice of augmenting the material culture of death is spreading to the marketing of individually customized cremation urns which use computer-assisted design and 3D imaging and printing technologies. A U.S. company called Cremation Solutions brings the individuation of commemoration to a new level by using these technologies to manufacture commemorative urns shaped to look like the head of the deceased person.[30]

Using 3D imaging techniques based on photographs and facial recognition software, the company is offering a small "keepsake" version for US$600, or a life-sized head urn for $2,600. On their website, the company promotes this customized urn as a means to ensure, "You will never again have to worry that you might forget what your loved one looked like." Nor are these customized cremation urns limited to replicas of the deceased, but can also be customized "in the image of your loved one or favorite celebrity or hero, even President Obama!"[31]

Alongside these individual commercial products is the growing use of global positioning system (GPS) and geographic information system (GIS) technologies within cemeteries to produce digital and interactive maps to assist the management and exploration of burial plots (e.g., http://www.cimscemeterysoftware.com/). A GIS uses computer technology to manage, analyze, and visualize spatial data. GISs are used in a wide range of application and contexts, such as urban planning and traffic management, and are now being applied to the geography of cemeteries.

GIS is predominantly being used in cemeteries to map the location of graves of the dead and to assist with cemetery organization. Typically, the coordinates of graves are mapped, and data gleaned from the headstones, such as name, age, and sex, are tagged. However, this mapping and visualization are also being enhanced with additional information, such as historical or personal narratives relevant to the site or deceased. As a data management tool, GIS is also being used to assist with preservation and to help manage maintenance and conservation of the site.[32]

These systems are used, too, by cemetery visitors to search for the plots of loved ones as well as for genealogical research. An example of such a system is in the U.S. Arlington National Cemetery, where GIS has been used to create an interactive map available on a website or mobile app for visitors to search and locate specific grave markers.[33] According to the Cemetery's official announcement, in the future, the ANC Explorer app will offer features such as emergency and event notifications, restroom, and water fountain locations, shuttle stops, and self-guided tours.[34]

These spatial information systems are not limited to cemeteries, however, with applications extending to a Roadside Memorial Marker Project: "The Roadside Memorial project is an online photo-journal data-base of roadside memorial displays from the U.S.A. around the world, so that the lives represented by these memorials may be honored, and the stories told."[35] This project is also collaborative, with users able to submit information, images, and stories about loved ones who have died in traffic accidents. Thus, it does more than map the coordinates of the death, but it also annotates that location with digital content.

While there are different kinds of traditional cemeteries (e.g., churchyard, monumental, and lawn) and while customs for treating the body of the dead vary historically and across different cultures and religions, cemeteries, in general terms, can be characterized as spatially located places and defined areas for burying or interring the dead. Within the cemetery, the locations of the dead are typically marked, presenting inscriptions of brief biographic information and tributes to the deceased. In a sense, then, the cemetery is a database of the dead in which the dead are organized in a collective and managed fashion. It is not surprising, then, that digital management systems such as GIS have been applied to different cemetery sites in order to assist with this database management.

Materialities of Death

Graves and related artifacts are not only sites for storage of the dead, but they also provide a material and geographic focus for mourning and remembrance. Consequently, it is not surprising that traditional headstones or gravestones have been made of durable material such as granite, marble, bluestone, and the like; nor is it surprising that inscriptions are carved directly into the stone and are often made more legible with gold-leaf, the most stable of metals. The materiality of gravestones is designed to last for a very long time.

Yet, traditional inscriptions carved on graves were, and remain, limited in their mediating capacity. They are oriented primarily at identification, providing, in most cases, familial context, dates of birth and death, and perhaps religious affiliation. Grave inscriptions provide a stranger (as opposed to a family member or friend) with few clues, prompts, or props that might guide their response to the memorial and thus their response to the deceased. The grave's inscription is an identifier, providing a formal link to the dead, but relating relatively little instruction on the life that was lived. By and large, the inscriptions in themselves are formal in tone and do not call upon the visitor to emote.

The inscriptions on a gravesite memorial may be minimalist, but they are important and serve to position the deceased in relation to social structures of long standing—most commonly, family and religion. The individual is gone, but their place in society, its institutions, and its structures remain marked. The inscriptions speak to the world of the deceased, reminding the world of the deceased, and they are, in this sense, outward looking and objectified; they contextualize the deceased by positioning him or her in the context of important and ongoing institutions not of the deceased's making. They also tell us, the visitor, something about what family members value generally and, more particularly, what they valued about the deceased. The gravesite mediates memorialization through carved stone, minimal inscriptions, and position in place, to imply a mode of relations that is structured, objectified, formal, and intransient.

In contrast, online memorials have a different approach to temporality in that they are made of materials that are deliberately impermanent. Websites, internet hosts, domain names, network protocols, mark-up languages, software, and electronic hardware are all artifacts that have relatively short life spans. They are all subject to more frequent and more radical change than stone. Online memorial sites also differ from traditional gravesites in that they comprise extensive inscriptions that range across many medias and genres. They are animated rather than in repose. At their most extensive, the memorial site animates the dead through the presentation of thousands of words of biography, hundreds of images, poems, stories and anecdotes, music tracks, and video clips. The memorial site buzzes with sensory and emotional stimuli. Many clues and prompts are given to the life that was lived. Visitors to the site, strangers and friends alike, are encouraged to emote. The text is dialogical rather than formal, particularly on "comments" and "tributes" pages, and the deceased is often addressed directly, in the first person, rather than simply being publically identified and introduced.

Like the headstone, web memorials also pay due regard to family connection, religion, and profession, but in addition to this objectified, structured orientation, web inscriptions also serve to position the deceased in an individualized network of subjective and intersubjective relations. The inscriptions in online memorials will typically be authored by many people and do not remain static once authored but continue to evolve over time through more collective contributions. Family may well retain editorial control over the site, but all family members, intimates, friends, workmates, acquaintances, and, in some case, strangers, will each be invited to contribute to the inscriptions. In addition to family relations, the web memorial will reference and detail these extensive networks of friends, workmates, acquaintances, pets, hobbies, sporting interests, musical tastes, and the like, providing a subjective and intersubjective context for identity memorialization that is informal rather than formal, interpolates social agency rather than social structure, and is subjective and intersubjective rather than institutional. Online memorials, therefore, imply a mode of relations that is quite different—a mode of relations that is networked, distributed, individualized, subjective, and fluid. Yet, the durability of online memorials, through servers, platforms, storage, and administration, is not guaranteed. The online memorial is temporal—it is both secular and transient.

As we have seen, however, these two quite different environments are capable of being hybridized, and, in the near-future, may no longer be separate. At the same time as people call for the creation of a sequestered space for mourning the dead separate from the practices of the living within social media platforms such as Facebook,[36] the digital-material hybridization of the cemetery has consequences for the ways cemeteries and material memorials such as headstones are understood and experienced.

From Requiem and Repose to Restless and Raucous

The word *cemetery* comes from the Greek word meaning "sleeping place," and the rituals and metaphors attending the burial and commemoration of the dead are infused by this etymology. For example, a Requiem or Requiem Mass (aka Mass for the Dead) is celebrated for the repose of the soul of the deceased. The Requiem comes from the Latin noun noun *requies*, to "rest, repose," and it begins with the words *Requiem aeternam dona eis, Domine*—"Grant them eternal rest, O Lord."

Similarly, studies of material anthropology of death have shown that the iconography of the cemetery heavily emphasizes sleep.[37] The anthropological work of Elizabeth Hallam and Jenny Hockey describes the prevalence and style of sleep symbolism in the material culture of death:

> "[S]leep" is the domain that many Westerners draw upon, metaphorically, to think about and manage death. In this context, material cultures of death include churchyards full of the stone "beds" in which the dead lie in their

white nightdress shrouds, stretched out on their backs in familial proximity to those they shared a bed with in life. The coherence of this system of metaphoric entailments is extended to the behaviour of living visitors who keep their voices down and take care not to step on the graves' flowery coverlets.[38]

The examples of digital mediation and augmentation of the cemetery and the material culture of death begin to challenge this understanding. The image of the dead in sleep or repose is challenged by the intermingling of traditional commemorative spaces and places with lively, dynamic, digital technologies that deploy many and multiple media. This mediation results in a vast increase in information and media forms (text, image, sounds) as well as their networking within and beyond the cemetery, creating a more raucous site and a more restless afterlife. The use of rich multimedia may help "bring to life" that person at the grave, but it also disturbs the traditional and sequestered notions and associated imagery of rest and repose.

Conclusion: The Material and Symbolic Mediation of Remembrance

The material and symbolic mediation of remembrance, or memory-ializing the life lived, has evolved from the narratives of traditional epitaphs and eulogies, wakes and funerals, inscription in stone, on gravestones in cemeteries, all of which go back through the millennia, through to centuries-old obituaries printed and circulated in newspapers, using text and images to provide a richer though often formulaic narrative. They have evolved to today's social media, which can be seen as the latest phase in this process of remediating memories of the dead.[39] And, like general-purpose communication online, commemoration online offers a far more extensive range of audiovisual media for constructing narratives of the dead, as well as varied platforms providing affordances for collaboratively storing, transmitting, distributing, and circulating these memories.

The examples we have presented in this chapter reveal a range of ways digital technologies are mediating the physical space of the cemetery. In many ways, it is to be expected that such novel technologies would be adapted for different contexts including cemeteries, yet, despite the wide range of services and technologies, they are a novelty at this point of time. These hybrid forms are largely at the fringe, the companies developing the hybrids are speculative, and their products are curiosities rather than mainstream. The history of product innovation suggests that most are as likely to disappear as takeoff; however, it is also clear that these hybrids will be subject to ongoing innovation and will continue to appropriate new technologies in this space.

Despite their current novelty, we argue that, as a collective of design interventions, they provide a glimpse of the potential for a reconfigured and hybrid digital cemetery, all of which speaks to forms of commemoration that are increasingly individualized, temporal, and animated. Here, the rituals associated with interring the dead so that they may rest or repose within the cemetery for an eternity shift to an increasingly restless posthumous existence. The restless dead are emerging through these hybrid interfaces of digital and physical, materializing in more lively forms of media, and exhumed within a network of social and technical connections previously delimited by biological death, social institutions, cemetery geography, and physical inscription in stone.

Notes

1. This research was supported by funding from Australian Research Council (DP140101871).

2. "The Internet of Things" is a term used to refer to emerging systems for connecting everyday objects such as cars, electrical appliances, environmental sensors and controls, traffic lights, and road sensors to the Internet with an IP address and allowing them to communicate with other Internet-enabled systems and devices.

3. Paul Anderson, *What Is Web 2.0? Ideas, Technologies and Implications for Education* (JISC Technology and Standards Watch, 2007).

4. Martin Gibbs, Joji Mori, Michael Arnold, and Tamara Kohn, "Tombstones, Uncanny Monuments and Epic Quests: Memorials in World of Warcraft," *Game Studies* 12, no. 1 (2012).

5. Pamela Roberts, "Here Today and Cyberspace Tomorrow: Memorials and Bereavement Support on the Web," *Generations* 28, no. 2 (2004): 41–46.

6. Evan Carroll and John Romano, *Your Digital Afterlife: When Facebook, Flickr and Twitter are Your Estate, What's Your Legacy?* (Berkeley, CA: New Riders, 2011); Martin Gibbs, Craig Bellamy, Michael Arnold, Bjorn Nansen, and Tamara Kohn, "Digital Registers and Estate Planning," *Bulletin of Retirement and Estate Planning Bulletin*, September 2013, 63–66.

7. Miriam Moss, "Grief on the Web," *Omega: Journal of Death & Dying* 49, no. 1 (2004): 77–81; Kylie Veale, "Online Memorialisation: The Web as a Collective Memorial Landscape for Remembering the Dead," *Fibreculture* 3 (2004); Amanda L. Williams and Michael M.J. Merten, "Adolescents Online Social Networking Following the Death of a Peer," *Journal of Adolescent Research* 24, no. 1 (2009): 67–90.

8. Jed R. Brubaker and Gillian R. Hayes, "'We Will Never Forget You [online]': An Empirical Investigation of Post-Mortem MySpace Comments," in *Proceedings of Computer Supported Cooperative Work CSCW* (2011), 123–32; Tero Karppi, "Death Proof: on the Biopolitics and Noopolitics of Memorializing Dead Facebook Users," *Culture Machine* 14 (2013); Alice E. Marwick and Nicole B. Ellison, "'There Isn't Wifi in Heaven!' Negotiating Visibility on Facebook Memorial Pages," *Journal of Broadcasting and Electronic Media* 56,

no. 3 (2012): 378–400; Patrick Stokes, "Ghosts in the Machine: Do the Dead Live on in Facebook?" *Philosophy & Technology* 25, no. 3 (2012): 363–79.

9. Kirsten Foot, Barbara Warnick, and Steven M. Schneider, "Web-Based Memorializing after September 11: Toward a Conceptual Framework," *Journal of Computer-Mediated Communication* 11, no. 1 (2005): 72–96; Tamara Kohn, Martin Gibbs, Michael Arnold, and Bjorn Nansen, "Facebook and the Other: Administering to and Caring for the Dead Online," in *Responsibility,* ed. G. Hage (Melbourne: University of Melbourne Press, 2012), 128–41.

10. Tim Hutchings, "Wiring Death: Dying, Grieving and Remembering on the Internet," in *Emotion, Identity and Death: Mortality across Disciplines,* ed. D. Davies and C. Park (Farnham: Ashgate Publishing, 2012), 51.

11. Ibid.

12. Jed R. Brubaker and Janet Vertesi, "Death and the Social Network," Presented at the CHI 2010 Workshop on HCI at the End of Life: Understanding Death, Dying, and the Digital, Atlanta, GA, USA (2010); Michael Massimi and Ronald M. Baecker, "A Death in the Family: Opportunities for Designing Technologies for the Bereaved," in *Proceedings of the CHI 2010* (ACM Press, 2010), 1821–30; William Odom, Roger Harper, Abigail Sellen, David Kirk, and Richard Banks, "Passing On & Putting to Rest: Understanding Bereavement in the Context of Interactive Technologies," in *Proceedings of CHI 2010* (ACM Press, 2010), 1831–40.

13. Adriana de Souza e Silva and Jordan Frith, "Locative Mobile Social Networks: Mapping Communication and Location in Urban Spaces," *Mobilities* 5, no. 4 (2010): 485–505.

14. Adam Greenfield, *Everyware: The Dawning Age of Ubiquitous Computing* (New Riders Publishing, 2006).

15. Jesus Carretero and Daniel García, "The Internet of Things: Connecting the World," *Personal and Ubiquitous Computing* 17 (2013): 545–59.

16. Kevin Ashton, "That 'Internet of Things' Thing, in the Real World Things Matter More than Ideas," *RFID Journal* (2009), http://www.rfidjournal.com/articles/view?4986.

17. Beth Coleman, "Everything Is Animated: Pervasive Media and the Networked Subject," *Body & Society* 18 (2012): 79–98.

18. Mark Weiser, "The Computer of the 21st Century," *Scientific American* 265, no. 3 (1991): 66–75.

19. Greenfield, Everyware.

20. Gary Gumpert, *Talking Tombstones and Other Tales of the Media Age* (Oxford: Oxford University Press, 1988).

21. Kathleen Garces-Foley and Justin Holcomb, "Contemporary American Funerals: Personalizing Tradition," in *Death and Religion in a Changing World,* ed. K. Garces-Foley (Armonk, NY: ME Sharpe, 2005).

22. Tony Walter, Rachid Hourizi, Wendy Moncur, and Stacey Pitsillides, "Does the Internet Change How We Die and Mourn? Overview and Analysis," *Omega* 64, no. 4 (2011): 275–302.

23. Kathryn Vercillo, "QR Codes on Tombstones Provide Info about the Deceased," *Mobile Phone Reviews* (2011), http://www.dialaphone.co.uk/blog/2011/03/16/qr-codes-on-tombstones-provide-info-about-the-deceased/.

24. Einar Sneve Martinussen and Timo Arnall, "Designing with RFID," in *Proc. TEI 2009* (ACM Press, 2009), 343–50.

25. Living Headstones, "QR Code Turns Headstone into Interactive Memorial," (2013), http://www.monuments.com/living-headstones.

26. Pause Ljudbild, CataCombo Sound System by Pause #hifi4ever, YouTube (2012), http://www.youtube.com/watch?v=SDpC5ZYcA7M.

27. Pause Ljud & Bild, *CataCombo Sound System* (2012), http://catacombosoundsystem.com/.

28. Jam Kotenko, "This Casket Streams Spotify So You Can Keep on Shuffling into the Afterlife," *Digital Trends* (2013), http://www.digitaltrends.com/social-media/you-can-get-a-coffin-to-play-your-funeral-songs-via-spotify/#ixzz2qcaPW8Q3; Jan Pollak, "Swedish Man Designs Surround-Sound Coffin," *Time Magazine* (2013), http://newsfeed.time.com/2013/01/20/swedish-man-designs-surround-sound-coffin/#ixzz2gRt4gBGL.

29. Pause Ljud & Bild, *CataCombo Sound System.*

30. Sarah Marsh, "Store Your Loved One's Ashes in a 3D-Printed Urn in the Shape of Their Head," *Wired Magazine,* 2012, http://www.wired.co.uk/news/archive/2012–07/27/cremation-urn-3d-head.

31. Cremation Solutions, www.cremationsolutions.com.

32. Sharon Mollick, "Mapping the Dead. Presentation at the ESRI Conference," (2005), http://proceedings.esri.com/library/userconf/proc05/papers/pap1008.pdf.

33. U.S. Army, Arlington National Cemetery website, http://www.arlingtoncemetery.mil/ancexplorer.

34. http://www.arlingtoncemetery.mil/ancexplorer.

35. The Roadside Memorial Project, http://www.friendsalongtheroad.org/markers.htm.

36. Chris Matyszczyk, "Does Facebook Need a Cemetery?" *CNET News,* 2013, http://www.cnet.com/news/does-facebook-need-a-cemetery/.

37. Elizabeth Hallam and Jenny Hockey, *Death, Memory, and Material Culture* (Oxford: Berg Publishers, 2001).

38. Ibid., 28.

39. Joanne Garde-Hansen, Andrew Hoskins, and Anna Reading, eds., *Save As . . . . Digital Memories* (Palgrave Macmillan, 2009); Jose van Dijck, *Mediated Memories in the Digital Age* (Stanford, CA: Stanford University Press, 2007).

Chapter 7

The Social Value of Digital Ghosts

Pam Briggs and Lisa Thomas

Introduction

The meaningful objects and memories we collect over a lifetime are increasingly taking a digital form. People are now "as likely to inherit a loved one's collection of hard drives, USB keys, SD cards, and e-mail accounts as we are collections of papers, journals and photographs."[1]

Over the past few years, a growing collection of designers and researchers have begun to consider this digital legacy, asking questions about the nature and provenance of digital ghosts that survive our corporeal lives.[2]

In this chapter, we present a critical review of contemporary services and artifacts designed to facilitate the preservation and transmission of memories and experience *postmortem* and ask what the social value of such digital ghosts may be. Work is considered that discusses attitudes and sensitivities to a digital afterlife, asking what is technically feasible and socially palatable. Findings are reported from a study uniquely assessing attitudes of older adults toward new technologies and services provided in this space, which show that context is key—people *do* want to pass on information to loved ones; however, privacy concerns and usability issues may stand in the way of adoption. It is summarized that there is little going on in terms of public discussion around the social value of digital legacies, but that they are an inevitable outcome of our growing technological dependence and should therefore be given more in-depth considerations for the future.

Our Digital Footprint

A significant number of daily activities are now conducted in the digital sphere. Many individuals work online, using technologies for data sharing, e-mail for communication, and the cloud for collaboration and improved mobility. But people also play online: uploading photographs and videos, using social media to access and sometimes create news, listening to a personalized, cloud-based music collection that travels with us, and accessing an individual collection of books and other reading material anywhere anyplace via digital services. This ever-changing data, our digital footprint will reflect many different facets of a life, but this can make for a complex digital legacy.

Digital footprints are small in those societies where access to technology and wireless services is limited, but they can be extremely large when the technological infrastructure is readily available to all. In the United States, for example, 72 percent of all online adults use social networking sites,[3] with two-thirds of American adults using Facebook as their dominant social network.[4] Not surprisingly, then, given the capabilities of such social media sites, we find that over half of American adults (54%) have posted original photos or videos online. This trend is also growing with new photo-sharing applications for mobile phones (such as Instagram and Snapchat) gaining a hold on the younger market.[5] However, the use of social media is also growing in the older population, with a 2013 Pew survey reporting that social media use in 43 percent of adults aged 65 and older.[6]

Citizens are surrounded by new tools that allow for the relatively seamless capture and curation of their everyday lives. The term "lifelogging" has come to mean the act of recording and shaping the multifaceted aspects of our digital selves—a practice that has been demonstrated most dramatically by Microsoft's Gordon Bell who tries to digitally capture all documents, photographs, and sounds he has experienced in his lifetime in his *MyLifeBits* project.[7] The idea of such "total capture" may seem somewhat extreme, but there is a growing awareness that lifelogging practices can be used to complement the activities of daily living[8] and potentially offer a useful service in compensating for the fallibility of human memory.

A more critical perspective would see lifelogging as a form of digital hoarding—the indiscriminate practice of keeping every digital record "just in case" it may be useful later. Researchers recognize that such hoarding practices may be counterproductive and lead to massive information overload ultimately resulting in something that is simply too large and complex to be useful. Such problems are likely to become more pressing as we move from systems that support the active and considered processes of digital curation to those that allow for passive capture of everyday places, events, and experiences. As an example, the new location tracking service Placeme.com can automatically publish daily timelines that describe where you are at different times of the day, store this data as a record of daily activities, and/or stream it to select others. Such systems show how it is becoming easier to simply record everything, but this then begs the question: *What might I do with all the stuff I collect?*[9]

Until now, there have been relatively few attempts to assess what people might want to do with this mass of information. While some progress has been made in the design of technologies that might aid in the bequest of data (e.g., Microsoft Memory Box), there is not yet an agreed mechanism or model which provides a suitable way to prepare for digital information bequests.[10] However, there is growing recognition that new digital hoarding practices will lead to serious problems in managing one's digital legacy.

Our Digital Legacy

Bizarrely, our digital footprints are simultaneously ephemeral and persistent. A paradox, but one that is easily resolved: for all sorts of reasons (as will be discussed momentarily), many find it hard to keep hold of digital data. We create a digital record but then find we cannot fully lay claim to it, constrain it, label it, or find it, which, in turn, means that we cannot effectively delete it, edit it, or bequeath it. It can linger in cyberspace, joining a growing digital diaspora that may become useless to us as individuals but is increasingly useful to commerce or government in feeding the new "big data" machine.

One contributing factor to the problem of managing our digital data is the fact that there are so many different data types, each with very different provenance. Researchers at California's Naval Postgraduate School, Simson Garfinkel and David Cox,[11] for example, define four types of digital footprint: (i) publicly identified footprints comprising digital data that is explicitly linked to an individual by name and that is relatively accessible and identifiable; (ii) organizational footprints that include company documents, web pages, e-mails, and calendars; (iii) pseudonymous footprints, where the author uses a false name consistently, or anonymous footprints, where the author has attempted to disguise his or her contribution and which may become lost *postmortem;* and (iv) private footprints that are typically held behind a password or other authentication mechanism or that are held on private machines.

So, the data itself can be complex, but there are other contextual factors also at play in at least four overlapping ways:

First, digital artifacts are often invisible and as such are seen as less valuable than their physical counterparts.[12] Digital intangibles are less easily claimed and they don't lend themselves to the physical acts of sorting through possessions that might be practised as a family. In researching "a digital death in the family," Michael Massimi and Ronald Baecker, exploring technology adoption in death at the University of Toronto, describe the process of siblings laying claim to the paintings of their deceased mother—by the simple act of writing their names on the back—and contrasts this with the problems inherent in laying similar claim to files: "There is no equivalent claiming affordance for digital files [. . .] it is conceptually more difficult to earmark many files spread across a file system than it is to claim a handful of physical items kept in a household."[13]

Second, individuals don't always own the rights to their own data, so access to what one has come to think of as his or hers can be denied. This may be at the corporate level, where companies storing data "in the cloud" could rescind the access rights to that data.[14] But, even within a family, the origins of digital artifacts can be forgotten or ownership can be shared, either of which can make it very difficult when issues of inheritance are discussed.[15]

Third, digital memories are often associated with particular access privileges that themselves require authentication, so forgetting a password itself becomes problematic. Accessibility issues also arise because of changes in technology itself. Family memories stored on videotape become inaccessible as new forms of digital storage take hold. Massimi and Baecker describe the ways in which something as simple as a password can prevent people from inheriting the assets associated with an account, quoting one of their participants as follows: "We just left it, I couldn't get into [my brother's] account . . . his school account was deleted obviously, but I left his personal account."[16]

Finally, digital memories can become lost or inaccessible as a function of failure to properly file or organize the information—it simply gets lost in the vast data space. People are not only reluctant to delete personal information,[17] but they also fail to organize it effectively.[18] Moreover, there are not many tools available to support them in this.[19]

Thus, a vast hinterland of orphan data is created. As William Odom at Carnegie Mellon University and colleagues from Microsoft Research note, "Posting something online, in today's world, can mean *relinquishing control* over the things that you care about, but also *losing awareness* of what exists, where it is, who has access to it, who is accountable for it, and what is being done with it."[20] No doubt, the vast majority of e-mails, tweets, spreadsheets, and messages that are exchanged in any one day are highly relevant to one particular time and place but irrelevant thereafter, leaving a garden of digital weeds that no one values but persists despite the neglect.

The need for systems that can both forgive and forget is important in this space, and a number of researchers are calling for such reparation as part of a new research agenda that can also help with the problems of digital overload described earlier. Will digital archives shed too harsh a light on the ways people live their lives? Digital curation can certainly carry some unintended consequences,[21] and lifelogging systems—particularly those more passive systems—illustrate our mistakes and misjudgments. While people may wish to share their "average" or "best" behavior, they can often promote themselves at their worst.[22] There are also times when a digital legacy seems inappropriate. The long-term storage of digital possessions after a relationship breakup can cause distress,[23] and it is easy for the bereaved to come across digital records that were never intended for their eyes.[24] Liam Bannon, working at the University of Limerick, reminds us that there is genuine value in the ability to forget information and wonders whether technologies used to support our digital selves should also support the act of forgetting as a means of avoiding digital overload. Bannon[25] also features the development of new applications that have an inbuilt "forgetting function" (e.g., the photo-sharing communication app Snapchat claims to delete data after around 10 seconds).

Dealing with Digital Legacy

The problems of digital legacy are slowly becoming recognized, and there are relatively few systems available to facilitate the inheritance of digital assets. The phrase "digital asset planning" has been used to describe the actions one might take to determine what will happen to digital data,[26] and big companies such as Facebook and Google have systems that support legacy processes. More dedicated commercial sites such as Legacy Locker[27] are appearing, offering the means to ensure personal, digital information to be accessed by others in the event of death or unexpected illness.

A number of authors have described the psychological burden accompanying the inheritance of digital devices—such as phones and laptops— where the digital data is somehow inaccessible, but where the promise of untold stories or links of strong emotional significance means that the bereaved cannot bear to throw those devices away.[28] The issue of what to do with digital information following the death of the creator is now a pressing issue for families,[29] and people are increasingly being advised to consider how they may want others to access their digital selves should anything happen to them.[30] Naturally, the issue of death is a sensitive topic, and there are many papers that discuss the need for "thanosensitive" design around the appropriate management of data postmortem.[31]

A number of approaches have begun to address the question of essential principles for thanosensitive design, beginning with a better understanding of the preparatory processes for digital inheritance. Three main activities have been identified when preparing a digital legacy: (i) curation, the active process of taking family records and annotating them so that someone else can make sense of them; (ii) creation of mementos by collating those curated materials in order to produce an artifact such as a scrapbook for family; and (iii) active reminiscence where people tell stories about the past based on their own memories.[32]

Some solutions to managing digital legacy involve the curating of data to form tangible objects—sometimes referred to as a "technology heirloom."[33] A technology heirloom is similar in many ways to a traditional heirloom, but can encapsulate computer files, mobile phone data, and any other digital information someone may wish to store. The heirloom can then be bequeathed to somebody in the event of death and used to support memories of that person. The form and function of such heirlooms can vary, with recent examples including tilting picture frames and mourning stones to support the grieving process.[34] Three heirloom designs, Backup Box, Timecard, and Digital Slide Viewer, all of which enable the archiving and reviewing of sensitive personal information, have been explored recently.[35] Timecard is a wooden photo frame that can be used as a personal timeline of the deceased. The Backup Box automatically backs up Twitter feeds in ways that might later acquire the same meaning as diary entries. Digital Slide Viewer is a physical device that could potentially contain online photo collections of the deceased, making them accessible to relatives, while The Family Archive was developed to enable the digitization of everyday objects in the home, displaying their photographs.[36] These projects highlight the fragile and temporal nature of physical objects, creating an important digital trace that could outlive their material shelf life.

Tangible and intangible heirlooms have very different properties. The former has a more natural propensity to decay over time, and so researchers have been interested in the value of such decay processes (in an argument similar to that discussed previously on the value of forgetting). Should both types of object—digital *and* physical—be allowed to decay over time? In response to such considerations, a number of websites have been developed that allow for the uploading of photographs that gradually decay (BlackBox, DataFade, and BitLogic), although these have not been universally welcomed. Participants, while happy to accept decay processes around physical objects (e.g., the clothes of the deceased) couldn't understand the point of digital decay, believing the main purpose of digital archiving was unlimited, high-quality storage.

Digital Memorials

The practice of offering online memorials to the dead began in the early days of the internet, when the bereaved would create commemorative web pages capturing the life and achievements of the deceased.[37] These were succeeded by more dynamic, cyber-memorials that allowed visitors to post messages of respect and condolence.[38] In both cases, these memorials were crafted in the period following death, when those most affected were able to come together and celebrate a life passed. Social media developments such as Facebook allowed for the living to create their own online identities that could be repurposed as memorials by friends and family.[39]

This repurposing included using the profile pages of the deceased as memorials[40] and promoting these memorials via social networks.[41] Brubaker and Hayes have noted that such memorials are unusual in that they have effectively been created by the deceased themselves and almost seem to offer a voice from beyond the grave. As such, it may not, therefore be so surprising that such profiles can provoke comments and expressions of remorse from friends and family and can effectively create a vehicle that gives the bereaved the sense that they can continue the digital conversation—that is, speak directly to the dead.[42]

A number of authors have explored the content of social media postings by the bereaved in order to understand more about the conversations provoked by such "virtual cemeteries." An ethnographic study of 200 Myspace comments made during January to April 2008[43] found that the most common form for posts were simple expressions of a shared loss: "*cursory comments that could be thought of as virtual black armbands, veils, or flowers left at a gravesite—symbolic and public expressions of loss and solidarity*"[44] although other, lengthier and more carefully crafted tributes were also posted—more akin to a speech made at a funeral. The authors also noted that site acted as a means to create a biography in which friends and family could share moments from the past in order to build a more elaborate picture of the person they'd lost.

Using a similar approach to data gathering, Brubaker et al. collected posts made to 1,369 deceased Myspace users during April 2010, although their study explored the utility of sentiment analysis in this space and focused on those contributions with clear expressions of emotional distress. In particular they noted the pain felt by those speaking directly to the deceased noting that "for these authors, the comment space serves more as an environment for conveying individual yearning or pain."[45] They acknowledge the writing of others in this space, noting in particular the finding that people can express their distress in comments posted over long periods of time[46] and recognizing the difficulty faced by survivors who must eventually take action to remove the deceased from their network.[47]

Digital Ghosts

The work on memorials shows that people have a need to be able to "speak" to those recently deceased, so it is perhaps unsurprising that new services are paving the way for the dead to respond posthumously. New applications such as LIVESON[48] use the tagline, "When your heart stops beating, you'll keep tweeting," and present their services as a social afterlife. Similarly, the website DeadSoci.al allows individuals to prepare goodbye messages and deliver them in a timely manner after death, as well as posting messages to sites such as Facebook. This is a theme that is premediated by fiction and film: In 1995, Bios discussed the idea of keeping someone "alive" by collating mannerisms and familiar speech patterns—at a time before digital lives were well established. One step further and television shows such as *Black Mirror* encourage us to think about the physical as well as digital reconstruction of a deceased loved one, relying on resurrection from online blogs, e-mails, and social network activity.[49]

The notion that someone can speak from "beyond the grave" is a well-rehearsed trope and one that has been used in the design of technologies surrounding death for some time. A 2005 study, for example, addressing the design of a cemetery in Atlanta, asked visitors to tour the cemetery with an audio guide narrated by a historian who led participants to his own grave.[50] It is not unusual for museums to use a known history of an individual to provide an engaging means of bringing the past to life, but it is only now, with the weight of digital information pressing upon us, that we might like to reflect on some of the values assumed by such practice.

Just because there is enough information to reanimate someone, does that mean we should? The company Ziggur invites visitors to consider such issues by posing the following questions on its website:

What happens to your ads on auction sites if you are no longer here? How do you prevent your birthday notices being sent to your friends via Facebook, telling them that you will be another year older "in a few days"? Or how do you prevent business contacts being reminded that they should get in touch with you through LinkedIn? What happens to money in your PayPal account? Or the heartfelt appeal to the love of your life to make themselves known to you?[51]

Such issues bring to the fore the notion that as citizens, careful attention should be paid to our digital selves, particularly when contemplating the possibility of a digital afterlife. But how can these issues be addressed in a sensitive way? Who should be consulted in order to ensure that there is a value agenda around such issues? A number of researchers have established the importance of value sensitive design (VSD) in the creation of any new technologies and this kind of approach is creeping into the digital legacy space.

Socially Sensitive Design around a Digital Afterlife

Within the bereavement and digital legacy space, VSD asks us both to understand the value of digital legacies and to and honor the wishes and the reputation of the deceased in tandem with the needs of the living. It is an agenda in which some practical problems must be solved while at the same time acknowledging a new landscape in which social mores and personal beliefs play an important role. In the previous section, for example, new technologies and future visions were explored. But what should be made of such possibilities as the deceased continuing to have an online presence postmortem and indeed even having a digital proxy that actively communicates from a VSD perspective? Massimi and Baecker[52] describe a "poltergeist" moment for Betty, a woman in her 20s who had lost her mother to cancer:

> I got a call a couple of months from her office after she died, but it was her phone number, and I thought I was having some surreal poltergeist kind of moment . . . I recognized she passed away and thought "My mom's calling me" and I froze and freaked out there. I remember that terrified me, but how excited I was at the potential to talk to her.[53]

In this and other stories, Massimi and Baecker point to the role of technology in "reanimating" the dead, but, to date and despite the volume of new research in this field recently, there has been little attempt to assess how a nonbereaved population might view such posthumous practices.

Indeed, very few researchers have asked people about how they may wish their legacy to be maintained. Strikingly very few systems have considered digital legacies from the perspective of the older adult. Those closest to death have rarely been consulted on the principles they would like to see enshrined in digital legacy, although there have been studies that have consulted those who have recently experienced bereavement.[54] In the remaining part of this chapter we summarize some of our own work, particularly our work with older adults, which addresses this omission. Our work not only uses a VSD approach in recognition of the fact that digital legacies will have a significant long-term impact on society but also specifically reflects a conversation with older people, those closest to death, in order to challenge some digital legacy and heirloom designs in terms of "what they think of as important in life."[55] We conducted a study with older adults (ranging in age from 56 to 76) from the local community in the northeast of England. In this study, we presented them with films capturing different aspects of digital legacy in order to prompt discussion on the social value of those digital technologies designed to support some kind of posthumous memorial or social presence. The films were selected from a scoping exercise provided a number of examples of legacy technologies, including art projects such as Mission Eternity,[56] commercial developments such as Asset Locker, as well as academic projects including Microsoft's Technology Heirloom work. From this sample, we selected two films that captured different elements of curatorial practice underpinning digital legacy: self-curation (lifelogging) and other-curation (memorialization). For each film, we provided a verbal description and at each showing we asked a facilitator to use the film to prompt a process of *envisionment* (generally considered important in value-elicitation practices)[57] and discussion of social values around digital legacy.

Self-curation was introduced to our older adults via a film clip of Gordon Bell's MyLifeBits project in which he is shown gathering digital data from every aspect of his life, including e-mails, phone calls, web pages, and conversations with people. Our participants also watched a film explaining the idea of the quantified self,[58] examples being where cameras placed on the chest are used to take regular photos, and how wearable devices such as watches and activity monitors collate a large amount of data about one's own activities.

Our older adults were asked to describe their feelings toward such scenarios and asked to consider the value of such data. They were encouraged to talk freely and exchange ideas with others. Data was collected in the form of audio-recordings of the discussions that took place; these were transcribed and analyzed thematically, revealing interesting themes pertaining to the older adult digital legacy perspective.

Other-curation was introduced via a promotional film for Living Memorials,[59] a company in Ireland that has created a way for relatives of the deceased to memorialize them by attaching a QR code to their gravestone. This QR code, when scanned with a smartphone, provides information about the deceased, usually as a blog or web page. Older adults were asked to watch the Living Memorials promotional video, depicting a family member attending a gravestone and scanning the QR code with their smartphone. The video explained how the information on the device can be modified by family members and friends.

Family Values

Our first observation was that both curation practices were viewed quite positively when discussed *within a family context*. The ability to access a digital record was seen as valuable, particularly when contrasted with the paucity of information accessible in previous years. This was acknowledged by at least one participant: "I did my family ancestry thing a few years back and my eldest sister helped. Now she has died, I've lost that line of contact and we never got round to putting very much on tape, and that information now has gone forever." Our older adults could also see the benefit for people outside of the family having some access to the data generated from lifelogging or memorial practices as a means to evoke memories: "It would be a nice sentimental touch to look back when somebody's grown old, to look back on their past life."[60]

However, participants worried that, *outside of the family context*, legacy and lifelogging technologies were open to misuse. There was a sense that information meant to be kept private may subsequently be released, and they argued that not everybody needed to know or should have the right to view such personal information. They also questioned the value of technologies that didn't directly support face-to-face contact with others who were sharing the grieving process. They explained that the opportunity for a family to be together is central to providing emotional and practical support—and, although they recognized that a process of discovery and fun was crucial to a family legacy, they weren't sure that a digital inheritance would feel the same.

We also found strong support for the idea that digital legacies wouldn't be valuable unless they could support forgetting. Our older adults expressed significant concern about a digital collection that would include those moments in a lifetime that we would rather forget:

"I have times in my life when I think, 'Oh my god, I wish I hadn't done that,' and, with the passage of time, you can file it into the background and forget about it. If you've got it there in front of you, movement by movement, you can't forget, you keep living it over and over again." Others talked of the value of forgetting in the grieving process, and they felt that remembering may not always be helpful, "I mean another word for forgetting is letting go and that's a very, very important process."

Who Controls a Posthumous Life?

Beyond the core values of what might be shared within and without the family, there were a number of more general themes that were considered important around the ideas of who controls the digital legacy. Three issues were discussed: technological exclusion, business practice, and digital vandalism.

Digital exclusion was a major worry, and our participants asked what would happen if people lacked the technological capabilities required to set up and maintain memorials. Older adults felt they had neither the technical means nor the understanding required to use digital systems, and they commented that this left them feeling vulnerable and overwhelmed. There was a sense that people might be at a disadvantage when presented with legacy-enabling technologies, if they weren't already familiar with them. The feeling of being overwhelmed by uncontrollable data was strongest when discussing the idea of lifelogging and dealing with the massive amounts of data involved. One participant said, "Just answer one question, will this computer burst?" This statement made people in the workshop laugh, but the participant genuinely didn't understand how the computer might store a decade's worth of information. Others commented that some of the processes involved in curating information, such as setting up a website or blog, were simply "too technical" for them.

Our participants realized that new businesses could support those who lacked the technical ability to do such things themselves. But they raised a number of issues, asking whether such legacy businesses were acting in the best interests of the bereaved or whether they were in the best of taste. For example, there was a strong consensus that accessing information on the life of the deceased via a QR gravestone was in decidedly "bad taste" and was exploitative. Such a means of prolonging the memory of someone was considered crude.

Finally, participants worried about what would happen when memories simply got into the wrong hands and were subject to acts of digital vandalism. The notion of "trolling," the act of posting a deliberately provocative online message with the aim of inciting an angry response, was a familiar enough concept. Participants had read various news reports in the media. They talked of trolling as a real threat and believed it would be even more damaging to an individual because of the sensitive nature of death: "There's a risk of people hacking that information as well. So, say there's someone I really didn't like; I could hack into it and say he's a pedophile or whatever, and it would come up on your gravestone. It's stuck there forever, then."

Summary

In this chapter, we have tried to review some of the new technologies and systems that support digital inheritance and that, essentially, create a diaspora of digital ghosts. We also discussed the importance capturing public values in this space, describing a brief study which uniquely assessed some of the attitudes of older adults to new technologies and services provided in this space.

We found that such technologies were valued by older adults provided they are used *in the right context.* Within the family, the act of passing on historical information was seen as important, and participants acknowledged that new legacy technologies could add value to the process of dealing with an inheritance, a process recognized as being difficult but often overlooked at the end of life.[61]

However, both inside and outside of the family context, legacy and life-logging technologies typically evoked privacy concerns in our older participants and, for our older participants, the protection of privacy, particularly within the family context, is paramount. For many, digital legacy systems are seen as unusable, simply because of issues of control, information leakage, privacy breaches, and the new threat of digital vandalism. A sense of exclusion was also prevalent in many discussions, brought about by their relative inexperience with existing technologies (e.g., QR codes having to be explained to everyone).

Feelings and emotions ran high in this population; our participants had, unsurprisingly, thought a lot about legacy issues and were fully prepared to discuss designs from an experiential but unsentimental standpoint. They were keenly aware of the importance of memories that could be circulated within the family but were quick to argue that such memories were not for public consumption, raising a number of privacy issues surrounding the broadcasting of private data and the unnecessary sharing of data from strangers: That came too close to being an unwanted personal invasion. Our older participants also worried that technologies might become the barrier, rather than the vehicle, for shared memories between generations because of the new knowledge or technical expertise required in the adoption of new legacy systems.

Digital legacy is a development space that is moving quickly: as noted, our digital footprints are growing rapidly, and the digital legacy issues associated with that growth are pressing. Yet, there has been relatively little public discussion around the social value of such legacies. Such a discussion is important, but the stakeholders are many and varied. Though we have brought an older adult perspective to bear, this is an issue that connects us all and of any age. We should be looking beyond the application of these technologies to specific groups such as the bereaved or those with memory deficits, and explore how technology can be utilized to manage and share digital collections belonging to the wider community.

Notes

1. Michael Massimi and Andrea Charise, "Dying, Death, and Mortality: Towards Thanatosensitivity in HCI," *Proceedings of the International Conference on Human Computer Interaction,* Boston, MA, USA, April 4–9, 2009, 5.

2. "Bequeathing the Keys to Your Digital Afterlife," *The New York Times,* http://www.nytimes.com/2013/05/26/technology/estate-planning-is-important-for-your-online-assets-too.html?_r=0. Accessed March 31, 2014.

3. "72% of Online Adults Are Social Networking Site Users," Pew Research Internet Project, http://www.pewinternet.org/2013/08/05/72-of-online-adults-are-social-networking-site-users/. Accessed April 15, 2014.

4. "Coming and Going on Facebook," Pew Research Internet Project, http://www.pewinternet.org/Reports/2013/Coming-and-going-on-facebook.aspx. Accessed April 15, 2014.

5. "Photo and Video Sharing Grow Online," Pew Research Internet Project, http://www.pewinternet.org/Reports/2013/Photos-and-videos.aspx. Accessed April 15, 2014.

6. "72% of Online Adults Are Social Networking Site Users," Pew Research Internet Project.

7. Jim Gemmell, Gordon Bell, and Roger Lueder, "MyLifeBits: A Personal Database for Everything," *Communications of the ACM* 49, no. 1 (2006), 1–18.

8. Abigail Sellen and Steve Whittaker, "Beyond Total Capture: A Constructive Critique of Lifelogging," *Communications of the ACM* 53, no. 5 (2010): 70–77.

9. Mary Czerwinski, Douglas W. Gage, Jim Gemmell, Catherine C. Marshall, Manuel A. Pérez-Quiñonesis, Meredith M. Skeels, and Tiziana Catarci, "Digital Memories in an Era of Ubiquitous Computing and Abundant Storage," *Communications of the ACM* 49, no. 1 (2006): 45–50.

10. Wendy Moncur, Jan Bikker, Elaine Kasket and John Troyer, "From Death to Final Disposition: Roles of Technology in the Post-Mortem Interval," *Proceedings of the International Conference on Human Computer Interaction,* Austin, Texas, USA, May 5–10, 2012, 531–40; Wendy Moncur and Annalu Waller, "Digital Inheritance," in *Digital Futures '10* (Nottingham, UK, October 11–12, 2010).

11. Simson Garfinkel and David Cox, "Finding and Archiving the Internet Footprint," Invited paper presented at the First Digital Lives Research Conference: Personal Digital Archives for the 21st Century, London, England, February 9–11, 2009.

12. David Kirk, Shahram Izadi, Abigail Sellen, Stuart Taylor, Richard Banks and Otmar Hilliges., "Opening up the Family Archive," *Proceedings of Computer Supported Cooperative Work,* Savannah, Georgia, USA, February 6–10, 2010, 261–70.

13. Michael Massimi and Ronald M. Baecker, "A Death in the Family: Opportunities for Designing Technologies for the Bereaved," *Proceedings of the International Conference on Human Computer Interaction,* Atlanta, Georgia, USA, April 10–15, 2010, 1821–30.

14. William Odom, Richard Banks, Richard Harper, David Kirk, Siân Lindley and Abigail Sellen, "Technology Heirlooms? Considerations for Passing Down and Inheriting Digital Materials," *Proceedings of the International Conference on Human Computer Interaction,* Austin, Texas, USA, May 5–10, 2012, 337–46.

15. Serge Egelman, A. J. Brush and Kori Inkpen, "Family Accounts: A New Paradigm for User Accounts within the Home Environment," *Proceedings of Computer Supported Cooperative Work,* San Diego, California, USA, November 8–12, 2008, 669–78.

16. Egelman, Brush, and Inkpen, "Family Accounts."

17. Ofer Bergman and Simon Tucker, "It's Not that Important: Demoting Personal Information of Low Subjective Importance Using GrayArea," *Proceedings of the International Conference on Human Computer Interaction,* Boston, MA, USA, April 4–9, 2009, 269–78.

18. Steve Whittaker, Ofer Bergman, and Paul Clough, "Easy on that Trigger Dad: A Study of Long Term Family Photo Retrieval," *Personal and Ubiquitous Computing* 14, no. 1 (2009): 31–43.

19. Elise van den Hoven, Wina Smeenk, Hans Bilsen, Rob Zimmermann, Simone de Waart and Koen van Turnhout, "Communicating Commemoration," *Proceedings of the Simulation Technology Conference,* Cambridge, UK, November 20–21, 2008.

20. William Odom, Abigail Sellen, Richard Harper and Eno Thereska, "Lost in Translation: Understanding the Possession of Digital Things in the Cloud," *Proceedings of the International Conference on Human Computer Interaction,* Austin, Texas, USA, May 5–10, 2012, 5.

21. Studying U.S. undergraduate student Facebook posts, Moore and McElroy found feelings of regret over inappropriate content were associated with personality traits. Kelly Moore and James C. McElroy, "The Influence of Personality on Facebook Usage, Wall Postings, and Regret," *Computers in Human Behavior* 28, no. 1 (2012): 267–74; Yang Wang, Saranga Komanduri, Pedro Giovanni Leon, Gregory Norcie, Alessandro Acquisti and Lorrie Faith Cranor., "I Regretted the Minute I Pressed Share: A Qualitative Study of Regrets on Facebook," *Proceedings of the Symposium on Usable Privacy & Security,* Pittsburgh, PA, USA, July 20–22, 2011.

22. Kieron O'Hara, Mischa M. Tuffield, and Nigel Shadbolt, "Lifelogging: Issues of Identity and Privacy with Memories for Life," *Proceedings of Identity and the Information Society,* Arona, Italy, May 28–30, 2008.

23. Corina Sas and Steve Whittaker, "Design for Forgetting: Disposing of Digital Possessions after a Breakup," *Proceedings of the International Conference on Human Computer Interaction,* Paris, France, April 27–May 2, 2013, 1823–32.

24. Massimi and Baecker, "A Death in the Family."

25. Liam J. Bannon, "Forgetting as a Feature, Not a Bug: The Duality of Memory and Implications for Ubiquitous Computing," *CoDesign* 2, no. 1 (2006): 3–15.

26. Gerry W. Beyer and Naomi Cahn, "When You Pass On, Don't Leave the Passwords Behind: Planning for Digital Assets," *Probate & Property* 26, no. 1 (2012): 40–43.

27. "Legacy Locker," http://legacylocker.com/. Accessed February 15, 2014.

28. William Odom, Richard Harper, and Abigail Sellen, "Passing On & Putting To Rest: Understanding Bereavement in the Context of Interactive Technologies," *Proceedings of the International Conference on Human Computer Interaction,* Atlanta, Georgia, USA, April 10–15, 2010, 1831–40; Massimi and Baecker, "A Death in the Family."

29. Michael Massimi, Wendy Moncur, William Odom, Richard Banks and David Kirk, "Memento Mori: Technology Design for the End of Life," *Proceedings of the International Conference on Human Computer Interaction,* Austin, Texas, USA, May 5–10, 2012.

30. "Estate Planning Is Important for Your Online Assets," *The New York Times,* http://www.nytimes.com/2013/05/26/technology/estate-planning-is-important-for-your-online-assets-too.html?_r=0. Accessed August 27, 2013.

31. Michael Massimi and Ronald Baecker, "Dealing with Death in Design: Developing Systems for the Bereaved," *Proceedings of the International Conference on Human Computer Interaction,* Vancouver, BC, Canada, May 7–12, 2011, 1001–1010; Moncur et al., "From Death to Final Disposition."

32. Siân Lindley, "Before I Forget: From Personal Memory to Family History," *Human-Computer Interaction* 27 (2012): 13–36.

33. Richard Banks, David Kirk, and Abigail Sellen, "A Design Perspective on Three Technology Heirlooms," *Human-Computer Interaction* 27 (2012): 63–91.

34. Van den Hoven et al., "Communicating Commemoration."

35. Banks, Kirk, and Sellen, "A Design Perspective," 63.

36. Kirk et al., "Opening up the Family Archive."

37. Jed R. Brubaker and Gillian R. Hayes, "We Will Never Forget You [online]: An Empirical Investigation of Post-mortem MySpace Comments," *Proceedings of Computer Supported Cooperative Work,* Hangzhou, China, March 19–23, 2011, 123–32.

38. Pamela Roberts and Lourdes A. Vidal, "Perpetual Care in Cyberspace: A Portrait of Memorials on the Web," *Journal of Death and Dying* 40, no. 4 (2000): 521–45.

39. Brubaker and Hayes, "We Will Never Forget You [online]."

40. Ibid.

41. Alice Marwick and Nicole B. Ellison, "There Isn't Wifi in Heaven!" Negotiating Visibility on Facebook Memorial Pages," *Journal of Broadcasting & Electronic Media* 56, no. 3 (2012): 378–400.

42. Robert Dobler, "Ghosts in the Machine: Mourning the MySpace Dead," in *Folklore and the Internet: Vernacular Expression in a Digital World,* ed. Trevor J. Blank (Logan: Utah State University Press, 2009).

43. Brian Carroll and Katie Landry, "Logging In and Letting Out: Using Online Social Networks to Grieve and Mourn," *Bulletin of Science, Technology, and Society* 30, no. 5 (2010): 341–49.

44 Ibid.

45. Jed R. Brubaker, Funda Kivran-Swaine, Lee Taber, and Gillian R. Hayes "Grief-Stricken in a Crowd: The Language of Bereavement and Distress in Social Media," *Proceedings of the Sixth International AAAI Conference on Weblogs and Social Media,* Dublin, Ireland, 2012, 42–49.

46. Brubaker and Hayes, "We Will Never Forget You [online]."

47. Jed R. Brubaker, Gillian R. Hayes, and Paul Dourish, "Beyond the Grave: Facebook as a Site for the Expansion of Death and Mourning," *The Information Society* 29, no. 3 (2013): 152–63.

48. "Liveson: Your Social Afterlife," http://liveson.org/. Accessed April 16, 2014.

49. "Review of Black Mirror 'Be Right Back,'" *The Independent,* http://blogs.independent.co.uk/2013/02/11/review-of-black-mirror-be-right-back/. Accessed August 29, 2013.

50. Steven Dow, Jaemin Lee, Christopher Oezbek, Blair MacIntyre, Jay David Bolter and Maribeth Gandy., "Exploring Spatial Narratives and Mixed Reality Experiences in Oakland Cemetery," *Proceedings of the International Conference on Advances in Computer Entertainment Technology,* New York, USA, 2005, 51–60.

51. "Ziggur. What Is Your Online Legacy?" http://ziggur.me/en/about.aspx. Accessed April 3, 2014.

52. Massimi and Baecker, "A Death in the Family."

53. Ibid.

54. Odom, Harper, and Sellen, "Passing On & Putting to Rest."

55. Batya Friedman, Peter H. Kahn, and Alan Borning, "Value Sensitive Design and Information Systems," in *Human-Computer Interaction in Management Information Systems: Foundations,* ed. Dennis Galletta and Ping Zhang (New York: Armonk, 2006), 348–72; Lisa P. Nathan, Batya Friedman, Predrag Klasnja, Shaun K. Kane and Jessica K. Miller., "Envisioning Systemic Effects on Persons and Society throughout Interactive System Design," *Proceedings of Designing InteractiveSystems,* Cape Town, South Africa, 2008, 1–10.

56. "Mission Eternity," http://www.missioneternity.org/summary/. Accessed April 16, 2014.

57. Theresa Satterfield, "In Search of Value Literacy: Suggestions for the Elicitation of Environmental Values," *Environmental Values* 10, no. 3 (2001): 331–59.

58. "Logging Our Lives with Wearable Technology," *BBC News,* http://www.bbc.co.uk/news/technology-22767096. Accessed April 16, 2014.

59. "Living Memorials," http://www.livingmemorials.ie/. Accessed April 16, 2014.

60. Lisa Thomas and Pam Briggs, "An Older Adult Perspective on Digital Legacy," *Proceedings of 8th Nordic Conference on Human-Computer Interaction,* Helsinki, Finland, October 26–30, 2014: in prep.

61. Massimi and Baecker, "Dealing with Death in Design."

Chapter 8

Mythopoesis, Digital Democracy, and the Legacy of the Jonestown Website

Rebecca Moore

Introduction

Regina Duncan died in Jonestown, Guyana, on November 18, 1978, at the age of 14. When her birth father, who had been estranged from the family, started an online search for information about her in 2013, he found the first photos of her that he had ever seen. He learned that she attended Opportunity High School in San Francisco before moving to the agricultural project developed by Peoples Temple. He found out that he was a grandfather, that Regina had had a daughter who also died in the murder-suicides that occurred in Jonestown. He was able to hear her voice on Peoples Temple audiotapes that have been digitized by Special Collections at San Diego State University. He could see when she arrived in Jonestown, where she lived in the community, and what she was doing (attending school). He discovered that Regina was a typical teenager: headstrong, rebellious, and wanting to leave Jonestown so she could perform with the group's dance team in Georgetown, the capital of Guyana. He was also able to write a memorial and post it online, as did three other relatives.

Alternative Considerations of Jonestown and Peoples Temple (http:// jonestown.sdsu.edu) is both a digital archive for historical documents pertaining to the group and a cyber memorial for those who perished in 1978. The website presents a list of the 918 individuals who died, their photos (if available), personal comments and reflections, and a wealth of additional information compiled by volunteers who have searched various documents to create a picture of life in Jonestown. I started *Alternative Considerations* in 1998, when I was teaching at the University of North Dakota, as an academic website for disseminating information and research about Peoples Temple. My husband, Fielding McGehee, currently manages all aspects of its content. It is now hosted on the server sponsored by Library and Information Access at San Diego State University, and it is the most comprehensive digital archive of primary source documents, digitized audiotapes, and personal and scholarly articles of any website dealing with Jonestown and Peoples Temple.

Most remarkable to us is the insatiable interest from strangers, friends, and relatives. Each year brings new visitors to the Jonestown Memorial List:[1] children named after deceased aunts and uncles; adults searching for parents who died; friends who, failing to find former college roommates on Facebook, learn from an online search that they died in Jonestown; and visitors who experienced a painful loss in their own lives and who are drawn by the magnitude of the Jonestown tragedy. Anyone can leave a short remembrance on the website, although we review each one to ensure respect and dignity. We do not upload remembrances that state "May you rot in Hell," or otherwise denigrate the person being memorialized. In addition, *the jonestown report*, the online annual publication of the site, includes a number of extended remembrances of individuals.[2]

While death is the great leveler, private graveyards and public monuments still reveal the hierarchy of value placed upon individual lives. Size, scope, weight, height, and location of markers and memorials all indicate the status of the deceased. A memorial and museum to those who died in two attacks on the World Trade Center (September 11, 2001, and February 26, 1993) opened in May 2014, at a cost of $700 million.[3] In contrast, it took more than 30 years for a permanent monument consisting of four simple granite plaques—listing the names of all who died in Jonestown—to be installed in a cemetery in Oakland, at a cost of about $15,000.[4] Monuments do seem to suggest merit.

At the same time, the cyber memorial at *Alternative Considerations* has expanded over time as more people discover the website and as a new generation of individuals—born after 1978—learns about the social movement that was Peoples Temple. The people once depicted only as decaying bodies lying face down in a jungle encampment have now become persons with names, faces, and histories.

The *Alternative Considerations* website demonstrates the democratizing power of the internet. Those who died have more individuality today—through photographs and remembrances—than they had as the corpses shown in the initial news coverage of the deaths. This is partly due to the mythopoetic role played by the website. Mythopoesis, or myth-making, is a narrative process that allows people "to represent and make sense of life, with all of its joys, mysteries and hardships," according to Peter Willis, Senior Lecturer, and Anne Morrison, Research Associate, both at the University of South Australia.[5] "The loss of traditional myths and the place of one's own story within a larger story," writes Meg Hegarty, a palliative care nurse and faculty member in the School of Medicine at Flinders University, "can entail freedom from the limits of old religious and cultural structures, but also the loss of strong structures of support."[6] Through mythopoesis, individuals create a story—a narrative—that addresses existential questions of meaning, yet which retains the ambiguity of real life at the same time. This mythopoetic activity is evident on *Alternative Considerations.*

This chapter first addresses the stigmatized deaths in Jonestown and the need for an outlet for the grief that was disenfranchised. Cyber memorials, in general, and the Jonestown website, in particular, provide such outlets. The mythopoetic task of constructing biographies serves the process of healing after a death has occurred, and researchers have observed this process in cyber memorials. Although some scholars criticize the archival nature of these memorials, as I will discuss in the following, the Jonestown website demonstrates that the creation of narrative lives not only serves the task of mythopoesis, but also democratizes memorialization of the dead.

The Stigmatized Deaths in Jonestown

Because of the tragic nature of the events in Jonestown—a mass murder-suicide in which hundreds of children, women, and men died after ingesting a poisonous cocktail—the deaths in Jonestown were highly stigmatized. The gruesome decomposition of the bodies in the jungle awaiting recovery and removal further distanced the victims from sympathetic consideration. David Chidester identified rituals of exclusion enacted against the Jonestown dead once they were repatriated to the United States. "These were bodies no one wanted," he remarked, describing the way the bodies were "thingified" by those processing the remains.[7] The deaths themselves remain in dispute, with many believing that the majority of victims were murdered, while others asserting that able-bodied adults killed themselves after sacrificing their children.[8] For many black families, the high number of African American victims (more than 70%) suggested racial motivations for the killings.

These notorious deaths inevitably disenfranchised the grief experienced by relatives.[9] Bereaved families were afraid to mourn publicly, given the sensational way that the news media covered members of the "suicide cult" who had assassinated a congressman and then participated in an "orgy of death."[10] Those in African American churches felt shame that their relatives had been led astray by white pied pipers, while black church leaders explicitly disavowed any connection between Peoples Temple and the black church.[11] Surviving members of Peoples Temple faced discrimination and hostility when they returned to the United States, with employers and even social workers assigned to assist in their reentry calling them "baby killers."[12]

The intense dehumanization of the dead and the disenfranchisement of the bereaved made an online memorial website a key element in the ability to mourn openly. Although the *Alternative Considerations* website did not begin with the purpose of memorialization in mind, ongoing research led to the compilation of the only comprehensive list of those who died. In 2002, personal details were added to the initial list: the names of family members, occupations in Jonestown, and other information fleshed out the bare names and birth dates comprising the initial directory. In 2005, site visitors were able to add remembrances to each individual listing. Finally, in 2008, the addition of photographs to the listings restored humanity to the iconic corpses by giving them living faces.

The fact that it took 30 years to produce a complete online catalog of all 918 people who died in Jonestown demonstrates the extent of stigmatization. Cyber memorials immediately emerged after the shooting deaths at Columbine High School in Littleton, Colorado, in 1999 and after the terror attacks on the World Trade Center and the Pentagon in 2001. More recently, web commemoratives and Facebook remembrances went online instantly to memorialize the first responders and others who died in a fire at a fertilizer factory in West, Texas (April 2013); those killed by tornadoes in Moore, Oklahoma (May 2013); and the "Hot Shot" firefighters who perished during the Yarnell Hill Fire (June 2013).

The delay in recognizing the Jonestown dead online can be partially explained because internet use was not widespread until the 1990s, with cyber memorials first beginning to appear in 1995.[13] Even taking that into account, however, the creation of a timely memorial would have been impossible due to the ignominious deaths in Jonestown. Within a few weeks of November 18, 1978, the U.S. Department of State prepared a list of those who died, but it was incomplete, providing the names of about 600—or two-thirds—of the people whose family members had been notified of their deaths. The lack of an official and complete list of the dead seems rather shocking in light of worldwide interest in the group and its demise. But those who died in Jonestown did not meet the criterion of being "worthy victims," an expression introduced by Noam Chomsky and Edward

Herman in their analysis of media bias.[14] It took the work of volunteers who were either related to the dead or committed to properly identifying those who died to finally generate the complete list that currently appears online. This resource is used today by lawyers, private investigators, and government officials, as well as by family members, because it is comprehensive and thorough. In late 2014, for example, the Coroner's Office for the State of Delaware used the Jonestown Memorial List to track down relatives of Jonestown victims, whose cremated remains had been found in a defunct funeral home.

Cyber Memorialization

Antiapartheid leader and South African President (1994–1999) Nelson Mandela died during the fall 2013 semester of my Religious Studies course in "Death, Dying, and the Afterlife." Students instantly learned of his death through Facebook. One commented in our online discussion: "It is a shame to realize that the reason I heard about his death was because of Facebook. It seems that a lot of news is broken to our society through the use of social media such as Facebook." Another wrote: "I was very shocked by Nelson Mandela's death. Unfortunately, the first thing I thought about was how long will it take for Facebook to blow up about RIP Nelson Mandela posts, or who will be the first to put a picture of Morgan Freeman up and say RIP Nelson Mandela." Freeman played Mandela in the popular film *Invictus*.

These anecdotes supplement the evidence found in a large body of research that examines the ways that the internet has changed traditional rituals of death and mourning. Doctoral candidate Jed R. Brubaker and Professors Gillian R. Hayes and Paul Dourish in the Donald Bren School of Information and Computer Sciences at the University of California, Irvine, note how Facebook has expanded opportunities to learn about death, provided information about the deceased, and continued the memorialization process.[15] They observe that cyber memorials enlarge temporal, spatial, and social opportunities for mourning. First, people learn of deaths more quickly; second, they do not need to cross geographical boundaries in order to discover sites of memorialization; and finally, they find information about the deceased. Moreover, friends share memories and content on these Facebook memorials, fashioning postmortem identities that may be artificial constructs that do not necessarily reflect the true nature of the deceased.[16]

A study of Myspace and Facebook by Brian Carroll, Associate Professor of Communication at Berry College, and Berry College then-student Katie Landry Branham, reports a similar problem, with conflicting narratives about the deceased appearing online.[17] Yet, the advantage of online memorials is their energetic and shifting character, with the opportunity for discourse and dialogue continuing in ways that monuments of stone deny. "Unlike gravestones or urns, these memorial pages are dynamic and inclusive."[18] Pamela Roberts, Professor of Human Development at California State University, Long Beach, also points out the ever-changing nature of memorial websites, which can be updated, altered, and transformed. "In a display of continuing bonds with the dead," she writes, "one can care for the memorial much like one tends a grave."[19]

The artist and writer Nicholas Grider's examination of the *Faces of the Fallen* website assesses the "dematerialization" of traditional war memorials.[20] During the Iraq War, *Faces of the Fallen* provided names and photos online of soldiers who died, bringing home the deaths at a time when media coverage of casualties was restricted. Yet, a vivid reminder of the ephemeral nature of such websites exists in the fact that this memorial is no longer online; it, too, has dematerialized.

Taking the opposite stance to Grider's is Maya Socolovsky, Professor in the Latin American Studies Program at the University of North Carolina, Charlotte, who argues that online memorials *materialize* the dead in photographs, narratives, poetry, and other visible ways. This materialization concretizes loss, and, as a result, the bereaved lose the "unknowability of absence and the otherness of death."[21] Online memorials fill in the gaps left by stone monuments and, indeed, overdetermine the deceased, leaving nothing to the imagination. Socolovsky cites historian Pierre Nora's observation that "modern memory is, above all, archival," noting that computers have virtually replaced human memory, at least for the middle classes.[22] Traditional physical monuments, in general, "are usually read as relieving us of the burden of remembering," although it would seem that Maya Lin's Vietnam War Memorial is a notable exception in its failure to narrate a heroic story of that war and thus allow us to safely forget our losses.

Socolovsky criticizes the archival impulse implicit in internet memorials, which she calls museums for ordinary people. They present a variety of types of information: everything from grief counseling to inspiring words to political messages. "Like a museum artifact or object, the images and photographs of the deceased who are ordinary members of the public, affirm the significance of the life lost."[23] This archival function can be clearly seen on the *Alternative Considerations* website. Both the Jonestown Memorial List and the larger digital archive presented on the site create a nonhierarchical, democratic organization in death that did not exist for members in life. They do indeed affirm the significance of the lives lost in Jonestown.

The Jonestown Website

Most people remember Jonestown as a tragedy which began when a U.S. congressman was assassinated on a remote jungle airstrip. The murder of Leo J. Ryan, along with three news reporters and one escaping resident of Jonestown, was followed by a carefully rehearsed suicide plan in which community members lined up and drank a poisoned fruit punch. Parents killed their children before taking the poison themselves. Jim Jones, the group's founder, became a symbol for the power-mad cult leader, and his last image alive, along with images of the sea of bodies in brightly colored clothes, signifies the potential dangers of new religions.

Because my sisters Carolyn Layton and Annie Moore died in Jonestown, along with my nephew Jim-Jon Prokes and many other people I knew, I felt a personal responsibility to understand how and why they died. This led to the filing of many Freedom of Information Act (FOIA) requests with government agencies that had contact with Peoples Temple in the United States and in Guyana in an effort to recover as many documents as possible. These requests, coupled with three FOIA lawsuits,[24] resulted in the release of thousands of pages of Temple records: passport applications, drug inventories, handwritten letters to Jim Jones, photographs and audiotapes, and much, much more.

Initially, we maintained files in our home, but in an effort to make the items accessible to a wider audience, we donated them to the California Historical Society (CHS), located in San Francisco. We then donated additional materials to Special Collections at the San Diego State University (SDSU) library. Place-bound libraries subject to the vagaries of public and private funding still have some limitations. While academic researchers might secure funding for travel to the libraries at CHS or SDSU, most people interested in conducting Jonestown research, either formally or informally, would find travel difficult. Therefore, when we inaugurated the *Alternative Considerations* website in 1998, we began to collect documents all over again in order to post them online so that the access problem would be ameliorated.

The *Alternative Considerations* website somewhat addresses this issue by providing an extensive online archive. Indeed, it is the largest digital archive pertaining to a single new religion—and a cult disaster—that we know of. Researcher Mark Swett once hosted a research-oriented website on the Branch Davidians and the tragedy at Waco, Texas, in 1993, but that has since gone offline. Another researcher, Matthew D. Wittmer, maintains a site dedicated to memorializing the Branch Davidians. He posts current news and information about Mount Carmel, home of the Branch Davidians, as well as models and diagrams he created which show the facilities—now destroyed—in three dimensions.[25] The World Religions and Spirituality Project hosted by Virginia Commonwealth University does provide links to the archives about several new religions, such as Scientology and the Branch Davidians (http://www.has.vcu.edu/wrs/index.html). And the anticult activist Rick Ross maintains an "Internet Archives for the Study of Destructive Cults, Controversial Groups and Movements," but this site collects only negative or critical information (news articles, letters, reports) about new religions.[26]

In addition to hosting the Jonestown Memorial List, *Alternative Considerations* archives Temple documents, photographs, and audiotapes. A section called "Primary Sources" organizes documents from the earliest days of Peoples Temple in Indianapolis, through its heyday in San Francisco, to life in Jonestown, the deaths there, and the aftermath. The "Jonestown Research" section reconstructs the history of the movement, presenting maps of where people lived in Jonestown, family trees indicating who was related to whom, and street addresses and family groupings for those who lived in San Francisco. It also provides a detailed analysis of the journals of Edith Roller, a 63-year-old former college professor and member of the Temple who died in Jonestown. Roller's day-to-day account of life in San Francisco and Jonestown presents a unique insider's view. Volunteer researcher Don Beck, a former member of Peoples Temple, has mined these accounts in order to describe what people ate in Jonestown, where they slept, what they did, who visited the community, who left the community, and whatever other features occurred in daily life.

Peoples Temple rather obsessively maintained records of its activities: membership rolls and photos of those living in San Francisco; censuses of who was living in Jonestown; and audiotapes of meetings, telephone calls, sermons, and special events. The Special Collections at the SDSU Library has digitized approximately 700 audiotapes and placed these MP3 files on the Jonestown website. By far the most popular tape is the so-called death tape (Q042) made by Jim Jones as people were lining up to ingest poison mixed with tranquilizers.[27] Other tapes are more revealing, however. Sermons and speeches given by Jones over the years show how the organization changed, moving from Pentecostal Christianity, to progressive mainline Christianity, to secular utopian communitarianism. Audiotapes made in Jonestown capture the voices of residents declaring their willingness to die—and to kill their children—in the event of an attack by American or Guyanese forces. Tape summaries and transcripts, also prepared by volunteers, present the names of all those speaking whenever they can be identified, and thus visitors can track down relatives on tape by using the site's search function. They can also conduct queries to find information on any individual: from their place on the Memorial List, to their relationships to other people in family trees and community organization charts.

A growing and contemporary archival function performed by *Alternative Considerations* consists of articles written by former members of Peoples Temple and remembrances written about individuals who died. The "Personal Reflections" section features stories covering a variety of topics: everything from sex in Jonestown, to reactions to the expression "drinking the Kool-Aid," to ways people have found healing from the trauma of loss. This section, as well as *the jonestown report*—which was published annually from 1998 to 2013—includes memory works (or remembrances) about the diverse individuals who lived and died in Jonestown: children, relatives, lovers, friends, and others. Some of the memorials are written by survivors of Jonestown and former members, but many are written by outsiders who remember their childhood friends, their high school sweethearts, and their students, employees, or coworkers with love and affection. Like the online memorials noted by Pamela Roberts, these too appear as letters to the deceased, poems, reflective commentary, and humorous anecdotes.[28] The story of a group of kids, for example, pooling their resources to share rides at the county fair, resonates with many readers, and brings Gladys Meadows Smith, who died in Jonestown, back into mainstream American society.

Mythopoetics: Constructing Biographies of the Dead

Professor Tony Walter of the University of Bath describes the quiet revolution occurring in grief counseling which once emphasized "detachment achieved through the working through of feelings," but now emphasizes "the continued presence of the dead and a continuous conversation with and about them."[29] This paradigm shift has occurred, in part, due to contemporary religious pluralism, which challenged both the Victorian era accent on the self in grief and the Modern era stress on the biology of death. Instead, indigenous practices of reincorporating the dead into existing community, the Jewish practice of sitting shiva and reminiscing about the deceased, and other customs in which a narrative or biography of the dead is created all resist conventional advice about "moving on" after a death. "Ritual is replaced by discourse," according to Walter, because individuals have become "disembedded" from place, traditions, and family.[30] Longevity and geographical mobility have meant that bereaved friends, coworkers, and neighbors may not know the particulars of the deceased's life. These factors account for the need to talk about the deceased and to construct a meaningful biography that enlarges the dimensions of an individual's life, since acquaintances know only a part of his or her life story.

It seems clear that internet memorials support this mythopoetic process by publishing such biographies. Carroll and Landry observe that "in some ways the most interesting theme concerns the way many posters contribute to and therefore author or coauthor biographies or narratives of the deceased's life, biographies that evolve over time and that in important ways are contested or negotiated by the post writers."[31] Roberts notes that visitors to online memorials form communities in which they can share their grief and learn more about the deceased. She gives the example of a father who said he learned a great deal about his son by reading the postings to his memorial page.[32] Our experience with the *Alternative Considerations* site confirms these observations, especially since the victims are humanized through accounts given by friends, family, and associates.

In the case of Jonestown, the mythopoetic remembrances, written by a number of people from vastly different walks of life, undermine the media frame which demonized those who died. Dr. Larry Schacht, for example, has been vilified as an evil genius who oversaw the deaths in Jonestown; yet the remembrance of Schacht written by Sherrie Tatum describes a teenager encountering romance, intrigue, and cool, a different portrait than that found in other accounts.[33] In "Judy Stahl, My First Love," Eddie Patterson provides an account of his efforts to maintain contact with his adolescent girlfriend who eventually died in Jonestown.[34] Patterson went on to write and self-publish the book *Forces of God, Faces of Evil*, which began as an account of his encounters with the Stahl family in Indiana and California but soon became an autobiography that "culminates with an explanation of how the small ripples in our lives push us towards a destiny that may be different from what we expect."[35]

Alternative Considerations has published these and many other mythopoetic narratives that offer reflections on "a destiny that may be different from what we expect." Is this rewriting history, as some critics claim who see any attempt to humanize the Jonestown victims as an apology for their actions? We, rather, would agree with those who see the narrative construction "as a complementary paradigm to science's analytical one."[36]

Indeed, the history of Jonestown and Peoples Temple is still being written. Given the contested nature of what happened throughout the course of the group's 25-year life span—clearly evidenced at *Alternative Considerations*—the more narratives and counternarratives available, the closer the approximation to the truth, or truths, of what happened.

The Efficacy of Cyber Memorialization

Socolovsky, however, questions the efficacy of online bereavement sites. "As a highly interactive, continually replaceable, reader-oriented medium," she writes, "we have to ask what kind of consoling space the Internet can provide for our collective and private memories."[37] Andrew Stark, Professor of Strategic Management at the University of Toronto, discerns a different problem: virtual immortality is meaningless unless an individual has accomplished something worth remembering. Although some websites, and thus some memorials, may remain online indefinitely, the individuals so immortalized will be forgotten within a generation.[38] Only family members will remain interested in the details of a life. Yet all that this really means is that cyber memorials may one day resemble 17th-century graveyards: of genealogical and historical interest, but not much else.

Because interest in Jonestown—and all that the single word has come to signify—remains high even after more than three decades have elapsed, Stark's prediction seems moot. Moreover, our experience managing *Alternative Considerations* for 15 years does not support Socolovsky's contention that the internet does not provide the means for consolation. An unexpected result of going online has been the creation of an *ad hoc* community of people interested in Jonestown: survivors, relatives, journalists, students, scholars, and a few who seem mainly interested in the notoriety or celebrity of Jonestown. Relatives have been able to locate living family members through the Jonestown Memorial List because extended family members are identified. Former members have gathered together at face-to-face reunions, thanks to the connections made online. "I wish to thank the Alternative Considerations website for being a vehicle for people that have been torn apart by the Peoples Temple experience to be able to find each other once again," wrote David Parker Wise upon being reunited with his former wife and mother of his child.[39]

Perhaps the most concrete example of community created by *Alternative Considerations* was the outpouring of financial support given to erect a stone monument that listed the names of all 918 people who died on November 18, 1978. A single granite gravestone located at Evergreen Cemetery in Oakland, California, had marked the hillside where more than 400 Jonestown victims were buried in May 1979. Relatives and former Temple members had long wanted something more substantial, however. In early 2011, a committee comprising three volunteers who had lost relatives in Jonestown raised $20,000 from more than 120 individuals and families in just a few weeks.[40] The simple monument consists of four large plaques set flat—rather than vertically—into the ground. Controversy arose over the fact that they include the name of James Warren Jones, the group's leader. The three-member Jonestown Memorial Fund agreed that the marker commemorated a historical event in which everyone, from Leo Ryan to Jim Jones, should be remembered. Including Jones's name on the monument had the paradoxical effect of reducing his power and making him no more important than anyone else. "Where he is—lost in a sea of names, stuck between a child named James Arthur Jones and an elderly woman named Jesse Weana Jones—he is neither elevated nor ridiculed," observed Fielding McGehee, a relative of Jonestown victims and one of three members of the Jonestown Memorial Fund. "He is just there, an equal among the others."[41] This equality is even more striking in the digital archive, where personality is reduced to texts and photographs rather than symbols.

Archive Fever and Digital Democracy

Socolovsky also argues that the process of archiving is an effort to maintain control over a life. Jacques Derrida's *Archive Fever* makes a similar point.[42] The deconstructionist observes that usually it is the powerful in society, those with "publicly recognized authority," who control the archives with the purpose of managing and interpreting information for everyone else. Controlling the archives is also controlling memory of the past. Unexpectedly, however, preserving our memories in an archive actually leads to forgetfulness, according to Derrida: We can set aside our recollections because they are safely ensconced somewhere else. This seems to be, in part, Socolovsky's concern over losing the mystery and measure of a life by reducing it to pixels on a screen. Derrida might call this a "prosthetic experience."[43]

Is visiting a cyber memorial a different experience from going to the cemetery with a bouquet of flowers? Of course it is. But, this does not make it prosthetic or fake. On the contrary, palliative care and bereavement counselors find the creation of biographies—and their dissemination in a variety of places, including the internet—important parts of the mourning process.[44] The passage of time has brought out more mourners for those who died in Jonestown, rather than fewer, because the site has destigmatized the dead and provided a convenient locus for memorialization. More than one visitor to *Alternative Considerations* has written of the tears they shed, especially over the children, as this anonymous message to a two-month old infant indicates: "I saw this the first time when my son was your age. I cried for hours for your placement in this life with a parent who not only didn't save you, but fed you the poison that caused your transition in the next life. Hope karma has left you better protected this time around."[45]

Furthermore, the process of mythopoesis seems to require some sort of archiving for it to be meaningful, and in today's world, that means the internet. It is true that there is a flattening effect caused by the overload of information. Yet, this overload seems required for a democratic society. "Effective democratization can always be measured by this essential criterion," writes Derrida: "the participation in and the access to the archive, its constitution, and its interpretation."[46] The internet democratizes not only access to the archive but also its very creation.

Finally, the digital archive that is *Alternative Considerations* pays much more attention to the members of Peoples Temple in death than they received in life. It shifts the emphasis once placed on the leader—the focal point of initial as well as continuing media coverage—to the followers by making them real through the construction of mythopoetic narratives. The deaths of the 917 others now demand the attention once given to the one. On the internet, as on the granite markers in Evergreen Cemetery, everyone becomes an individual in the democracy of death.

Notes

1. "Jonestown Memorial List," *Alternative Considerations of Jonestown and Peoples Temple* [henceforth *Alternative Considerations*], http://jonestown.sdsu.edu/?page_id=690. Accessed January 25, 2014.

2. See, for example, *The Jonestown Report* 14 (2012), *Alternative Considerations*, http://jonestown.sdsu.edu/?page_id=34370. Accessed January 25, 2014.

3. David B. Caruso and David Porter, "WTC Memorial Magnificent, but at a Steep Price," Associated Press, http://news.yahoo.com/wtc-memorial-magnificent-steep-price-132938429.html. Accessed February 20, 2014.

4. Fielding McGehee, "The Campaign for the New Jonestown Memorial: A Brief History," *the jonestown report* 13 (2011), http://jonestown.sdsu.edu/?page_id=34364. Accessed February 20, 2014.

5. Peter Willis and Anne Morrison, "Introduction," in *Spirituality, Mythopoesis and Learning,* ed. Peter Willis, Timothy Leonard, Anne Morrison, and Steven Hodge (Mt Gravatt, Australia: Post Press, 2009), 2.

6. Meg Hegarty, "Learning to Die, Learning to Live: Mythopoesis in the Baby Boomers' Search for Wisdom," in *Spirituality, Mythopoesis and Learning,* ed. Peter Willis, Timothy Leonard, Anne Morrison, and Steven Hodge (Mt Gravatt, Australia: Post Press, 2009), 247.

7. David Chidester, "Rituals of Exclusion and the Jonestown Dead," *Journal of the American Academy of Religion* 56, no. 4 (1988): 684, 685.

8. See "Was It Murder or Suicide: A Forum," *the jonestown report* 8 (2006), *Alternative Considerations,* http://jonestown.sdsu.edu/?page_id=31981. Accessed January 25, 2014.

9. Rebecca Moore, "The Stigmatized Deaths in Jonestown: Finding a Locus for Grief," *Death Studies* 35, no. 1 (2011): 42–58.

10. For "suicide cult" see Marshall Kilduff and Ron Javers, *The Suicide Cult* (New York: Bantam Books, 1978); for "orgy of death" see Clare Crawford-Mason, Dolly Langdon, Melba Beals, Nancy Faber, Diana Waggoner, Connie Singer, Davis Bushnell, Karen Jackovich, and Richard K. Rein, "The Legacy of Jonestown: A Year of Nightmares and Unanswered Questions," *People Magazine,* November 12, 1979, http://www.people.com/people/article/0,20075018,00.html. Accessed February 20, 2014, now offline.

11. See "Consultation on the Implications of Jonestown for the Black Church and the Nation," in Rebecca Moore, *Understanding Jonestown and Peoples Temple* (Westport, CT: Praeger, 2009), 115.

12. Chris Hatcher, "After Jonestown: Survivors of Peoples Temple," in *The Need for a Second Look at Jonestown,* ed. Rebecca Moore and Fielding M. McGehee III (Lewiston, NY: The Edwin Mellen Press, 1989), 135.

13. Brian Carroll and Katie Landry, "Logging in and Letting out: Using Online Social Networks to Grieve and Mourn," *Bulletin of Science, Technology, and Society* 30, no. 5 (2010), 343.

14. Noam Chomsky and Edward Herman, *Manufacturing Consent: The Political Economy of the Mass Media* (New York: Pantheon, 1988).

15. Jed R. Brubaker, Gillian R. Hayes and Paul Dourish, "Beyond the Grave: Facebook as a Site for the Expansion of Death and Mourning," *The Information Society* 29, no. 3 (2013): 152–63.

16. Ibid., 161.

17. Carroll and Landry, "Logging in and Letting out," 344.

18. Ibid., 347.

19. Pamela Roberts, "Here Today and Cyberspace Tomorrow: Memorials and Bereavement Support on the Web," *Generations* 28, no. 2 (Summer 2004): 43.

20. Nicholas Grider, "'Faces of the Fallen' and the Dematerialization of US War Memorials," *Visual Communication* 30, no. 6 (2007): 265–79.

21. Maya Socolovsky, "Cyber-Spaces of Grief: Online Memorials and the Columbine High School Shootings," *JAC* 24, no. 2, Special Issue Part 1: Trauma and Rhetoric (2004): 471.

22. Pierre Nora, quoted in Socolovsky, "Cyber-Spaces of Grief," 467.

23. Socolovsky, "Cyber-Spaces of Grief," 472.

24. *McGehee v. CIA* resulted in the release of heavily-redacted CIA documents in 1983, which nevertheless indicated that the agency was monitoring life in Jonestown closely even before the deaths. *Moore v. FBI* unsuccessfully attempted to challenge national security exemptions used to withhold documents about my sister Carolyn Layton. Filed in 2001, *McGehee et al. v. U.S. Department of Justice* has not been settled as of this writing, although the FBI has released additional documents and photographs as a result of court orders.

25. Matthew D. Wittmer, "Memorializing Mount Carmel Center East of Waco, Texas," http://www.stormbound.org/waco.html. Accessed August 16, 2013.

26. Rick Ross, "The Ross Institute Internet Archives for the Study of Destructive Cults, Controversial Groups and Movements," http://www.culteducation.com/. Accessed August 16, 2013.

27. Tape numbers (e.g., Q042) were assigned by FBI personnel who listened to them and briefly logged their contents in their investigation of the assassination of Congressman Leo Ryan. A summary of Q042 appears at http://jonestown.sdsu.edu/?page_id=29078; a transcript is located at http://jonestown.sdsu.edu/?page_id=29079; and an MP3 file appears at https://archive.org/details/ptc1978-11-18.flac16.

28. Roberts, "Here Today and Cyberspace Tomorrow," 41–46.

29. Tony Walter, "A New Model of Grief: Bereavement and Biography," *Mortality* 1, no. 1 (1996): 7–25.

30. Ibid., 15.

31. Carroll and Landry, "Logging in and Letting out," 345.

32. Roberts, "Here Today and Cyberspace Tomorrow," 44–45.

33. Sherrie Tatum, "Remembrance of Larry Schacht," *the jonestown report* 11 (2009), *Alternative Considerations,* http://jonestown.sdsu.edu/?page_id=30878. Accessed January 25, 2014.

34. Eddie Patterson, "Judy Stahl, My First Love," *the jonestown report* 11 (2009), *Alternative Considerations,* http://jonestown.sdsu.edu/?page_id=30880. Accessed January 25, 2014.

35. Edward Patterson, "Forces of God, Faces of Evil," *the jonestown report* 14 (2012), *Alternative Considerations,* http://jonestown.sdsu.edu/?page_id=34315. Accessed January 25, 2014.

36. Margaret Byrne, "Let Me Tell You a Story: An Example of the Mythopoetic in Palliative Care Education," in *Spirituality, Mythopoesis and Learning,* ed. Peter Willis, Timothy Leonard, Anne Morrison, and Steven Hodge (Mt Gravatt, Australia: Post Press, 2009), 259.

37. Socolovsky, "Cyber-Spaces of Grief," 469.

38 Andrew Stark, "Forever-or Not," *The Wilson Quarterly* 30, no. 1 (Winter 2006): 58–61.

39. David Parker Wise, "Re-United after 35 Years through the Alternative Considerations Website," *Alternative Considerations,* http://jonestown.sdsu.edu/?page_id=31955. Accessed January 25, 2014.

40. Fielding M. McGehee III, "The Campaign for a New Memorial: A Brief History," *Alternative Considerations,* http://jonestown.sdsu.edu/?page_id=34364. Accessed January 25, 2014. Approximately $15,000 was spent on the stone markers and the remaining $5,000 was spent on costs incurred during fundraising, such as printing and mailing of an appeal,

printing and distribution of a program, travel scholarships for those wishing to attend the dedication, and other business-related expenses. No funds were spent on any stipend, salary, or honorarium for members of the organizing committee.

41. Fielding M. McGehee III, "Jim Jones' Name on the Marker: A Discussion of the Committee's Decision," *Alternative Considerations,* http://jonestown.sdsu.edu/?page_id=29418. Accessed January 25, 2014.

42. Jacques Derrida, *Archive Fever: A Freudian Impression,* trans. Eric Prenowitz (Chicago and London: University of Chicago Press, 1995). I am not going to address Derrida's analysis of Freud and the death drive here.

43. Ibid., 25.

44. Walter, "A New Model of Grief."

45. http://jonestown.sdsu.edu/WhoDied/bio.php?Id=1344. Accessed January 25, 2014.

46. Derrida, *Archive Fever,* 4, no. 1.

Part III

Virtual Worlds beyond Death

Chapter 9

Remembering Laura Roslin: Fictional Death and a Real Bereavement Community Online

Erica Hurwitz Andrus

Introduction

The *RememberLaura* community on the *LiveJournal* website was created in March 2009 as the television show *Battlestar Galactica* (*BSG*) came to an end. In the finale of the series, one of the main characters, Laura Roslin, finally succumbs to cancer, and peacefully departs from life. The first post of the *RememberLaura* community reads:

Welcome to the Laura Roslin Memory Wall.

We all knew it was inevitable, yet many of us still hoped for some miracle, for some magical storyline that would let Laura have her happy ending.

When she died, as beautiful and graceful as it was, it was hard to come to terms with the loss of her character.

The emotions we have are very real—we felt like she was a close friend, that we connected with her in some way. So losing her was hard, and this community was set up for people to realize that 1) you're not alone, and 2) there are ways you can get through this.

We'd like people to post any kind of memorial they wish. Pictures, picspam, fanfic, letters to Laura, poems, essays, even posts asking for some sort of guidance on how to accept our loss. Also, **please don't feel like your tributes have to be somber.** Happy posts—remembering the good times, remembering all the awesome things about Laura, even your favorite *BSG* moments that featured her—are not only welcome, they are encouraged.

[...]

There's so much life. Let's celebrate her life in the best way possible—by not letting her memory die.[1]

This online community represents possibly the best example of how the vast and complex realm of cyberspace can provide a safe, warm, and creative "place" for fans to work through their emotional reactions to not only the death of a well-loved fictional character, but the end of an entire (televisual) universe. Because it is explicitly addressing the death of a character, the tone of respect, honor, and support is established from the outset, and it fosters the positive side of internet communities, in which people feel free to joke, disagree, and share their emotions, knowing they are all there with one common shared element: love for that character and that show.

In his classic book *Textual Poachers,* Henry Jenkins writes that there are some fans who "move beyond the status of criticism and interpretation" to satisfy the "oft-voiced desires of the fan community" through creative acts of writing and assemblage of videos, music, and digitally altered photographs, not to mention handcrafted works of art.[2] The fans involved in *RememberLaura* mostly fall into Jenkins's category, and the *LiveJournal* social network is oriented toward this kind of fan creativity. Fans create new stories, or "fanon," to add to the stories presented in the official productions, known to fans as "canon." As an academic and a fan, I feel my own involvement does not rise above the level of "criticism and interpretation" so I participate in the site primarily as a "lurker"—a member who reads and enjoys the contributions posted there but doesn't make her presence known overtly. I do participate in the occasional surveys posted by the moderators, but, beyond that, my posts reflect only my opinions and do not enlarge the boundaries of "fanon" (a portmanteau of fan-canon indicating widely accepted fan fiction) as more literary contributions do. For this chapter, I drew on the thousands of posts and comments that are publicly available to anyone who can access the *LiveJournal* site. The community consists of around 364 members and another 300 or so who "watch" the community, as well as two moderators. In the years since it started, the site has had over 1,800 entries, and more than 38,000 comments. Usually, the moderator posts something, and a few people will respond. On certain days, the number of responses rises above 100, but the majority of posts have between 4 and 20 comments.

Who Was Laura Roslin?

One fan described her as:

> A president. A teacher. A formidable protector. A loving mother figure. Beloved. A hedonist. A statist. A visionary. A savior. She is the reluctant warrior, the self-sacrificing politician. She is the general who carries no weapon but her mind. She is the childless woman who is mother to all of humanity. She is the martyr who fights for her life. She is the frail and dying hero. She is a woman of noble character, and her worth is far above jewels.[3]

Roslin was a fictional character from the reimagined *BSG* television series, a post-9/11 "space opera" based on the premise and characters of the hokey 1970s television series of the same name. In this 21st-century reenvisioning of the show, the creators, or "show runners," David Eick and Ronald D. Moore sought to create a world in which the fears, dilemmas, and traumas of viewers' own world could be explored in a gritty and unflinching portrayal of human responses to destruction and revelation. The dark nature of the series was in part a response to 9/11.[4] The entire show itself can be understood as a meditation on death, from the scale of planetary genocide, to an examination of the morality of abortion in the face of human extinction, to the question of what it means for a machine to die. (The enemies in the show are a race of cyborgs, called "Cylons" who have a seemingly endless supply of backup bodies, both human-looking and mechanical, into which one can be downloaded when one dies).

On the day I discovered the *RememberLaura* online community, it happened to be early March 2012. I was researching a paper on religion in *Battlestar Galactica* or *BSG* for short. I was searching for a good quote to illustrate how Laura Roslin, the character who is catapulted by disaster from the role of education minister to president of all human beings, inspired strong feelings of admiration and loyalty in her fans. The show inspired many websites, including an exhaustive wiki created by fans.[5] In the course of my search for testimonials about Laura Roslin, I came across the *RememberLaura* community displaying this message: "And here's a poll about our anniversary party. It's a little over two weeks away (March 23). Majority rules on these, though if we end up having a week of festivities, I'll pick the most popular options."[6] The next day the results were posted, indicating how 28 people voted to celebrate the third "anniversary" of Laura Roslin's death. As an introduction to the community, it brought me up short. How could you have an anniversary for a person who had never lived, not in the same time or universe as the creators of the site at any rate, and therefore never died? How did they determine the date of her death, when in the *BSG* story-universe, it happened millennia ago in some remote prehistoric past? How do you have a party online anyhow? And most importantly, what is going on here? I immediately signed up on the site and have been a "lurker" there ever since, enjoying the photos, stories, and discussions they continue to host, occasionally contributing responses to prompts and polls, and realizing over time that this community offers something special—it shows us how we turn to each other to remember the ones we have lost, even if they only existed as fictional characters.

Transmission of Culture: Mourning

Human beings as individuals, and societies have a fascination with death, being creatures who are cognizant of their own finitude. Every society must create and practice ways of acknowledging and transcending the death of people, and often, unfortunately, the deaths of whole groups of people due to diseases, natural disasters, and, of course, violent human actions. For societies to continue and to maintain their sense of identity, the culture they embody must be taught and shared, from one generation to the next, from established members to newcomers. The ways we handle the paradoxes and challenges of mortality must be part of the culture we pass on, or as French scholar Régis Debray describes it, the culture we *transmit*. Debray, the creator of the term "mediology" and a philosopher of communication theory, sees media, including now the internet, as a primary form, not simply to communicate ideas, emotions, or information, but of the transmission of culture, a longer-term and more sublimated process.[7] In particular, the medium of cyberspace, when it becomes a venue for a community of fans devoted to the maintenance of a world created by television, can function to facilitate the transmission of techniques of embracing the life and memory of those individuals who have passed on. This *LiveJournal* community, *RememberLaura,* is a perfect example of this transmission process, a fan community dedicated to the memory of Laura Roslin, the fictional president of the Twelve Colonies in a recent version of *BSG*.

Debray writes that

> transmission takes its course through time (diachronically), developing and changing as it goes. A thread plus a drama, it links the living to the dead, most often when the senders are physically absent. Whether configuring the present to a luminous past or to a salvific future, mythical or not, a transmission arranges the effective force of the actual with reference to the virtual [...]. Communication excels by cutting short; transmission by prolonging.[8]

The "senders" in the virtual community are always physically absent, and the character being honored is triply absent, not only because of the virtual nature of the community, but through death, as well, and through the tacit fact of her fictionality. In addition, the entire site's purpose is to prolong the participants' engagement with the stories and the characters. Debray expresses the idea that "[w]e transmit meanings so that the things we live, believe, and think do not perish with *us* (as opposed to *me*)."[9] In the case of the demise of a television series, the "us" undergoes a transformation from a fictional culture, to the (cyber) community of fans who maintain the memories, values, and stories that the fictional community embodied (although never literally). When the "powers that be" cease to create the world in question, fans like the members of this *LiveJournal* community step in and pick up the burden of transmission. Other venues like the Battlestar Wiki, numerous Tumblr blogs, and a variety of other *LiveJournal* communities exist for maintaining the *BSG* 'verse, but this one stands out because it was created to be an outlet for expressions of grieving to be aired in a socially acceptable virtual setting.

Thus *RememberLaura* illustrates how the internet creates genuine communities of fans who can embrace the emotions and practices associated with grief as well as admiration, not only transmitting but also adapting cultural values and practices surrounding death to a virtual context.

Why Remember Laura?

In the midst of the grand scale of death and destruction that forms both backdrop and premise for *BSG,* the character of Laura Roslin represents death in a more intimate, more ordinary, and deeply more poignant way. Within the first 15 minutes of the very first episode, Laura Roslin is given the news that she is suffering from a terminal form of breast cancer. In a rare scene of quiet, early in the series' first episode, we see Roslin sitting in a spacious, cathedral-like room. The walls and ceiling are glass, and she gazes out at the city around her—including a variety of transit airships that remind the viewer we are on a place that is Earth-like, but not Earth—and she waits in an austere but comfortable looking armchair. The camera revolves around her seated figure, and we see that the sound of a door opening makes her jump and flinch a little in her seat. The camera pans back, and a man in a white lab coat strides into the room and sits down at a desk across from her. He has a full head of silvery hair, and a serious, kindly face. He leans forward across the desk and says matter-of-factly, "I'm afraid the test is positive. The mass is malignant." We see Laura's face accepting the news as though she had tried to prepare herself for the worst, and for the first time in the scene, it seems that music begins, drowning out the remainder of the doctor's speech. As the scene ends, though, the sound is revealed to be the noise made by preparations for departure by an airship.[10] So, from the beginning, the audience knows that this important main character is going to be struggling with a death sentence, if not dying before the show is over. In a brief, but poignant moment, viewers are introduced to a woman they know is embarking on a terrible journey through illness. Some fans in the *RememberLaura* community cite this as an important moment in their relationship with the character, like when one writes: "I caught her face in her first scene in the miniseries in the doctor's office, and she touched my heart . . . but it was a brush. An infatuation. All I knew was that I was going to pay attention to her."[11] Before her day is over, she will learn of the attack on her home worlds including the death of all 42 people who were ahead of her in line for the presidency, at which time she will assume the office of president of the Twelve Colonies herself.

Throughout the arc of the show, Laura Roslin proves herself to be a strong, willful, loving, stubborn, devious, and shrewd leader. Her flaws and her strengths are both emphasized as she makes a journey from being a minister of education, with a basically agnostic religious perspective, to being the civilian leader of the remnant of humanity that survived the attacks, and the "dying leader," prophesied in the Colonies' polytheistic religious texts, destined to lead the people through the stars, away from the enemy, to a new Edenic home on a lost planet (called Earth incidentally)—where she would die of her affliction before seeing humanity established in its new home. The religious implications in this plotline are too numerous to follow up in this chapter, but the resonance between Laura's story with a fictional religion from within the *BSG* universe as well as with the real-world Abrahamic tradition of Moses leading his people through 40 years of wandering in the desert and arriving at the banks of the Jordan to see Canaan but never live there cannot be missed. Like Moses, Laura Roslin has troubling visions and encounters resistance to her religious message when she begins to use the scriptures as the basis for decisions concerning the movements of the fleet. In contrast with Moses, Laura Roslin is constantly aware of her mortality because she knows she is being consumed by breast cancer, which is paradoxically a source of power as well as weakness: her authority as a leader and a prophet is confirmed by the disease that marks her as the "Dying Leader" of scripture.

The creators of the show consciously chose to "give" Laura Roslin cancer, as opposed to some other disease or something alien as appropriate to an alien world, so that the full emotional impact of the disease would be understood and felt by the audience. As the writer and producer, Ronald D. Moore says in the commentary that accompanies the miniseries DVD,

> Cancer being a sort of a recognizable Earth problem, something the audience can relate to, was where I wanted to go, as opposed to giving her some made-up sounding, you know, bizarro, exotic disease that doesn't matter to anyone. When you say that someone has cancer it means something, it brings an emotional response from the audience, it grounds you in the reality of it, you've suddenly put yourself into Laura's predicament.[12]

Many if not most of us know first- or secondhand the fear, anger, and grieving that accompany a diagnosis and treatment of cancer. The ordinary horror of cancer makes her character's other challenges more poignant, as we watch her step into her role as leader and then as lover in her relationship with the admiral of the fleet. In her emotional journey through the uneven progress of her disease, the audience sees her in the most intimate moments of strength and weakness, watching as she weathers the effects of chemotherapy, as she makes devastatingly questionable moral decisions about how to treat prisoners, when to change laws, and how to rig an election in order, she feels, to save humanity. These are moments we could never share with an actual friend, coworker, family member, or teacher, but there we are, where Moore and Eick have put us, just inches from her soulful gaze, as she gives the shockingly cold order to open the airlock and execute a prisoner. And there we are, too, in the cockpit of the little shuttlecraft at the end of their journey, as her beloved admiral daydreams out loud of the house he'll build for her, and she quietly slips into death.

The arc of the series is coterminous with her life as a cancer patient: it begins with her diagnosis and ends within minutes of her death. The accumulation of intimate moments in between created a powerful bond for and a strong sense of the reality of this character, this person, named Laura Roslin. For over five years (or four episodic seasons), viewers learned to respect, understand, and ultimately love her, in all her frightening complexity—although it would be disingenuous not to acknowledge that the character and the actress who played her had detractors as well as devotees, an inevitable outcome, given the role she plays as a female leader who does not always conform to gendered expectations of nurturing and compassion. For example, her decision in the beginning of the series to take all the ships capable of "faster than light" propulsion to an undisclosed place of safety, leaving thousands of civilians on less technologically advanced ships to die in an attack, made her seem "cold" and heartless to many viewers who expected a woman to be more emotionally vulnerable. On the other hand, her ability to be calculating proved one of her strengths over the course of the series; and the challenge to expectations also added to her appeal as a more human, well-rounded character. Some of the fans on *RememberLaura* report that one reason they liked her so much was because of her hard edge, for example, when one fan described how Laura's response to the question of who put her in charge demonstrated this no-nonsense attitude that allows her to be a powerful leader. The fan starts with a quote from the miniseries:

> Doral: "W . . . wait a minute, who put you in charge?"
>
> Laura: "Well, that's a good question. The answer is: no one. But, this is a government ship, and I am the *senior* government official so that puts me in charge . . . so, why don't *you* help me out and go down into the cargo area and see about setting it up as a living space."
>
> Laura then does a freakin' 180-degree heel-pivot, effectively dismissing the little weasel. This is **the** moment where I fell in love with Laura. This is SUCH a classic teacher move—"If you have time to complain, then you're not busy enough". I already knew I was going to like her, but this moment shot me straight into Roslin-worship.
>
> Hehe, I should've included this one in the "favorite scene" thread, but I just rewatched the mini yesterday and was reminded of the absolute kick-ass-ness of this scene.:)[13]

When the series ended, viewers were left to mourn the death of the beloved "mother" as well as the end of the story-world. Her character had no children, but she represented a nurturing role through her association with teaching, and as a romantic partner for "the Old Man" (as Admiral William Adama was known to his close friends and crew) who was both a literal and symbolic father. Although the series ends with the transcendent discovery of the "Promised Land" (or planet in this case), the experience of viewers is that the *BSG* 'verse has come to an end, at least on television. The world that has been so meticulously and lovingly constructed for the previous five years can now only be visited through the creative efforts of the fans themselves (as well as, of course reviewings of the special edition DVDs complete with commentaries, short features, and the webisodes that give viewers insight into plotlines that just couldn't be included in the main series due to time constraints).[14] Although *BSG*, like many television shows and films, became the source for many licensed products—games, comic books, novels, collectables—the focus of this particular online community seems to be fiction, both "canon"—part of the official story line of the show—and "fanon"—story lines created by fans, but consistent with the official plotlines.

"All of This Has Happened Before, and All of This Will Happen Again"[15]

If Americans search the airwaves either for the reenchantment of this world or the creation of new and engaging alternate worlds, the question of what to do when a fictional world ends seems unresolved. There are a number of options for fans of a show to engage when the finale comes around. The network usually creates a certain amount of buzz around the show's final airdate. This seems to happen most in cases where a show has run for a number of years and the characters have attained an iconic pop cultural status, like *Seinfeld* and *Cheers,* and more recently *Breaking Bad, House,* and *The Sopranos.* Because of their genres and settings (i.e., sitcoms, hospital procedurals, gangster antihero drama), the shows could have, in theory, continued indefinitely. Other shows seek to build into their narrative structure a logical end, like *Alias, Lost,* or *BSG.* These shows' finales function as a kind of "reveal" in which certain mysterious plot elements are finally resolved, along with the relationships between main characters, usually. Those types of shows logically create a great deal of hype around their final episode, whose secrets are closely guarded, in some ways even after they are aired, so that people who watch them in the next week or so are not inadvertently subjected to "spoilers."

All of these sorts of season finales (predating the recent shows produced for a streaming audience and delivered as complete seasons available for viewing at the discretion of the consumer) are freighted with cultural significance, to the extent that a person might ask: do you remember who you were with for the *Seinfeld* finale? Do you remember where you watched the last episode of *Lost?* Websites spring up offering advice for hosting finale theme parties, complete with menu, décor, and costume suggestions. One web channel even offers a generic "how-to" video on hosting a TV series finale party, using *Gray's Anatomy* as an example. The tone of such parties is usually lighthearted, and not meant to resemble rituals of mourning, but the video does draw on religious language (in a somewhat satirical manner) when the narrator suggests that "instead of sulking alone on the couch, you can escort those memorable characters into rerun heaven" by hosting a party.[16]

The proliferation of fanfic, as documented by cultural studies scholar Henry Jenkins,[17] offers another, more long-term, answer to the dilemma of how to carry on in the absence of new episodes. Fanfic, fictional stories based on characters and plots established in the television shows, creates new knowledge of the world in question, and allows members of the community to continue to "play" in the universe of their choosing. Mary Kirby-Diaz, who studied fan communities devoted to the *Buffy the Vampire Slayer* television series, identifies different levels of fan commitment and interaction. Those fans whom she calls "story oriented," find outlet in writing "fanfic"—they are fans for whom the stories offered by the television show (and any webisodes) are only the beginning.[18]

RememberLaura: An Online Memorial Community

One of the many *BSG*-fan websites to come into being after the end of the show is the *LiveJournal* community called *RememberLaura. LiveJournal* provides a platform for fans of any media or celebrity to create online virtual communities of like-minded fans. It seems to be especially oriented toward fans who actively extend the worlds of their chosen shows through "fanfic" and the creation of icons, banners, music video collages, and so on. These fans of Laura articulate and examine their interest in continuing the story lines of Laura Roslin's character themselves. For example, in October 2012, the moderator posted a prompt referring specifically to fiction that expands Roslin's romantic life: "why do we feel the desire to enhance Laura's storyline with affairs that we don't think really happened in the series?" to which one particularly eloquent contributor described different pairings she had explored in her writing and why, ending with the explanation that "I utterly adore Laura as a character, and I want to know everything there is to know about her, so this lets me figure all of that out."[19]

RememberLaura is only one of many sites dedicated to *BSG*, and even to Laura Roslin. As far as I have been able to discover, it is, however, the only website that exists as a place for *BSG* fans to actively memorialize the life of a fictional character. As such, this cyber-memorialization differs from sites that are created in memory of actual people, celebrities or not. Because no one alive was actually related to the deceased, the ways that fans discuss her life do not have to take into account the possibility of trespassing on someone else's more "legitimate" grief over the death of Laura Roslin. All fans have equal access to her life, both interior and observed. The affection fans feel for her is based on emotional experiences that are subjectively real, and which are acknowledged freely to be based on interactions with a person who is objectively not real, a fiction. Likewise, the grief inspired by watching a beloved fictional character die feels like real grief and in-spires responses of sincere desires to reach out to others to share that grief and celebrate the "life" of the character in ways that reflect social norms about grieving and mourning the life of any celebrity. In fact, early in the community's history fans report sometimes responding more emotion-ally (crying more) in response to thoughts about Laura Roslin's death than to the deaths of extended family members, and turning to the *LiveJournal* community for understanding because family and friends respond that it was "just a show."[20]

Why Mourn a Fictional Person with a Virtual Community?

Since the 1950s, when Donald Horton and R. Richard Wohl published their influential article "Mass Communication and Para-Social Interaction" in the journal *Psychiatry*, researchers have studied the phenomenon of televi-sion viewers developing "parasocial relationships" with fictional television characters or celebrities. In these relationships fans form emotional bonds with people who cannot reciprocate because the relationship is formed through the medium of television.[21] Keren Eyal and Jonathan Cohen de-scribe these relationships as "a set of feelings viewers develop toward media characters that allow viewers to think and feel toward characters as if they know and have a special connection with them."[22] In their study of the phe-nomenon they call "parasocial breakup," these communications research-ers found that the end of a show (in this case, the sitcom *Friends*) did cause a kind of distress but not to the same degree as a breakup with a romantic partner or a falling-out with an actual friend might do. They acknowl-edge, however, that the amount of distress felt by a person who developed a parasocial relationship with a television character might be different in different contexts, a soap opera character versus one from a sitcom, for example.[23]

The kinds of shows that create entirely new or alternate universes, it might be predicted, could result in a more profound sense of loss when the show ends. S. Brent Plate explores the concept of "world-making" as part of the process of re-creation/recreation that television performs in our lives. He argues that science-fiction films, particularly, create entire worlds through narrative but also *mise-en-scène* and the use of cosmically sym-bolic images, such as the stars, planets, and other celestial bodies frequently found in the opening frames of both film and television. The depth and complexity of these worlds increases their ability to absorb the viewer in an alternate universe and experience the emotions and passage of time that is only subjectively "real" due to the constructed world of the television show or film.[24] The popular press, for example, reported a rash of depression amongst viewers of the film *Avatar* who felt despair after seeing the film and being confronted with the fact that they could not live in the world of the film on a permanent basis.[25] Perhaps the fanfic approach is a creative and highly adaptive way of grappling with the phenomenon of the parasocial relationship and its inevitable demise. Further research on this question is necessary.

The *LiveJournal* website both takes advantage of the internet's ability to facilitate the creation of community and blends it with the powerful urge to continue to create and play in this fictional world. Although the very first post, inviting participants to sign up and share both grief and joy in relation to Laura's life, refers to the site as a "memory wall," that metaphor did not stick. The memory wall concept is familiar to all viewers of *BSG*, as it plays a prominent role within the series to memorialize lost crew and civilians in the fleet. The show also uses the memorial wall as another mirror of our own society and its ritualized communal reaction to tragedy and loss, made familiar through iconic media coverage of memorials at Ground Zero in Manhattan after 9/11 and at Buckingham Palace after the death of Princess Diana. But in the *LiveJournal* community, simply posting pictures of ones who are gone is not satisfying to the community as a whole, and the ongoing practice of communicating thoughts, desires, and alternate universes changes this wall into a gallery, living room, lounge, debate hall, or any number of more interactive and flexible sites. As found through casual browsing of *LiveJournal,* most often the participants simply refer to it as a "comm"—shorthand for "community."

Lorne Dawson, in his "Religion and the Quest for Virtual Community," delineates six characteristics that allow us to identify an actual online community, as opposed to a more ephemeral or random form of online communication. These six include: "1) interactivity; 2) stability of membership; 3) stability of identity; 4) netizenship and social control; 5) personal concern; 6) occurrence in a public space."[26] The *RememberLaura* site fulfills all of these criteria. The site is highly interactive, as it solicits responses from participants on an almost daily basis. The users of the site return regularly enough to become familiar with each other's usernames, and to offer each other "gifts"—a sign of "netizenship" according to Dawson.[27] So the membership is generally stable (although declining in activity as time passes) and made up of people who consistently return under the same user ID. Because the stated purpose of the site is to offer support in the face of emotional distress, the posts do tend to show a concern for the feelings of others on the site and a desire to encourage people to express themselves and be creative in their engagement with the world of Laura Roslin.

Most posts focus exclusively on Roslin and the ideas people have about her tastes, life outside the *BSG* canon, and other creative speculation, but on some occasions, people post comments expressing their emotional connection not just to Roslin, but to the site and other members of the community itself. One such occasion took place in January 2013, when, after almost four years, the moderator announced she was going to be closing the community. Within days, two members had volunteered to take over, and within a week they had done so. The announcement inspired a number of grateful posts to the three people involved, including statements like:

> But I want to thank you for creating this community. Not only was I devastated by Laura's death, but I also wasn't ready to stop fangirling over the show in general, and this was the only community that kept posting regularly after *BSG* ended. So it really helped me on both fronts.

And:

> Thank you so much for all the work you've done here. I really enjoyed this comm and for me it was what made the difference into actually participating into the fandom instead of just reading fics.
> *hugs everyone in the comm*[28]

Fan Communities and Created Universes

The universe of *BSG*, like the life of Laura Roslin, has a distinct beginning, middle, and end, if you approach the show as a television event—a series of discrete episodes, produced in units of seasons, each season having its own story arc, and the entire show having a larger arc, consisting of many interwoven personal stories making up the larger story of the conflict between Colonials and Cylons. In watching the show, a person becomes immersed in this fictional world. The availability of DVDs creates the possibility of extended immersion in the *BSG* experience. For a viewer, every episode begins, not with the show itself, but the iconic turning globe of Universal Studios, and the brass fanfare of the network's theme. As S. Brent Plate describes, the creators of television and film worlds signal the holistic nature of each new creation with symbols of cosmic significance. He writes, "world making, like filmmaking, is an active intervention into the space and time of the universe."[29]

In online, intentional fan communities like this, we can find the strongest argument for the idea of online religion embodied in a pop culture form if we follow classical definitions of religion such as those proposed by Geertz and Durkheim—symbolic systems and culturally constructed meanings based on shared emotional experiences. These definitions, like Plate's world making, allow us to overcome the perceived dichotomy between what is serious and what is play by understanding that the symbolic significance of the worlds we invent in our play reflects the deeper assumptions of our everyday lives. Rachel Wagner's work on the religious aspects of online gaming in *Godwired* also addresses this process of continuing to build a world after its commercial life span is over. Approaching the *RememberLaura* community from the perspective of play allows us to explore the created television world's ability to function through "make-believe" as a source of meaning in life. Wagner writes: "Both games and religion can set a mode of being in place for us, color our values, give us stories that provide meaning to our lives, make us promises, give us interpretive grist for storytelling and identity formation, and create in us a deep desire to enter into the other worlds they evoke."[30] The serious play that people engage in with transmediation, in this case the virtual *RememberLaura* community and fanfic, allows people in a "secular" world to experience a kind of faith. Participants can simultaneously acknowledge the fantasy of the created world and its fictions, and the reality of the emotional sway it holds over us. The fictional life of Laura Roslin thus becomes a vehicle for individuals to care—about her, about each other, about art, music, the sanctity of a life itself.

How Do Fans Remember Laura?

While holding these two opposing thoughts in their heads—this is real, this is make believe—authors of fanfic approach *BSG* as they may approach other aspects of life. Like the fans of soap operas as discussed in Nancy K. Baym's research, the people who participate in the *RememberLaura* community find their own emotions stimulated by the connection they have developed with the characters, and use the internet to share that emotional experience with others who empathize.[31] Even on July 17, 2013, almost 10 years after the show premiered, one participant responded to the photo of the day with a post that expressed her emotional response:

sniffles
As time goes on I think I miss Laura even more!

Is that sad? She's a fictional character, Mary has moved on, so have the fans! But I miss her!:-([32]

One particularly fruitful prompt from the moderator asked "When did you first fall in love with Laura? Which episode, which scene, which quote or quirk caught your heart?" to which many responded with descriptions that evoked feelings like being "smitten" or "heartbroken" or "captivated." One fan described a "three-step process" and another wrote that it began with:

Her first on screen appearance. At first I thought that it was one hell of an ugly colour for a business suit and then I saw her face and I think I literally went "damn you're going to break my heart, aren't you?"

I tend to always be drawn to the middle-aged woman in a show or film and I immediately liked her. I think her reaction [to learning of her cancer diagnosis] on the ship [in the series premier episode] when she escapes from Billy [her aide] and just tears open her blazer had me nearly in tears, which rarely happens. I knew I was doomed in the best possible way.

33 [The first regular episode] only cemented my love for Laura and started my never-ending love for Mary.[33]

This fan's description of being "doomed in the best possible way" evokes the draw that we feel to this type of return over and over to a show that causes us to love a person and then takes her away from us. The community is an expression of the yearning to ignite feelings not simply of passion, excitement, adventure, and adrenaline that we associate with science-fiction war dramas but also with the grief that accompanies the deaths that are the requisite sacrifices to the events that inspire those emotions. The internet opens space for experiencing these emotions safely, when and where we desire them, and still in the company of others who understand and empathize.

According to Johanna Sumiala in her book *Media and Ritual: Death, Community and Everyday Life,* anthropologists have described four ways in which death rituals serve communities, all of which must face loss. These are: to "help individuals and societies cope with the loss," to "serve as the trajectory from dying to afterlife"; "to help individuals and societies cope with the fear of death"; and "help individuals and societies cope with the social and cultural consequences of death."[34] We can address each of these as they are transformed in the context of the real experiences of this virtual community. In the first case, the site was explicitly created to satisfy this need on the part of individual fans. In the second, the fanfic generated on the site, and linked to the site, creates a virtual "afterlife" for this fictional character, allowing her to live on after the show and its world have come to an official end. The "canon" of *BSG* can be an analog for "this life" where the "fanon" becomes the afterlife of the characters from the show.

The third function, helping people "cope with the fear of death," is perhaps less applicable. Fans, after all, do not have to fear their demise due to cancellation or the end of a series. In addition, the show offers little in the way of answers when it comes to questions of afterlife. The characters in the show are just as uncertain what happens after we die as most Americans. The unwillingness to provide a definitive answer to what happens after death, of course, reinforces the realism of the show. However, Roslin herself does have a vision, at a certain point in her illness, of traveling in a boat over a river to meet the members of her family who had died before, including her mother, thus opening up a possibility of an afterlife that resonates with many Christian themes of heaven.[35] Although many ideas about the afterlife are discussed by characters on the show, or depicted in their rituals or actions, I have not seen them discussed on the site.

Fourth, I would argue that the *RememberLaura* community does open up a space for people to explore the "social and cultural consequences" of both death and the end of a fictional world—the posts and discussions on the website explore not only Laura's death and absence, but the many deaths she caused or was responsible for over the course of the show, and their implications for "real life." Two examples of this stand out as topics of discussion on *RememberLaura:* an episode in which she is forced to go against her previous political stance of supporting women's choice in the matter of abortion to instituting a law against having or providing an abortion, a decision made to adjust to a new reality in which each human death represents a step toward the annihilation of humans, and each birth represents a defiance of extinction. Second, during a brief period of the show's story arc when the humans had slipped away from their Cylon enemies and found a mostly hospitable, uninhabited world to settle on, there is a scene in which Roslin discusses with Adama the value of enjoying the moment, even knowing that any threat to human lives could be the final moment for all humans. She says to him: "Let's get real. Cylons come back, we're dead. Disease strikes, we're dead. Earthquake, volcano, hurricane, today, tomorrow, five years from now, it's—And you know what I'm saying? Life's a bitch and then you die. . . . I think we should all look at every moment of every day as borrowed time." So Roslin's own reflections on death offer consolation for the fans that are searching for meaning in mortality.

One of the most striking aspects of the website is how often Laura's physical person is referenced in the posts. Her hair, legs, glasses, eyes, and smile are repeatedly remarked on, even to a poll on "which outfit is your favorite?" These references to the physicality of the character defy the ways that Laura Roslin does not exist in the real, nonvirtual world: first because she was a character acted out by the actress Mary McDonnell, and second because even in the story-world her death made her become absent. Elizabeth Hallam and Jenny Hockey examine the relationships between "death, memory, and material culture" in their book of that title, exploring "the capacity of material objects to bind the living and the dead, to hold a fragile connection across temporal distance and to preserve a material presence in the face of an embodied absence."[36] In this context, the materiality is transformed into a virtual reality, where "objects" are stories, pictures, and emoticons. Yet, the fascination with those things that created the seemingly living body of Laura Roslin (hair, legs, smile, etc.) evidences a desire to "keep her alive in our memory" not unlike the desires that actual bereaved family and friends may have when a loved one dies.

On the other hand, the memories that an individual has of a living person who has died are qualitatively different from memories created by watching a still-accessible DVD of a person whose entire life is known only through that medium. The finite nature of a scripted television drama—what can be considered "canon"—and Roslin's status as a created fictional character, give fans the freedom to create interstitial stories and knowledge that can then be shared with a community. As one fan posted in responding to the prompt asking why people like to write about Laura in relationships with other people:

> Part of it is I think that *BSG* canon is loose- as much as Laura was a lead, there are still so many spaces and threads of her story that were never dealt with in canon. Part of that is what makes it so easy to write fic, because there are all these places where there is time and story that can be filled in quite easily, expanded upon, etc. I mean, you have years between her Sean encounter and the start of the series, some episodes have weeks between them, a[nd] 16 months on New Caprica of which we saw 1 night pre-occupation and a few days right at the tail end of it, then again weeks and months between episodes till the end- it leaves for a lot of filling in.[37]

The site also allows fans to address the problem of the distinction between the beloved character and the beloved actress who plays her. Contributors acknowledge feeling conflicted about comparing one character to another, or developing loyalties to a new show based on the presence of the actress they liked in an old one. One discussion in August 2012 on the *RememberLaura* site started with this daily post:

> Mary has moved on to new roles since she played Laura, but the role of Sharon Raydor on Major Crimes is the most significant work she has done since Laura died.
>
> Since Major Crimes has started and we are now following Mary as Sharon Raydor, how is everyone dealing with it? Are you having a hard time disassociating Mary with Laura? Do you see Laura in the character of Sharon?
>
> Do you feel guilty loving Major Crimes or Sharon Raydor?
>
> Do you feel guilty shipping Mary's character with someone other than Eddie/Bill?
>
> Has Mary's evolution into a new character brought up old feelings about Laura's significance to you, or her death?
>
> I don't even need to say this, but be sure to be respectful of others' opinions, no matter how they differ or agree with yours.:)[38]

Clearly, these are questions that would never apply had the person in question been an actual person who lived and then died. The nature of fictive worlds like *BSG,* however, creates these kinds of situations, ones in which the fans of a show experience real emotions of sorrow, guilt, and loss, and still recognize the virtuality of the object of their feelings. On the *RememberLaura* site, they find a place to explore the unique opportunities for creative mourning offered by the loss of a fictional character. The confluence of television, the internet, DVDs, or streaming episodes allows for the development of new rituals of grieving that members of this community work out together and share with each other, thus adding to the cultural repertoire available for expressions of loss.

Concluding Thoughts

It could be argued that this site is no different from the many myriad communities where fans come online to share their fiction and artwork. However, the framing of the site as a memorial does make it a particularly potent example, especially in considering how media moves beyond communication into the process of transmission. The members of *RememberLaura* teach us how to transform rituals of passing on memory through material objects and memories into the transmission of virtual objects and memories.

The search to "know" a character is the heart of fanfic, and a creative response to the death of the character and the "death" of the show itself.

The *LiveJournal* "Remember Laura" community shows us how the phenomenon of transmediation—the multiplicity of media platforms all reinforcing the created universe of a particular show or book or film—creates new places to play at mourning and memorialization, places that are more satisfying because they can engage precisely that ambiguity between reality and fiction that is presented through these new universes. The emotions they elicit are real, and some fans want to return again and again to that well in order to experience the love, exhilaration, and, yes, even the grief that comes with loss.

Notes

1. *RememberLaura*, LiveJournal, 3/22/2009.

2. Henry Jenkins, *Textual Poachers: Television Fans and Participatory Culture*, Updated Twentieth Anniversary Edition (New York: Routledge, 2013), 155.

3. pocochina, "Laura Roslin: A Woman of Noble Character," LiveJournal.

4. Stacy Takacs, *Terrorism TV: Popular Entertainment in Post-9/11 America*, ed. Erika Doss and Philip J. Deloria, Culturamerica (Lawrence: University Press of Kansas, 2012).

5. *Battlestar Wiki*, http://en.battlestarwiki.org/wiki/Main_Page.

6. *RememberLaura*, 3/6/2012.

7. Regis Debray, *Transmitting Culture*, ed. Lawrence D. Kritzman, trans. Eric Rauth, European Perspectives (New York: Columbia University Press, 2000).

8. Ibid., 3.

9. Ibid.

10. "Miniseries," *Battlestar Galactica*, (2003), 1.1.

11. obsessive_a101, *RememberLaura*, 6/20/2013 and 1/15/2014.

12. Ronald D. Moore, David Eick, and Michael Rymer, *Audio Commentary*, *Battlestar Galactica: The Miniseries*. Universal Studios (2004).

13. Aka_plynn. *RememberLaura*, 4/3/2009.

14. The remarkable amount of "extras" available through the internet and on DVD special features in fact created a controversy about the extent to which the network and the show runners were attempting to control the "fanon"-inserting official stories and information into the interstices where fans usually find the space to practice their own creativity. See Suzanne Scott, "Authorized Resistance: Is Fan Production Frakked?" in *Cylons in America: Critical Studies in Battlesstar Galactica*, ed. Tiffany Potter and C.W. Marshall (New York: Continuum, 2008).

15. "Miniseries," *Battlestar Galactica*, (2003). In an interview transcribed on the Battlestar Wiki website, Ronald D. Moore explains that the phrase was originally taken from Disney's *Peter Pan*, but seemed to fit the religion of the Colonials (Humans) and is identified as the first line of the sacred scroll called *Pythia*.

16. "How to Throw a Series Finale Party," Videojug, http://www.videojug.com/film/how-to-throw-a-series-finale-party.

17. Jenkins, *Textual Poachers*.

18. Mary Kirby-Diaz, "So What's the Story? Story-Oriented and Series-Oriented Fans: A Complex of Behaviors," in *Buffy and Angel Conquer the Internet: Essays on Online Fandom,* ed. Mary Kirby-Diaz (Jefferson, NC: McFarland & Company, Inc., 2009).

19. Icedteainthebag, and astreamofstars. *RememberLaura,* 10/23/2012.

20 See, for example, *RememberLaura,* 4/9/2009.

21. Donald Horton and R. Richard Wohl, "Mass Communication and Para-Social Interaction," *Psychiatry* 19 (August 1956), 215–29. See also Cristel Antonia Russell and Barbara B Stern, "Consumers, Characters, and Products: A Balance Model of Sitcom Product Placement Effects," *Journal of Advertising* 30, no. 1 (Spring 2006), 7–21 for a review of literature parasocial theory in the fields of communications, psychology, and marketing.

22. Keren Eyal and Jonathan Cohen, "When Good Friends Say Goodbye: A Parasocial Breakup Study," *Journal of Broadcasting & Electronic Media* 50, no. 3 (2006), 504.

23. Ibid.

24. S. Brent Plate, "Filmmaking and World Making: Re-Creating Time and Space in Myth and Film," in *Teaching Religion and Film,* ed. Gregory J. Watkins, *Teaching Religious Studies* (New York: Oxford University Press, 2008).

25. see, for example, Jo Piazza, "Audiences Experience 'Avatar' Blues," CNN.com, January 11, 2010.

26. Lorne Dawson, "Religion and the Quest for Virtual Community," in *Religion Online: Finding Faith on the Internet,* ed. Lorne L. Dawson and Douglas E. Cowan (New York: Routledge, 2004).

27. Reflecting the patterns described in Karen Hellekson, "A Fannish Field of Value: Online Fan Gift Culture," *Cinema Journal* 48, no. 4 (Summer, 2009), 113–18.

28. *RememberLaura,* 1/15/2013.

29. Plate, "Filmmaking and World Making," 221.

30. Rachel Wagner, *Godwired: Religion, Ritual and Virtual Reality,* ed. Stewart M. Hoover, Jolyon Mitchell, and David Morgan, *Media, Religion and Culture* (New York: Routledge, 2012), 220.

31. Nancy K. Baym, *Tune in, Log On: Soaps, Fandom, and Online Community,* ed. Steve Jones, *New Media Cultures* (Thousand Oaks, CA: Sage Publications, Inc., 2000).

32. adarosbsg60, *RememberLaura,* 7/17/2013.

33. surena_13, *RememberLaura,* 6/20/2013.

34. Johanna Sumiala, *Media and Ritual: Death, Community, and Everyday Life* (New York: Routledge, 2013), 102.

35. "Faith," *Battlestar Galactica,* (2008), 4.6.

36. Elizabeth Hallam and Jenny Hockey, *Death, Memory and Material Culture,* ed. Paul Gilroy, Michael Herzfeld, and Danny Miller, *Materializing Culture* (New York: Berg, 2001), 18.

37. rococoms, *RememberLaura,* 10/23/2012.

38. *RememberLaura,* 8/29/2012.

Chapter 10

Necromedia—Reversed Ontogeny or Posthuman Evolution?

Denisa Kera

You'll scream with laughter. It's the craziest death in the world.[1]

What is a being? . . . The sum of a certain number of tendencies . . . Can I be any-
thing other than a tendency? . . . No, I'm moving towards an end . . . And what
about the species? . . . Species are only common tendencies towards an end ap-
propriate to them . . . And life? . . . Life, a series of actions and reactions . . . When
living, I act and react as a mass . . . when dead, I act and react as different mol-
ecules . . . So I don't die? . . . No, undoubtedly I don't die in that sense, neither I nor
anything that is . . . To be born, live, and pass away—that's changing forms . . .
And what's important about one form or another? Each form has the happiness
and unhappiness appropriate to it. From the elephant all the way to the flea . . .
from the flea all the way to the sensitive and living molecule, the origin of every-
thing, there's no point in all nature which does not undergo pain and pleasure.[2]

Nabokov's Poisonous Opus and Diderot's Dream

Dying in a culture immersed in science and media with shifting paradigms
of what it means to be human is anything but simple, both in technical and
moral senses. This is the main message of Vladimir Nabokov's last novel,
The Original of Laura, which will be read as a design manual, or rather
a manifesto, for creative ways of dying in the 21st century. This "hacking
kit" for the "craziest death in the world"[3] shows how various old and new
media, together with emerging neurosciences, transform the human existence into a set of experiments with both mortality and fame. Nabokov's

manifest summarizes the paradoxes involved in this strange fusion of technology, media, and death, leading us to the present obsession with digitally enhanced but also obliterated death to which we will refer as "necromedia." Here, we are extending the meaning of Marcelo Gorman's definition of necromedia as fusion of media and death to apply it to the phenomena of enhancement and obliteration connected to emergent technologies.[4] The novel reflects mortality and individuality as something that need to be constantly objectified by means of media and the neurosciences. Villains and heroes are reduced to neurotransmitters, which are as ephemeral and as eternal as anything else in the universe, and the various media immortalize everyone to 15 seconds of fame to let them perish into oblivion and void like some subatomic particles in a literary collider.

This strange combination of ephemerality, immortality, and even certain immorality and decadence defines the present necromedia and its online and technological forms as death-related design. Such design is a form of an *Ars Moriendi* manual, a reflection, but also a collection of self-help advices on how to die well in an age of emergent science and imploding media, where nothing remains sacred. It is a mereological meditation on molecules and bodies in which the relations between the ephemeral, newly defined biological and media fragments to some social and even cosmological unit are transient and often on a verge of collapse. Nabokov's necropolitical manifest embraces these experiments with biological and media fragments. It reduces the body to a network of interacting biological, social, political, and media fragments that are in need of some design principle that will save the "phenomena" and create meaning. The design principle organizes the emerging fragments, networks, bodies, and units, and redefines the possibilities of life and death.

Mereological reflection as a design principle for an age immersed in science and technology is already anticipated in the Denis Diderot's famous dream attributed to d'Alembert. The dream is an early attempt to resolve the paradoxes involved in a similar fusion of technology, media, and death. Both Nabokov's and Diderot's delirious works reduce their characters into biological, social, and cultural fragments that are in constant collisions forming hard-to-define hybrids. The most realistic and scientific reductions (humans as physiological and cell events) go hand in hand not only with the most ephemeral media constructions but also dreams and distortions. *Mementomori* becomes a spectacle of human physiological but also media fragmentation. Both authors couple them together in a strange marriage—also an important theme in these works.

Present necromedia, in which death-related online services explore the digital cycle of our personal data and various recycling technologies offering new ways of disposing of our physical remains, are a continuation of these literary experiments, which show the shifting definitions of life, death, and technology. They bring together death and design to transform our fragmented bodies and lives into changing and often monstrous units and networks. They explore death as a relation to our inorganic "base" and open a question as to whether science and technology, with their interest in the inorganic world, create conditions for reversed ontogeny and phylogeny to the inorganic past or if they explore potential posthuman future.

Designing Pleasurable and Creative Deaths

Philip Wild, the main character of Nabokov's last novel, is a lecturer in "experimental psychology" at the University of Ganglia where he experiments with death by shutting off his body from toes upward and restoring it again with the use of elaborate tools. The whole book is a "neurologist's testament"[5] of a "luxurious suicide,"[6] a "poisonous opus"[7] describing a process of dissolution and self-obliteration in which the main character mimics "an imperial neurotransmitter on awesome messenger carrying the order of self-destruction to (his) brain."[8] The innovative forms of destruction exploring a possibility of a pleasurable suicide and creative death are also a domain of interest for Laura, Philip's wife who uses media, books, and newspapers to experiment with various representations of her own death. The fragmented characters and the novel itself, written shortly before Nabokov's own death in 1977and published more than 30 years later, present a manifest of creative ways of dying with the use of science, technology, and media. The mediated fragments and scientific data betray any attempt for unity, identity, and meaning for sake of variety, experiments, and unexpected assemblages which are simultaneously literary, political, and biological. Death simply organizes the literary, political, and scientific discourses into meditation upon the relation between newly defined parts to a larger and more organized systems and units (e.g., body, family, society, media industry, cosmology).

Science, with its ability to define and construct new entities (e.g., cells, tissues, neurotransmitters), brings a political and social challenge of creating new units both in Nabokov's novel and in an earlier work, Denis Diderot's dream attributed to his estranged friend Jean le Rond d'Alembert (Le Rêvede d'Alembert, written in 1769). Diderot's scandalous and fragmented dream-talk was published only in 1830, almost 50 years after the author's death. Like Nabokov, Diderot also negotiates the complex and unsettling relations between political power and personal (neuro)-"sensitivity"[9] that bring together issues of personal, social, and biological unity. The difference between centralized and anarchic forms of what Diderot calls "sensitive networks" (réseauxsensibles),[10] defined as biological and political units (human bodies, but also political systems), is developed in terms of boundaries between normality and monstrosity, reason and dream, and interpretation and delirious speech. Diderot's discourse on politics, science, life, and death summarized by these networks leads to proliferating biological and political hybrids and metaphors, monstrous units, and decentralized organisms challenging our social institutions, like marriage and government.

The emergent neuroscientific view of the human body and its mortality voiced in these early Diderot's reflection on the "sensitive networks" lead to rather strange political and biological metaphors of "human polyps" describing our future. Once we define our body as a political and biological unity of emergent parts, which we need to manage with science and technology, we are also opening a space for creative forms of death. The passage, which leads to Nabokov's neurological manifesto of creative forms of dying and to the present new media involvements with death starts with a reference to a story from a popular Royalist weekly "Gazette de France" on the Siamese twins, which Mademoiselle de l'Espinasse calls "a really odd species" with "alternating periods of life and death" experiences by the twins.[11] d'Alembert's Siamese twins with their "double life and death of doubled being" have alternating periods of life and death, while another odd species we speculate on, the so-called human polyps,[12] are even reaching immortality. Bordeu speculates on the creative ways of killing such polyps by introducing a metaphor of the "imperceptible bees,"[13] which can be killed only by crushing rather by cutting, and two types of organic structures: "bees formed continuously and the group of bees formed contiguously."[14] It introduces a difference between "normal animals, like us, fish, worms, and snakes," and "animal polyps"[15] defined by extreme forms of life and death. This provokes Mademoiselle de l'Espinasse to hysterical laughter and speculation on "human polyps" and radical atomism as a form of immortality: "In Jupiter or in Saturn, human polyps! The males resolve themselves into males, females into females—that's an amusing thought. Man splitting himself up into an infinity of atomized men which we could keep between sheets of paper like eggs from insects which spin their cocoons, remain for a certain period in the chrysalis state, pierce through their cocoons, and escape as butterflies—a human society formed and an entire region populated by the fragments of a single individual—all that is very pleasant to imagine [. . .]." (Then the bursts of laughter started again) "If there's a place where the human being divides itself into infinity of human animalcules, people there should be less reluctant to die. It's so easy to make up for the loss of a person that death should cause little regret."[16]

These envisioned forms of life, politics, and death as configurations of the "network" of some newly defined (biological) parts present a blueprint of our present thoughts on; the necromedia and other explorations of the creative forms of dying. Diderot's networks, Nabokov's testament, and present necromedia use death as something that does not signify an end but a novel organization of parts defined by some emergent scientific insight or technological possibilities. These parts are biological and political at the same time and they form new units. The human form is just a type of a centralized network, which has to rule the "sensitive and excitable particles,"[17] defined by the scientific insight and emergent neurosciences. When the body loses control over its parts, we are transformed into a state similar to insanity and hysteria (an "anarchistic" nervous system)[18] and later death. Death is simply an anarchy of our constituents and a form of rebellion against a central authority, and our scientific insights enable us to imagine future "human polyps," which are immortal because they are politically and biologically dispersed.

Death shapes the discourse on the hybrid networks as an issue of centralized power over newly discovered parts. For Diderot death is close to dreams, insanity, but also anarchy and other instable configurations of networks reflected as these limits of what is organic and nonorganic, human and nonhuman. The same proto-cybernetic obsession with systems and networks and creative forms of death and immortality also defines Wild's experiments in Nabokov.[19] Nabokov's descriptions of pleasurable and spectacular deaths relate to the age of neurotransmitters and extreme objectification of the body as an alliance of various impulses and media phenomena. Death becomes an ability to overcome our tendency to anthropomorphize and to see everything through, as Diderot's Dr. Bordeu says to Mademoiselle de l'Espinasse, the "spectacles of our own system."[20] Death makes us free to imagine new forms of life, beings, and social organization; these new forms of biological, technical, and political networks based on new parts are always defining new ways of dying.

Sentimentality, Indifference, and Transgression of Necromedia

Pleasurable and creative deaths are a contradiction in terms that present an interesting design challenge for a Western society immersed in various technologies of enhancement of the living and life in general. Technological solutions offering pleasurable and creative deaths vary from online recipes and social networking strategies for painless euthanasia[21] to extreme green guerrilla movements supporting voluntary mass suicides.[22] While websites and organizations supporting euthanasia face challenges in terms censorship agendas, the extreme artistic projects looking into creative forms of suicide as an activist solution for saving the planet are conceptual projects supporting eco-fantasies of a healthy Earth ecosystem. Services offering euthanasia to individuals often deal with issues of privacy, pain, and illegality, and we can even witness special "hacking classes" for senior citizens in Australia to enable them to access information on euthanasia which are filtered.[23] The numerous design ideas on "green burials"[24] and eco-cemeteries[25] present less extreme projects that are nevertheless still scientifically, technologically, and socially challenging. To this account, we should also add the semi-serious online "Darwin Awards"[26] for the most impressive forms of deaths (with their infamous motto "Honoring those who improve the species by accidentally removing themselves from it!"), "Death Clocks" reminding us "that life is slipping away,"[27] various online suicide pacts and rings[28] that romanticize death, Twitter and social media live suicide notes that border with new forms of reality show, and so on. Creative or pleasurable forms of death explore various aspects: from romanticization and idealization of death, to a need to provoke, to even concerns related to some nonanthropocentric ideal of a healthy planetary ecosystem.

The creative death spectacle does not concern only one's physical bodies but also one's virtual existence; there are individuals who commit mass Facebook profile suicides or game avatar suicides as a form of an art performance,[29] and even game environments' massacres.[30] In the case of "virtual suicides"[31] targeting Facebook accounts,[32] the possibility is offered to free ourselves from our virtual doppelgängers. These growing numbers of solutions and design ideas that explore the possibilities of pleasurable and creative forms of deaths are probing the scope and depth of various data and traces we create as living beings in a mediated world. The purpose and function of all these creative explorations of our physical and virtual mortality vary from the more therapeutic to the more performative. People simply need a place where they can voice freely their thoughts, uncertainties, and various musings on death without being hospitalized and here is but one example from an online post typical of this genre: "It was so refreshing, so therapeutic to read the open discussion without the fear of people calling 911 or sending the emergency services on you and having you involuntarily committed."[33] The websites on death are discursive and fantasy playgrounds, which often start with questions such as "What would be a cool way to die?" or "The 10 manliest ways to die."[34]

The actual design ideas behind these suicide recipes connect death with a range of activities and situations ranging from the mundane to the extreme such as Empedocles's legendary jump into a volcano, or Kenji Urada's famous death-by-robot.[35] There is even "crowd sourced wisdom" related to Scott Christensen's classic blog-post, "Cool Ways to Kill Yourself,"[36] the less famous "Layman's Guides to Suicide,"[37] and a whole genre of fake YouTube suicides that give vivid instructions. Projects offering creative "design solutions" for death seem to give comfort from or make fun of our collective death-anxiety, and only some of them are also trying to work with the idea of immortality based on data.[38] The online public, constantly reduced to data, is searching for solutions that will preserve online lives, and resolve the anxiety we feel about the degradation of our physical bodies.

These design solutions and responses to death can be categorized into roughly three groups. First would be projects creating new forms of technological sentimentality, and even kitsch, which we can observe in the case of common online memorial sites, such as "Virginia Tech Second Life® Memorial Tribute."[39] The second category relates to projects that respond to the immense indifference of nature and the universe to human death and extreme movements supporting voluntary mass-suicides for the sake of the planet could be another good example of such attitudes. The third approach relates to the technological forms of the "apotheosis of the perishable"[40] in the form of not only various green burials but also virtual suicides that accept and even celebrate death with creative ideas on how to leave this form of existence.

These three paradigmatic responses to death in terms of sentimentality, indifference, and transgression point to the iconography of death starting with the sentimental motive of the "death of the maiden," the indifference behind the "dance of death," and the transgressive qualities of every "triumph of the death."[41] The traditional iconography related to death offers various perspectives on our mereological question of parts and units and how they define organisms and death in Nabokov and Diderot. These technological and design experiments, essentially, probe which parts of our existence are part of which units (i.e., individual, social, ecological, and even cosmological) and how to work with their redefinitions and transformations.

Nabokov's Neuropolitical Manifesto

Vladimir Nabokov's, *The Original of Laura,* summarizes well and anticipates these digital and technological types of deaths and the design choices involved in them. The extreme objectification of human existence and the loss of intimacy connected to death seem to define the transgressive forms of death both that we are starting to witness online and that are described in the novel. Nabokov, as one of the first designers of pleasurable and creative deaths as transgressions bordering between technological sentimentality and apotheosis of the perishable, anticipates our present and future forms of dying via new media and emergent technologies.

Nabokov's spectacular forms of death remind us that we are actually dying while alive. We can monitor, control, and make sense of every moment of our dying in a similar way in which the main character, Philip Wild, both becomes aware of the pain of dying on the level of his cells and tissues and tries to immunize himself from the fear of death. This almost-stoic but at the same time transgressive relation to death is a part of a strange, "ecological" wish to understand ourselves as a part of a larger system which is not spiritual nor religious but "material"—related to the ecosystem of the planet or the complex system of neurotransmitters in our body. We place ourselves in relation to some large-scale metabolism or even collective organism; we are part of a complex food chain and energy cycle that can encompass even the inorganic world to which we need to return.

The potential of this design approach to monitoring, experiencing, and immunizing ourselves to death is already present in the applications that monitor everyday life-functions used by the "The Quantified Self"[42] (QS) movement. While most QS applications try to improve quality of life, it would be interesting to rethink their approach to death. These measurements can help us develop the fantasies of pleasurable and entertaining forms of death in which we imagine or slowly experience and discover our inorganic "heritage" in terms of molecules and physiology that are doomed to return to their origins. *The Original of Laura* is in this respect something of a prototype that introduces the idea of a design for the "craziest death in the world," exploring these returns to our inorganic past. The neuroscientist Philip Wild, haunted by jealousy because of his young, unfaithful, and beautiful wife, decides to experiment with death by shutting off his body and restoring it again in order to experience the inorganic aspect of his being. This "mad neurologist testament" of a "luxurious suicide, delicious dissolution"[43] is transforming him into "an imperial neurotransmitter on awesome messenger carrying [the] order of self destruction to [his] brain."[44] This well-planned act of destruction develops elements of creativity and an almost Buddhist awareness of the inorganic end.

How can suicides be made into pleasure? What are the design principles for pleasurable and creative deaths? In order to answer these questions, the book plays with the difference between the human and the animal, the human and insect, or even the human and plant as the first steps in the understanding of our original and inorganic nature. These differences even define technology and science as that which brings us closer to the ultimate "inorganic" truth about our origin and destiny. The human characters in the novel are described in a very scientific, botanical, and even entomological way: the main character is Flora, her grandfather is called Lev Linde (linden being an ornamental tree sometimes referred to as a lime tree or basswood), and there are numerous other flowers and animals referring to the characters. Inanimate objects are often described as living (e.g., the clock on Flora's hand is an "onyx eye on her wrist";[45] the "telephone is ringing ecstatically"[46]), all in order to prepare us for their death. This almost-animistic insight which connects the human and the nonhuman defines contemporary design that enables humans to understand their symbiotic or ecological relation to the planet as a relation to their inorganic past and future.

Necrotechnologies as the Reversal of Human Ontogeny and Phylogeny

The whole novel is nearly a catalogue of various ways of dying related to various media and technologies. Flora's grandfather, a painter, is defined by a boring death: "What can be sadder than a discouraged artist dying not from his own commonplace maladies, but from the cancer of oblivion invading his once famous picture."[47] Flora's father, a photographer, is the first to explore the spectacular forms of death related to technologically mediated suicides:

> Adam Lind had always had an inclination for trick photography and this time, before shooting himself in a Montecarlo hotel (on the night, sad to relate, of his wife's very real success in Piker's "Narcisse et Narcette"), he geared and focussed his camera in a corner of the drawing room so as to record the event from different angles. These automatic pictures of his last moments and of a table's lion paws did not come out too well; but widow easily sold them for the price of a flat in Paris to the local magazine Pitch which specialized in soccer and diabolical *faits-divers* [*tidbits*].[48]

This scene, written by Nabokov in 1977, almost predicts the real-time, YouTube-style public suicides sometimes witnessed today. We have to give a credit to Nabokov for realizing the potential of any new media and technologies as not only that which enhances our lives but also our experience of death.

Technologies are simply defined as ways in which we explore our relation and connection with the animal, plant, and, later, even the inorganic world. The social and media impacts of our deaths are just aspects of a very complex system of reporting on death in this novel. The memoirs of Flora (Laura) are written by her lover in order to destroy her in the act of portraying her. Parallel to this, readers are witnessing the disturbing and strange diary of her mad husband that is trying to develop the same theme from a neuroscientific perspective. The first description of the "most creative suicide"[49] starts with a simulation of the neuroscientific jargon:

An enkcephalin in the brain has now been produced synthetically [. . .] It is like morphine and other opiate drugs [. . .] Further research will show and why morphine has for centuries produced relief from pain and feelings of euphoria [. . .] I taught thought to mimic an imperial neurotransmitter and awesome messenger carrying my order of self destruction to my own brain. Suicide made a pleasure, its tempting emptiness.[50]

The "tempting emptiness" of the creative suicide is further elaborated into a mental exercise in which the "student" who desires to die "projects the mental image of the way he imagines his suicide by slowly destroying the three divisions of the physical self: legs, torso and head" the "self-emblemizing"[51] process. This process of what might be termed "self-deletion" through amputation is in some moments even ecstatic: "deletion of my procreative system sweet death's ineffable sensation,"[52] "the process of dying by auto-dissolution afforded the greatest ecstasy known to man,"[53] "divine delight in destroying one's breastbone [. . .] Enjoy the destruction but do not linger over your own ruins lest you develop an incurable illness, or die before you are ready to die."[54]

The ecstatic descriptions of death are paradoxically close to Phillip Wild's scientific ideal of methodology related to what he calls "sophrosyne"[55]—the ideal of self-control stemming from man's rational core: "An act of destruction which develops paradoxically an element of creativeness in the totally new application of totally free will. Learning to use the vigour of the body for the purpose of its own deletion, standing vitality on its head."[56] It is an experiment and expression of scientific curiosity,[57] and it is a process of scientifically testing a discovery: "Now when it is the discoverer himself who tests his discovery and finds that it works he will feel a torrent of pride and purity."[58] The strong connection between death as an exploration of our inorganic nature and the scientific method as another type of close examination of the nonhuman reality summarizes the whole opus and its mission. Death defined by scientific curiosity means an interest in the "extravagant messages that reach the brain,"[59] and this neuropolitical approach based on self-objectification and discipline is almost morbidly reminiscent of the late Michel Foucault's "technologies of the self"[60] as: "In experimenting on oneself in order to pick out the sweetest death, one cannot, obviously, set part of one's body on fire or drain I of blood or subject it to any other drastic operation, for the simple reason that these are one-way treatments."[61]

Nabokov's and Wild's sketchy notes on the science of neurotransmitters express one of the most powerful reductionism of human beings to facts in recent times. In this respect, the whole novel defines the science and technology project as a type of a death manifest. This novel performs the "stuff of which our dreams and nightmares are made of,"[62] the neurotransmitters and the molecules as the bases of our identity (e.g., "the self-annihilation a deep probe of one's darkest self, the unravelling of subjective associations"[63]) and which leads us to accept our animal and, later even, inorganic past and future.

These extreme and posthuman ideas show how all of our technologies and sciences are actually a reversal of human ontogeny and even phylogeny. They are necrotechnologies and necromedia, simply ways in which we explore our return to the inorganic past and future. Nabokov's novel and the original connection of death with technology and media present a challenge to the popular transhumanist and posthumanist dreams of some future forms of evolution. Instead of creating a better and more complex human or a form of super being, we see these explorations into death and science as a form of "devolution" into inorganic nature, identifying with what we came from—star dust.

Sensitive Networks (RéseauxSensibles): Posthuman Evolution or Devolution?

This discussion of our relation to some nonhuman, inorganic, and non-alive world in terms of evolution or "devolution" has its blueprint in the Denis Diderot's dream. This "dream talk" paradoxically presents one of the first attempts for a materialist philosophy and has a form of a frivolous conversation between Mademoiselle de l'Espinasse and the famous doctor Bordeu. The whole conversation revolves around the concepts of *réseau sensible* and *milieu* (sensitive network), describing a decentralized agency of the senses or other elements (points) that have a potential to create new unity—organs or beings. These new units are not always standard, expected, or normal but often transgress into unexpected, strange, and monstrous organisms. The design of such unexpected new connections and networks is described as legitimate and even creative. The whole dialogue cherishes the ability of life to create such new connections and combinations between the points and the threads (networks, *fil délié, brin*), the new types of networks and unexpected units. The agency of different elements in these networks is discussed in terms of "infinity of human animalcules," as vibrating strings and sensitive fibers or living points successively conjoining a single living unity: "Each sensitive molecule had its identity (it's 'me') before the accumulation, but how did it lose that, and how, from all these lost identities, does one end up with the consciousness of a totality? How does it fuse with other? Sensitive and living molecule fuses itself with a sensible and living molecules."[64]

In order to explain this part of d'Alembert's dream, Dr. Bordeu makes an interesting, biological, and political distinction between congruity and continuity, between assembly and total unity. He defines several types of networks and forms of life and death: clusters, large hives, polyps, and animals of some (new) kind. "Sensitive molecules" either aggregate new units, like tissues of small sensitive beings, or create more centralized "unified systems" with an awareness of their own unity. In both cases, life and movement are absolute singularities—"In this immense ocean of matter, no single molecule resembles any other, and no single molecule resembles itself for more than a moment"[65]—that are interlinked in a perpetual flux. This means evolution into something more complex as much as it means devolution into something simpler: "All beings circulate through each other— thus all the species [...] everything is in a perpetual flux [...] Every animal is more or less human being, every mineral is more or less a plant, and every plant is more or less an animal. Everything is more or less something or other, more or less earth, more or less water, more or less air, more or less fire, more or less of one kingdom or another."[66]

These forms of nonhuman agency and inorganic existence define the *réseau sensible* and the *milieu* as a decentralized agency of our senses which reason as a tyrant tries to organize in order to claim some unity. The agency is based on sensory data related to our molecules rather than that unity we construct out of this material. These data which are the life of the molecules are used by our reason in order to organize the network into some unity, but that does not mean they are part of only one network and that they will disintegrate after some organism changes.

These sensory data related to the activity of smaller fragments and parts gifted with agency are the key issue in deciding on the meaning of death in relation to evolution and devolution. The word "data," in all its present omnipotence related to the rise of visualizations, data-analytics, and simulations, has a very modest genealogy. The original meaning of "data" is simply a gift or, rather, a precedent of an unequal exchange. Kenneth L. Schmitz summarizes the Middle Age discussions on the gift and creation as "the paradoxical character of a given which excludes a giver."[67] What is important is not the giver but the act of giving (the act of *praecisio*), the performativity involved in its unfolding in the presence of human observer which creates an exchange between unequals (gods and humans, slaves and masters). The original, Latin meaning of *donum* is a gift without obligation, as opposed to *munus*—a present which customs induce to make homage—and it is often related to the gift of freedom that a master can give to his slaves.

Scientific or any type of data have such potential to give freedom, to reconfigure both political and biological networks and create new units which Diderot describes in his dream as various monstrosities, oddities, and potential new types of beings. The scientific data open the network to new reconfigurations. The creative evolution rather than devolution into the inorganic past is the reason why, too, death of these new types of units and beings (twins, polyps) is more "creative" and complex. "Data" play an important role also in the recent discussions on sensor networks and the rise of online interaction over DNA, bio data, and other forms of sensor data related to our environments.

Communities of people monitoring, sharing, and making sense of such "objective" and "scientific" data in their everyday lives are already exploring the future symbiotic relations between various types of agencies and experimenting with these microlevel connections between various scales. They are the true cosmopolites exploring emergent, often surprising connections, networks, and mash-ups between different data across (unequal) scales. This design revives the original idea of a data as gift involving impossible exchanges in which life and death are just various phases in the reconfiguration of new networks, organisms, and units.

Notes

1. Vladimir Vladimirovich Nabokov and Dmitri Nabokov, *The Original of Laura (Dying Is Fun)* (New York: Alfred A. Knopf, 2009), 227.

2. Denis Diderot, *Rameau's Nephew/D'Alembert's Dream* (London: Penguin UK, 1976); Denis Diderot, *D'Alembert's Dream*, trans. Ian Johnston, http://records.viu.ca/~johnstoi/diderot/dalembertsdream.htm. Accessed April 16, 2014.

3. Nabokov and Nabokov, *The Original of Laura*, 227.

4. Marcelo Gorman, "What Is Necromedia?" *Intermédialités* 1 (Printemps, 2003): 155–64, http://cri.histart.umontreal.ca/cri/fr/intermedialites/p1/pdfs/p1_ogorman.pdf. Accessed April 16, 2014.

5. Nabokov and Nabokov, *The Original of Laura*, 3.

6. Ibid., 243.

7. Ibid., 3.

8. Ibid., 127.

9. Denis Diderot, *D'Alembert's Dream,* trans. Ian Johnston, http://records.viu.ca/~johnstoi/diderot/dalembertsdream.htm. Accessed April 16, 2014:

BORDEU: I was reflecting on the way great men are made.

MADEMOISELLE DE L'ESPINASSE: How are they made?

BORDEU: How? Well, sensitivity. . .

MADEMOISELLE DE L'ESPINASSE: Sensitivity?

BORDEU: . . . or the extreme mobility of certain threads in the network is a dominant quality in mediocre creatures.

10. Diderot, *Rameau's Nephew/D'Alembert's Dream,* 168, 193, 205.

11. Ibid., 138.

12. Ibid., 171–72.

13. Ibid., 171.

14. Ibid., 169.

15. Ibid., 171.

16. Ibid., 172.

17. Ibid., 176.

18. Ibid., 205.

19. Nabokov and Nabokov, *The Original of Laura.*

20. Diderot, *Rameau'sNephew/D'Alembert's Dream,* 199.

21. "Exit International," http://www.exitinternational.net/. Accessed April 16, 2014.

22. "The Voluntary Human Extinction Movement," http://vhemt.org/. Accessed April 16, 2014.

23. For example, "hacking classes" for seniors in Australia enable them to access information on euthanasia: "Exit International has held Hacking Masterclasses for Seniors wanting to circumvent the Rudd Government's proposed new mandatory internet filtering plan." The Masterclass was designed by one of the country's leading young IT gurus Davis Campbell of Newcastle and was prompted by the reported inclusion of Exit International websites www.peacefulpill.com on the government's secret Blacklist of banned websites. "The Clean Feed Policy Will See Older Australians Denied Access to Current End of Life Information." in *The Peaceful Pill Handbook,* http://www.peacefulpillhandbook.com/page/Internet+Masterclass. Accessed April 16, 2014.

24. "Green Burials . . . Return Naturally," http://www.greenburials.org/. Accessed April 16, 2014.

25. "Forest of Memories: Resources and Information Supporting Eco Burial in North America," http://www.forestofmemories.org/eco_burial.htm. Accessed April 16, 2014.

26. "Darwin Awards: In Search of Smart," http://www.darwinawards.com/. Accessed April 16, 2014.

27. "Death Clock: The Internet's Friendly Reminder that Life Is Slipping Away," http://www.deathclock.com/. Accessed April 16, 2014.

28. S. Rajagopal, "Suicide Pacts and the Internet," BMJ 329, no. 7478 (2004): 1298–99.

29. Brody Condon, "Suicide Solutions," YouTube.com, Uploaded May 10, 2008, https://www.youtube.com/watch?v=dbBmyWrxwXQ. Accessed April 16, 2014.

30. M. Luck, "Crashing a Virtual Funeral: Morality in MMORPGs." *Journal of Information, Communication & Ethics in Society* 7, no. 4 (2009): 280–85.

31. "Web 2.0 Suicide Machine," http://suicidemachine.org/. Accessed April 16, 2014.

32. Sepukko.com famously engaged in a legal battle with Facebook over its offering to assist Facebook users in terminating their accounts; a battle which Facebook won, and which Sepukoo.com now states has rendered their services useless as of 2011. http://www.seppukoo.com/. Accessed April 16, 2014.

33. "Belief in People," http://beliefinpeople.wordpress.com/2010/03/01/unusual-support-for-suicide/. As of April 16, 2014 the site is no longer available, indicating: "The authors have deleted this site." The post is available with a date March 1, 2010 http://web.archive.org/web/20120501054652/http://beliefinpeople.wordpress.com/tag/suicide/.

34. "10 Manliest Ways to Die," Oddee.com, October 17, 2008, http://www.oddee.com/item_96485.aspx. Accessed April 16, 2014.

35. "1001 Ways to Die," http://1001waystodie.blogspot.sg/. Accessed April 16, 2014.

36. Scott Christensen, "Cool Ways to Kill Yourself," Scribd.com, 1995, http://www.scribd.com/doc/49337763/100ways-to-Commit-Suicide. Accessed April 16, 2014.

37. Rob Cummings, *The Layman's Guide to Suicide: The Essential Handbook Guaranteed to Make Any Problem a Laughing Matter* (Boulder, CO: Paladin Press, 1995), http://www.keyword.com/cd/laymans_guide/pageone.htm. Accessed April 16, 2014.

38. Mission Eternity, etoy. Corporation, http://missioneternity.org/. Accessed April 16, 2014.

39. "Virginia Tech Second Life(r) Memorial Tribute," May 6, 2007, http://wn.com/Virginia_Tech_Second_Life%C2%AE_Memorial_Tribute_Video. Accessed April 16, 2014.

40. G. Bataille and A. Stoekl, *Visions of Excess: Selected Writings, 1927–1939* (Minneapolis: University of Minnesota Press, 1985).

41. E. Schuster, *Das Bild vom Tod: Graphiksammlung der Heinrich-Heine-Universität Düsseldorf* (Recklinghausen, Germany: A. Bongers, 1992).

42. "Quantified Self: Self Knowledge through Numbers," 2012, http://quantifiedself.com/. Accessed April 16, 2014. See also Yasmine Abbas and Fred Dervin, *Digital Technologies of the Self* (Newcastle: Cambridge Scholars, 2009); Anthony Elliott, *Concepts of the Self. Key Concepts.* 2nd ed. (Cambridge, UK: Polity Press, 2007).

43. Nabokov and Nabokov, *The Original of Laura,* 243.

44. Ibid., 127.

45. Ibid., 25.

46. Ibid., 39.

47. Ibid., 45.

48. Ibid., 50–51.

49. Ibid., 127.

50. Ibid., 128–29.

51. Ibid., 139.

52. Ibid., 145.

53. Ibid., 171.

54. Ibid., 181.

55. Ibid., 155.

56. Ibid., 213.

57. Ibid., 159.

58. Ibid., 161.

59. Ibid., 193.

60. Michel Foucault, L. H. Martin, H. Gutman, and P. H. Hutton, P. H., *Technologies of the Self: A Seminar with Michel Foucault* (Amherst, MA: University of Massachusetts Press, 1988).

61. Nabokov and Nabokov, *The Original of Laura,* 246.

62. Ibid., 69.

63. Ibid., 247.

64. Diderot, *D'Alembert's Dream.*

65. Ibid.

66. Ibid.

67. Kenneth L. Schmitz, "The Recovery of Wonder: The New Freedom and the Asceticism of Power," *McGill-Queen's Studies in the History of Ideas* 39 (2005): 31–32.

Chapter 11

Infinite Gestation: Death and Progress in Video Games

Stephen Mazzeo and Daniel Schall

Introduction

The idea of "permadeath," the permanent loss of a player's character in a video game, has been frequently discussed in gamer and game developer circles. For example, Jonathan Glater, in his *New York Times* article "50 First Deaths: A Chance to Play (and Pay) Again," discusses what seems at first glance to be an issue situated purely within the crosshairs of media ecology, player feedback, and good business: "If the 'death penalty' in the game is too severe and your character is permanently destroyed [...] you may stop playing the game and, even worse, stop paying the monthly subscription fee for it." As Glater notes, ultimately many companies opted to reduce the "sentence" for permadeath in online games. However, while the discussion of the business models surrounding permadeath is important for the continued success of online gaming models, surprisingly little interest seems to have been paid to the psychological and social effects of its reduction.

Part of the reason there seems to be a gap in scholarship on permadeath is that the term permadeath actually encompasses only a fraction of what should be a larger discussion of progress. In many video games, the main achievement in the game is attaining a well-developed character. Quests that are completed and items that are obtained by players all serve to progress the character toward greater skill and development. Thus, when permadeath occurs, it is traumatic to the player not necessarily because of losing a particular persona but because the particular persona is a marker of the overall progress that has been made in the game.

Even a cursory review of the history of video games shows a burgeoning tendency toward minimizing permadeath since the development of home console gaming. Most notably, this is done through the ability of the player to "save" his or her game, much like a document on a computer, and restore such a game back to a prior state in the event of failure or temporary termination of play. But what does the continual reinforcement of saving do to a player's conception of power and security?

This chapter aims to review not only the psychological effects of hedging against progress loss through saving in video games, but also the effects of catastrophic progress loss on players' interpretations of mortality despite this hedging. While prior arguments have suggested that saving manipulates game time and thus affects the player's overall conception of power,[1] we will argue that such concepts of power are dependent upon saving as a method of risk/loss aversion with regards to *progress* and investment of *real* time. Catastrophic loss, in this case, reinforces the presence of unexpected events which circumvent measures taken to mitigate loss. Catastrophic loss subsumes the previous function of death in video games as a mitigator of ballooning conceptions of power and control, which directly result from the blurring of both real and virtual spaces through the act of saving itself.

Games as Flow

The fact that games provide many or all of the components of enjoyment is one of the main reasons why people pursue them. Video games are no different, particularly in that they prompt what Mihaly Csikszentmihalyi, one of the foremost theorists of positive psychology, calls "flow"—that is, a cathartic experience of "enjoyment" and enrichment of self through purposeful activity. This chapter, when using the word *enjoyment*, will refer to the definition of the term as laid out by Csikszentmihalyi:

> First, the experience usually occurs when we confront tasks we have a chance of completing. Second, we must be able to concentrate on what we are doing. Third and fourth, the concentration is usually possible because the task undertaken has clear goals and provides immediate feedback. Fifth, one acts with a deep but effortless involvement that removes from awareness the worries and frustrations of everyday life. Sixth, enjoyable experiences allow people to exercise a sense of control over their actions. Seventh, concern for the self disappears, yet paradoxically, the sense of self emerges stronger after the flow experience is over. Finally, the sense of the duration of time is altered; hour pass by in minutes, and minutes can stretch out to seem like hours.[2]

The player of a video game, if the game is well designed and if the player achieves his or her goal, experiences enjoyment similar to what Csikszentmihalyi describes earlier: the player emerges from the gaming experience with a greater sense of fulfillment and contentment. Games, however, have different means through which players ultimately experience enjoyment. We must, then, discuss two different kinds of games that allow players to achieve enjoyment: *scoring games* and *completion games*.

Scoring Games

We define a *scoring game* as one whose main goal is to achieve the most valuable score within the parameters of the game world *in a single iteration of gameplay*. Such games may have different means by which they calculate or symbolize such a score (a racing arcade game may inversely track the score by having players attempt to record the *fastest* or *lowest* time, while a game of pinball may calculate success by recording the *highest* scores), but all scoring games share this trait. The player of a scoring game may have a varied number of "lives" or chances to attain this score, but all lives factor into a single iteration of gameplay which, after the lives have been expended (i.e., after the player "dies"), records the score for others to see, should it be notable enough to warrant such a display. Most arcade games fit the definition of a scoring game, but many home console or computer games also fit into this category, particularly arcade games like *Contra* (Konami 1987) that were transferred from arcade hardware to home gaming consoles, but also console originals like *Super Mario Bros.* (Nintendo 1985) and *Snood* (David M. Dobson 1996). Most scoring games have a screen which displays the highest attained score. What is important here is that this score is most often a numerical or symbolic representation of the player's progress in the game, a digital memorial that acts as curator of both player progress and status at the point of game "death."

Scoring games can be further broken down into two categories: games in which virtual time is fixed or variable. For example, in an arcade on a New Jersey boardwalk, a *Whak-A-Mole* game is one in which virtual time is fixed: the game runs for an exact amount of time for each player, and the measure of success in the game is the score that can be achieved within that static time frame. Variable scoring games, however, are ones like *Pac-Man* (Midway 1980), in which the achievement of a particular task is the means of achieving the score, which in turn is the measure of success: levels in *Pac-Man* do not end after a particular time period, but instead after all the objectives have been achieved or not.

Completion (Saving) Games

We define *completion games* as games in which the main goal is *not* determined by the player and is not a quantified score (points, time, etc.); instead the goal is the attainment of a particular *condition* in the game, which has been determined by the game designers. The desired condition almost always has some backing narrative. The strength of narrative in completion games varies greatly. For example *The Elder Scrolls* (Bethesda Game Studios) series is famous for epic sweeping narratives while many first-person shooters (FPS) consist of little more than killing the bad guys. Narrative strength is often a defining feature in video game genres, but the strength of the narrative element does not affect the game's standing as a completion game.

Completion games are also similar in that they almost all share the feature of saving the progress of the game. These stored, saved states can then be reloaded later to allow progress in the game to continue; in older games, the resume point was usually the beginning of a level, and in most newer games, progress usually continues from the exact point at which the game was saved.

The critical evaluation of these two branches of games might tempt some to aggregate variable scoring games into completion games, since these games usually advance through levels. However, the distinction should not be made in terms of the *means of advancement* in the game, but rather in the relationship of *real time* to virtual time. In completion games, as we will describe in the following, this relationship is not a one-to-one correspondence. But despite the separation of scoring games by their measurements of success, each scoring game, variable or not, still retains a one-to-one correspondence between real time invested and virtual time that has progressed in the game: the 30 seconds playing *Whak-A-Mole* are the same as 30 seconds playing *Space Invaders* (Midway 1978), which are the same as 30 seconds drinking a soda outside the arcade.

Progress and Enjoyment

In both scoring and completion games, progress is a determinant in enjoyment. How progress impacts enjoyment in each of these, however, is quite different. All scoring games, for instance, adhere to Csikszentmihalyi's criteria for enjoyment. Scoring games tend to focus on what Csikszentmihalyi terms: "the merging of action and awareness."[3] This is not based on the difficulty of the goal set, but the ability of the player. For scoring games, there is no separation between achievement and enjoyment: progress quite literally is both the delaying of eventual death, as well as the very goal.[4] Scoring is any way of achieving in a video game that has quantifiable results and a clear goal. The goal may be externally imposed by the player, a community of players, or by a competition. Types of scores include: *speed runs* (finishing a game in the fastest possible time), *max outs* (getting the most possible points a game allows), *high scores* (which could range anywhere from a score that is a personal best to competition for an entry into the *Guinness Book of World Records*), and *king of the hill* (being the best player on a particular day within a group of players).

Despite the tendency to think of them as rote responses to functional stimuli, scoring games generally adhere more to the conditions of what Csikszentmihalyi calls "creative activities"; in such activities, "where goals are not clearly set in advance, a person must develop a strong personal sense of what she intends to do."[5] When a player resets his or her goal in the play of a scoring game, depending on that goal, this shifts also the conditions for enjoyment. If the goal is set high enough, gameplay may be transformed from a casual experience into a competitive one. The player is not chasing a good score or decent score; players are generally chasing a personal best or the best score on a given machine or the best score amongst a group of peers. In some instances, a player may be chasing a world-record high score or even fastest completion time.

In the documentary film *Ecstasy of Order: The Tetris Masters* (2011), players are competing in the first Tetris World Championship. The film documents both the time leading up to the event and the event itself. Participants are all seasoned *Tetris* (Nintendo 1989) players, most of them having played for as much as 15 or 20 years. Several of the players hold or co-hold world records for most lines cleared or highest points (two men co-hold the world record for highest points total because the game has a score cap). In the case of *Tetris*, both lines and points totals count as scores. What is particularly interesting about the participants, however, is that before the competition they are interviewed and speak much the same way athletes do before or after an event. The players also actively train in a particular form of *Tetris* that the community has agreed upon as the consummate version of the game: the original 1989 Nintendo Entertainment System release. Unsurprisingly, scores that would please casual *Tetris* players, perhaps 75 lines cleared or a points total of 65,000, are utter failures to world-class players.

For these players to experience enjoyment, they need to perform at superhuman levels, because they have personally set such performance as their goal(s). That the gap between the max-out world record score of 999,999 and the third highest recorded score is over 250,000 points further highlights what is actually *Tetris*'s capacity to handle extreme ranges in player goals. Player modifications to the parameters of scoring games, however, never change the fact that the main goal of the game is to achieve or exceed the set goal determined by the particular community. And as the goals of the players become increasingly more challenging, the impact of the death in a scoring game becomes more traumatic as the player nears this achievement. However, most players at such levels in a scoring game are aware of the exponentially increased risk of playing in this way.

Of course, *Tetris* is not the only instance of a popular or lasting scoring game, nor is victory at the World Championship and inclusion in a documentary film the only important ramifications of scoring games. While completion games tend to generate communities quickly upon their release and then experience a sharp decline as the majority of players finish the game, scoring games tend to fulfill other emotional requirements in the lives of serious participants, such as social interaction via a sustained community. The Tetris World Championship has become an annual event with its own website, Facebook page, and so on. While we do not have the space here to elaborate, further research is necessary on the important social structures that surround scoring games and how they are perceived in the global gaming community, including perceptions of goals in such games.

Completion games, however, are unique in the kind of enjoyment they offer to players. Completion games, as their name implies, offer an intense kind of satisfaction upon the *completion* of the game. Thus, despite the likely uncountable number of deaths that will occur in order to progress in a completion game, progress is merely *the means by which the player completes the game*. The cathartic effects of the game itself are directly related to *completion*, not progress. In other words, if the point of a scoring game is to die the best death, then the point of a completion game is to memorialize progress through completing the narrative or character life in the game, regardless of the number of deaths and rebirths any character may experience.

Completion and Saving

Given that completion games primarily offer enjoyment upon the achievement of a final goal, and given that completion games usually have this goal woven into a complex and lengthy narrative in the game that requires many hours to complete, the advent of saving is a natural development in these games. Saving replaced less elegant solutions such as passwords, in which a player could restore the previous state of a completion game through the entry of a particular code. In terms of player action in games, we agree with Chuk Moran's claim that saving in video games has allows a shift in the *type* of challenge in the game from one of "performance" to one of "configuration."[6] Through greater precision in saving (i.e., being able to save more frequently and at any point in the game), video games have become increasingly detailed and demanding, without necessarily becoming more challenging.

Moran notes "undoing is not simply the restoration of a previous state, but also constitutes another form of action taken in the course of play."[7] Players enter into a game with the intent to save as a hedge against loss of progress. But there is an important difference between saving progress and saving time. Players are rarely concerned with the overall time a video game takes to complete. However, they are frequently concerned with how many attempts each individual task will take them. If that task requires a player to replay a level, or portions of a level, such repeated attempts compound player frustrations to impediments in progress. Without saving and other methods of undoing, the number of players willing to complete a video game would decrease at higher levels. This is simply because some levels are too difficult to be palatable or the frustration of repeated attempts breaks the notion of "flow" for the player: there is no point in continuing an activity one intends for enjoyment if the challenge is beyond one's means.

While a player uses precision saving to configure how they will progress through a game, the reasoning behind such a manipulation is usually emotionally motivated. For players in the process of playing a game, real time is often less valuable than in-game progress, provided that the progress does not need to be repeated due to in-game death. Moran echoes this sentiment by describing the loss-mitigation through saving used by players: "Linear models of time make it impossible to recognise the time of undoing, but loading a saved game to avoid death, taking back turns, and making choices that can be easily reversed have long been common in video games."[8] The act of saving, which may require player action or merely observation in the case of autosave functions, mitigates risk and makes in-game death more of an inconvenience, thereby encouraging players to attempt different or more difficult challenges while completing the narrative.

Conversely, when a game does not allow saving, a player is inclined to cut out as much gameplay as possible to complete the narrative as efficiently as possible, because progress in these games is completion of the narrative and not the completion of optional content or side quests. Take, for example,

Super Mario Brothers 3 (Nintendo 1988), which included two major short-cuts (i.e., "warp whistles") for players to utilize. The shortcuts allow play-ers to skip large amounts of the game's content without compromising the narrative.[9] This is, in part, because the narrative is very simple (rescue Princess Peach) and because the shortcuts are intentionally included by the game designers. *Super Mario Brothers 3* must be completed in one sitting (or at least without turning off the Nintendo console). This imposes a real-time clock on the game-time experience. The game could not offer a 100 hours of gameplay because such duration of continuous play was implau-sible. Not coincidentally, the same exact narrative was used in *Super Mario 64* (Nintendo 1996), a game with a precision save function. In *Super Mario 64*, players must collect stars. Once the required number (70) is collected, players can confront the end-game villain. Even if each of the 70 stars was collected on the player's first attempt, the game would likely take, at the very least, about 11 hours to complete, far longer than most players would be able to play in a single sitting or iteration. Furthermore, players are of-fered a second ending if they are willing to collect all the stars in the game (120), in essence completing every level of the game to the fullest extent. Again, even if the player is 100 percent successful and never chooses to load a saved game, the play time would reach at least 20 hours.[10] Saving, thus, not only mitigates loss of progress through death, but also allows the game to grow in complexity and length.

Real Time and Progress Time

As evidenced in the previous example, the ability to save a game has a sig-nificant impact not only on how a player goes about playing the game, but saving also affects how the player conceives notions of power in relation to the game.[11] The differences in objectives between the two types of games, along with the ability to save data in completion games, create a major dif-ference between scoring and completions games in terms of the player's investment of *real time*. Discussions of time in this context, however, are complicated by burgeoning scholarly consideration in the difference be-tween various kinds of time in both real and virtual settings. This has re-sulted in a complex, unstandardized vocabulary to describe the various temporal phenomena that accompany playing games.

Discussions of the relationships between time and playing games have historically been rooted in Johan Huizinga's seminal book *Homo Ludens: A Study of the Play Element in Culture*, which details the relationship between games and players. One of Huizinga's primary theories in the text is that of the "magic circle," a reserved space or location in which the logic and conditions of the game supersede existing social conditions.[12] This space is often physical, but does not need to be. For example, the space can be a chess board for playing chess, but also can be a virtual space, such as when one turns on a gaming console, or even an unspoken agreement between children when two or more decide to play "tag." The magic circle serves as a barrier between not only the game space and the surrounding world, but also these spaces' social conditions. In other words, the magic circle informs players who voluntarily participate that the social conditions within are about to change. Thus, actions that are often considered socially unacceptable (e.g., stealing, touching, tackling, etc.) are permissible within certain magic circles, because the circle allows the game rules to modify acceptable social behavior.[13]

More recently, Huizinga's theory of the magic circle has been disputed by a number of scholars. As supported by Juul,[14] Moran[15] and Consalvo,[16] the nature of the magic circle and its effects on the social spaces it inhabits within the time of a game have been increasingly recognized as the permeable barrier that it is, rather than an impassable boundary between real and virtual social structures. In particular, Juul's argument that game spaces are always contextual is one that has led to the perception of the magic circle as increasingly subject to the surrounding social conditions.[17]

This discussion of game sociology and space has naturally bled into various considerations of time in games. Juul delineates between a variety of relationships between "play time" and "fictional time."[18] These relationships can be 1:1 correspondences (such as what we might see in scoring games) or narratologically structured so that fictional time (also called *virtual* or game time) is experienced achronologically (such as what we might see in completion games). More recent treatments of virtual time, most notably Moran, have questioned the perception of virtual time as continuous and criticized theorizing game time as designers and players do during gameplay: Moran argues instead that game time, like real-world time, exists as a combination of various types of time, and these times stand in juxtaposition rather than coordination.[19]

When we first conceived the idea of this chapter, we intended to use one of the aforementioned terms (i.e., *virtual time, fictional time,* or *game time*) to describe what elapses in the game world of any given game. However, as evidenced previously by the developing scholarly discussion on this topic, the complexity of vocabulary and perceptions of time in virtual worlds requires a term that more precisely describes the time that contributes to the achievement of the goal in either a scoring or completion game. Therefore, we have settled on *progress time,* a term which reflects *time advancing the progress of the game.* This is a crucial distinction for us to make in this chapter, as prior descriptions of "virtual" or "fictional" time are all rooted in the fictional context of the game, while the time expended advancing the progress of the game remains rooted to the real-world consequences that result from the outcome of such a game.

Juul is correct in his assertion that "the player's time and actions are projected onto the game world where they take on a fictional meaning [...] corresponding] to a basic sense of *now* when playing a game."[20] Juul acknowledges, however, that "the objective, linear time described in the game time model feeds subjective experiences,"[21] this framing of experience still hinges on the monitoring of the artificial times discussed earlier that depend on *time elapsing in the world of the game.* Where Juul complicates the issue is his assertion that fictional/virtual/game time, rather than *progress,* is in any way proportional to the investment of real time. In other words, Juul's diagram, in which "a fictional time of a year takes a few minutes of play time"[22] is inaccurate: rather, a few minutes of play time result in a few minutes of *progress* in the game. Should the player make an error and reload the game, the player also forfeits any progress achieved since the last save state of the game.

Moran seems to follow a line of argument similar to ours against Juul's model of game time, noting:

> [I]n-game events are not just subjective experiences, but are the mutual adaptation between variations in a game's procedures and actions of the body playing. Juul's model subsumes these times: fictional time means clock time [...] There is, however, nothing inevitable about the habitual translation of other times into the solid line with an arrowhead whose width is meaningless ... the time within games is polymorphous, and translated into more than one other time. The clock's time need not be privileged.[23]

Moran here is closest to our argument in his assertion that "[s]aved games and everyday life both offer dramatic juxtaposition by which play's time can become a ray,"[24] in other words, both the normalizing experience of play within the "magic circle" and the reloading of saved games become epistemological reflexes which maintain fictional/virtual/game time as purely linear to the player. However, Moran's claims, like Juul's, hinge on the notion that such time can be phenomenologically translated into real time. This is not true. The only form of time that can be translated into real-world human experience is that of time spent advancing the *progress* of a particular game: *progress time*. This is important to note because when players die in games and reload a previous save state, they are not only experiencing a loss of fictional/virtual/game time, but more importantly a loss of game *progress*.

Loss and Power

The argument's crux begins to develop: Since progress time is unique because it has genuine real-world impacts, it is also subject to real-world events, including catastrophic progress loss such as permadeath.

The fundamental underlying psychological impact of influencing progress is a modification of the player's conception of power and control in the game. The power to influence the rules of the game space while within such a space greatly affects how the player not only views the game but also the magic circle surrounding the game. Though saving is such a power, its influence on the game space and magic circle is largely dependent on the inherent design of the system of saving. Take, for example, *Tomb Raider* (Core Design 1996), in which save portals were located in specific places throughout each of the game's levels. A player would need to "reach" the save portal (i.e., the player would need to progress far enough *without* the aid of a save function) before he or she was given the ability to save. Such a use of saving sits firmly within the rules of the game space. *Tomb Raider 2* (Core Design 1997), however, allows direct saving at any time through selecting an option in the menu. This type of saving, as even the metaphysical nature of a menu would imply, exists *outside* the rules of the game, yet it modifies the way the game is played: it is important to note that the physics and rules of the game world do not change, even if the player can save at any moment.

This distinction is important because it challenges what is perhaps a reductive categorization of "rules" and "game states" by Juul.[25] When the save feature is subject to the conditions of the game, it exists within the rules of the game. When it does not, it is not. Moran, indirectly, supports this idea when he discusses power relations *within* the game space:

> In the relaxed time made available by undo commands, configuration is privileged over performance, death is deferrable, interruption minimised, precision trained, urgency optional, uncertainty resolved, and some of games' harsh discipline sidestepped. The player thereby arrives in a different set of power relations, which are of control (Deleuze, 1992) rather than discipline (Foucault, 1977).[26]

We propose that what Moran really argues here is an increasing power of the player to modify the conditions *of the magic circle while still within its boundaries.* This is akin to, say, a child inventing a new and invincible option to perform in "Rock, Paper, Scissors." The idea, while technically not included in the accepted rules of "Rock, Paper, Scissors," is one that is employed frequently, and it often results in the "magic" nature of the circle being reduced to pure configuration. This is especially true when other players in the game accept the modification to the rules: should other players of "Rock, Paper, Scissors" decide that the new, invincible option in the game is acceptable, they may invent new options of their own. The social and creative "arms race" here becomes clear and extends to such a degree that it breaks the very foundation of the magic circle surrounding the game.

The ultimate effect of the magic circle losing its purported magic is that the conditions that govern it begin to bleed into real-world desires, conflicts, and events. Consalvo notes this from the perspective of factors external to the design of the game;[27] however, through the example of *Tomb Raider*, we can see that even intentional aspects of the functionality of the game can be considered "real-world" interferences. Moran's consideration of saving in this regard places it in a highly complex relationship between the external world and the world of gameplay:

> There are other ways to correct, fix, and change things in a game; undo features offer to entirely negate user action—including other fixes—in order to restore an earlier state, sometimes on a very small scale. This changes player behavior, yet is an optional extra in each game—no one has to undo.[28]

Moran's opinion that "no one has to undo" perhaps fails to account for what is a growing cultural acceptance for undoing. For example, in the online puzzler game *Bloons* (Ninjakiwi 2007), which tasks players with popping a certain number of balloons in each level in a fantastical world, the player has a specific number of darts (read: lives) available in each level to complete the task. However, should the player fail, the level simply starts over and the player tries again. Life renewed—but without progress or distinct development. This is an important difference to a game that gives players *the option* to try again: the repeat of the level with no other loss of progress is akin to an "undo" of the previous attempt, but the developers of this game have taken into account the cultural assumption that players will likely want to try the level again. Development of games with consideration to how they are going to be used is a strong indicator of changing cultural perceptions of power in games. It is not considered "cheating" to try the level in *Bloons* over and over after "dying" each time, because the game is programmed to allow you to do this (even flashing the words "TRY AGAIN" across the screen after a failed attempt before returning the player's to "life").

However, the aforementioned examples highlight just how complicated an action saving really is. Since there are times that precision saving is forced onto the player, this reinforces the cultural preconditions which prompt such saving even when it is *not* required. Thus, the cultural acceptance for precision saving has impacted the internal rules structures of video games, which in turn has influenced how players save even when saving remains an option.

Saving is one of the few complex interphysical actions that can be considered both within and without the magic circle simultaneously, highlighting precisely the kind of struggle between player and designer power described in Steinkuehler.[29] When real-world actions outside of the rules of the game space (such as player-driven precision saving) impact the game itself, the positive effect is an external hedging against death in the game world, and by extension loss of progress. However, just as such external modifications to the magic circle can provide positive effects, so can they provide negative ones. Because saving hedges against loss, and because saving is an action that is in both worlds, when saving fails, it has genuine repercussions in both worlds, as well. And since saving influences the player's notion of mortality and progress, catastrophic loss (such as permadeath or failures in save states) often significantly and traumatically shifts the player's understanding of the relationship between these values.

For the completion game player, events resulting in catastrophic loss are rare, but usually directly impact the *progress* of the game (e.g., permadeath, corruption of data, catastrophic game bugs, etc.). Since progress in completion games is almost always dependent upon save data, catastrophic losses are often the result of a problem outside the normal experience of save files and their interactions with the player and game worlds.

These events are usually catastrophic because saving, as a function, attempts to mitigate most other forms of progress loss, including death. Players save with high frequency or precision in order to prevent loss of even minor instances of progress. Thus, when the entire save file is damaged, corrupted, destroyed, or otherwise lost or inaccessible, *all* or *most* progress in the game is similarly damaged or negated. A concrete example in the video gaming world might go as follows: a player progresses about 50 percent of the way through *Final Fantasy IX* (Square 2000). Knowing that she has progressed significantly through the game, the player saves multiple versions of the game in order to prevent a corrupted save file from thwarting her progress. These files are saved to a memory card, which she then puts in her pocket after playing for the day. Later in the week, the player does laundry, putting her clothes in the wash with the memory card still in her pocket. When she realizes this and removes the card after the wash cycle, she finds that the memory card will no longer be read by her game console or any other game console.

For all intents and purposes, her progress in the game has been lost. This, in itself, is a kind of death that supersedes all other deaths that might occur in such a completion game. As an ultimate irony, the very system of protection that players might come to rely upon to mitigate death in the game world exposes those players to a form of death that is much more devastating, precisely because it straddles the line between real and virtual worlds: death of data. Not only is any character that a player might have created in a state of pure digital death, but also the digital progress, which has significant real-world impacts, also dies.

A crucial point here is that the player only recognizes the full investment of real time into the digital progress of the game in either of two circumstances: when the game is fully complete or when progress is catastrophically lost. Death in completion games is, therefore, complexly related to both progress and the investment of real time: death in completion games with precision saving is not a serious consequence of player failure, but death of *data* becomes catastrophic. Each death that has occurred in a completion game is revealed now for what it is: a piece of real-world time that the player can never recover.

The breakdown of the magic circle through the interphysical act of saving also creates a subsequent traumatic reaction in the event of catastrophic loss of progress in such a game state. Juul's formalist interpretation of the magic circle is perhaps the best indicator of a lack of consideration of this special interphysical space: "But in video games, the magic circle is quite well defined since a video game only takes place on the screen and using the input devices (mouse, keyboard, controllers), rather than in the rest of the world; hence there is no 'ball' that can be out of bounds."[30] Juul's assertion in *Half-Real*, while technically correct in terms of virtual space, does not account for saving nor for catastrophic events that genuinely impede the separation of real and virtual spaces.[31] For example, if a player of a video game drops the memory card—on which a save state of that game is stored—into a cup of water, thereby short-circuiting its memory, this has a real implication not only on the catastrophic loss of the save state but also on the perception of the game space: this is the equivalent of a ball leaving the playing field by virtue that its destruction not only impedes game progress but also destroys the notion of the magic circle by highlighting its existence as an artificial social space.

This is why catastrophic progress loss often results in players simply abandoning the game in question: continuing the game—that is, the mechanism for Csikszentmihalyieqsue enjoyment—becomes unlikely, because the game itself no longer serves as the means through which many of the elements of enjoyment can be fulfilled: progress loss impedes the feasibility of success, the ability to concentrate, and—most importantly—the ease of "involvement that removes from awareness the worries and frustrations of everyday life."[32] For example, if two players are deep into a game of checkers, and a child walks by and flips the board over, not only will those players not get the expected enjoyment out of playing the game, but they will be much less likely to set up the board again and start over. Death of data in video games is so devastating because it takes the very method of escaping the concerns of daily life and, in an extreme transposition, reveals the method to be yet another problem.

Thus far, we have discussed the impacts of catastrophic losses on save states in completion games. This is not to say that a loss at a later point of progress in a scoring game is not devastating but, rather, that it is less devastating than a catastrophic loss in a completion game due to the expected risk. In scoring games, the associated risk of the iteration of play is always a function of the goals set by the player: if, as in the earlier example, the player is playing for a personal best score, the ratio of risk to reward is significantly lower than if that same player is playing for (and could possibly achieve) a world record. However, all gameplay in scoring games, since gameplay and progress occur in a single iteration, has an inherent risk that is higher than that in most completion games, most importantly those that have allowed for precision saving. Saving mitigates risk in completion games, and precision saving specifically often lulls players into believing that risk is completely negated.

But since risk is *never* completely eliminated, there is a kind of trauma that results in the wake of a catastrophic loss of progress. We propose that the disappointment resulting from catastrophic progress loss in a game with a prior save state is greater than that in a scoring game because humans, by nature, are both loss-averse and perceive ownership of an object (such as a save state) to be an extension of the self.[33] Kahneman, Knetsch, and Thaler describe part of this phenomenon through what they call the "endowment effect": there is greater disappointment in losing something you already own than pleasure in gaining something you do not own.[34]

Particularly relevant to our point is research citing emotional preconditions in the effect[35] and also research challenging the rationale for the effect as a function of ownership and choice rather than loss aversion.[36]

The argument and framing of the endowment effect find an interesting nexus in the idea of saving in video games. A save state in a video game, as we have suggested earlier, occupies an interphysical space: it is a preserver of progress within the game environment, yet it also exists as hard data, which can be transferred, copied, moved, deleted, and lost. These dual natures of a save state situate it within the boundaries of both of the widely cited rationales for the endowment effect: it is something that is *owned* by the player in both digital (e.g., *my* save file) and physical (e.g., *my* memory card) forms, and yet it is also a representation of progress and gains by the player in the digital world. In either scenario, the save function effectively operates as a means to reduce loss, or the *perception* of loss through the choices the player makes. Saving both allows players to justify the choices made in the game environment (regardless of whether or not these choices were the most effective way to progress through the game), and simultaneously preserve the player-owned progress of the game.

This is the key distinction between losses that occur in scoring games and those that occur through catastrophic events in completion games. In other words, even if the loss of progress in each game might be relatively equal considering the length and complexity of the game, the loss of progress in a completion game is ultimately more devastating because of the player's comparatively reduced *expectation* of loss, combined with the players actual loss of the owned save state. Thus, the loss of a save state is not only death of the player's progress, but also death of part of a players' identity, both in the digital and real worlds.

We propose that the combination of these factors ultimately manages the psychological reactions of the player to lost progress in a completion game. The very act of saving somewhat dissolves the already permeable barrier created by the magic circle in gameplay, and the catastrophic loss of save states in completion games further breaks down or destroys completely the separation between game space and real space. Yet, catastrophic events that result in catastrophic progress loss are also subsequently rationalized as plausible and preventable by players. We theorize that such analysis is what ultimately corrects players' conceptions of power and control not only in the game state, but also in most ways in which such conceptions might have bled from the game state into real-world decision making.

Portions of this relationship between completion games and virtual time require further research. It is impossible within the space of this chapter, for instance, to offer insight on how catastrophic loss affects perceptions of real time and the social repercussions of that lost time in a *multiplayer environment*. Further, applications to Massively Multiplayer Online Role Playing Games (MMORPG) would require research that delves into *character-as-progress* video games, which may be considered completion games, but whose means of success may not be the completion of particular global objectives within the game environment.

Notes

1. Chuk Moran, "Playing with Game Time: Auto-Saves and Undoing Despite the 'Magic Circle,' " *The Fibreculture Journal* 16 (2010), http://sixteen.fibreculturejournal.org/playing-with-game-time-auto-saves-and-undoing-despite-the-magic-circle/.

2. Mihaly Csikszentmihalyi, *Flow: The Psychology of Optimal Experience* (New York: Harper Perennial, 1990), 49.

3. Ibid., 53.

4. It is worth noting that, because progress is the sole goal in each iteration of play in a scoring game, that the concept of permadeath becomes polarized: one either considers permadeath in scoring games to be nonexistent, or rather fully existent in each iteration of play.

5. Csikszentmihalyi, *Flow*, 55.

6. Moran, "Game Time."

7. Ibid.

8. Ibid.

9. It should be noted that in-game decisions made by the player that involves cutting out content but utilizes functions included by the game designers are not considered cheating, but elements of gameplay that are intended to affect the way the player plays the game.

10. Ryan Harrison and Nick Morgan, "Super Mario 64 Walkthrough," *IGN*, last modified January 1, 2006, http://www.ign.com/faqs/2006/shindou-super-mario-64-rumble-pak-vers-walkthrough-566275.

11. Moran, "Game Time."

12. Johan Huizinga, *Homo Ludens: A Study of the Play Element in Culture* (Boston: Beacon Press, 1950), 10–12.

13. Jesper Juul, "The Magic Circle and the Puzzle Piece," *The Conference Proceedings of the Philosophy of Video Games*, 2008, 59–60, http://opus.kobv.de/ubp/volltexte/2008/2455/.

14. Ibid., 63–64.

15. Moran, "Game Time."

16. Mia Consalvo, "There Is No Magic Circle," *Games and Culture* 4, no. 4 (2009): 411–15, doi:10.1177/1555412009343575.

17. Juul, "Magic Circle," 63–64.

18. Jesper Juul, *Half-Real: Video Games between Real Rules and Fictional Worlds* (Cambridge: MIT, 2005), 141–56.

19. Moran, "Game Time."

20. Juul, *Half-Real*, 143.

23. Moran, "Game Time."

25. Juul, *Half-Real,* 57–63.

26. Moran, "Game Time."

27. Consalvo, "There Is No Magic Circle," 412–13.

28. Moran, "Game Time."

29. Constance Steinkuehler, "The Mangle of Play," *Games and Culture* 1, no. 3 (2006): 205–11, doi:10.1177/1555412006290440.

30. Juul, *Half-Real,* 164–65.

31. Juul later claimed in "The Magic Circle and the Puzzle Piece" that the magic circle itself is subject to surrounding social influences, but more so in the terms of preexisting social conditions that might impact magic circle spaces. Our claim here focuses more on emergent external forces on the magic circle space.

32. Csikszentmihalyi, *Flow,* 47.

33. Bertram Gawronski, Galen V. Bodenhausen, and Andrew P. Becker, "I Like It, Because I Like Myself: Associative Self-Anchoring and Post-Decisional Change of Implicit Evaluations," *Journal of Experimental Psychology* 43 (2006): 229.

34. Daniel Kahneman, Jack L. Knetsch, and Richard H. Thaler, "Experimental Tests of the Endowment Effect and the Coase Theorem," *Journal of Political Economy* 98, no. 6 (1990): 1342–46.

35. Ying Zhang and Ayelet Fishbach, "The Role of Anticipated Emotions in the Endowment Effect," *Journal of Consumer Psychology* 15, no. 4 (2005): 322–23.

36. Carey K. Morewedge, Lisa L. Shu, Daniel T. Gilbert, and Timothy D. Wilson, "Bad Riddance or Good Rubbish? Ownership and Not Loss Aversion Causes the Endowment Effect," *Journal of Experimental Social Psychology* 45, no. 4 (2009): 950.

Chapter 12

The Death of Digital Worlds
William Sims Bainbridge[1]

Introduction

Simula Tion met her death bravely at midnight on December 15, 2011, standing with a score of comrades between the cantina and Mos Eisley Spaceport on the desert planet Tatooine. A Jedi knight, she had reached the maximum level 80 of status achievement possible in her world, but there were still things she wanted to do, given the freedom she enjoyed and the endless opportunities for creativity that life offered. Her friend, level-80 engineer Algorithma Teq, had decided to end her own existence in a wild farewell party held at the sarlacc pit in Carkoon. She joked that that anyone fed to that monster would suffer a thousand years of agony as she was digested, but at least that agony would be living. A third alternative would be to stay in their huge house, surrounded by the great variety of droids Algorithma had built, and not far from the boyhood home of Luke Skywalker. But they had decided to die at different funeral wakes so that they could compare their experiences if ever they met again in an afterlife.

Elsewhere, an individual known only as Bridgebain suffered his own intense frustration, trapped in the subway station at 23rd Street and Broadway in Manhattan, tantalizingly near the home and office he had owned for 50 years at 34 Gramercy Park. The date of his demise may have been February 28, 2009, when his entire world ended, or September 22, 1947, when he individually died for the first time. Yet it seemed to be some time into the 21st century, because the World Trade Center had already been built, destroyed, and replaced on his beloved New York skyline. After having battled his way across the galaxy, and collecting all the enshrined wisdom of the Eloh, he had returned home with the liberation forces, hoping to save his wife and children, not knowing whether they still lived. He recalled with excruciating pain his failure back in 1912, when all his skill as a surgeon failed to save his daughter Elizabeth, who died during her fourth day of life. Now a Korean corporation had decided his own life was insufficiently profitable, and they pulled the plug.

These two tragedies took place in *Star Wars Galaxies* and *Tabula Rasa,* respectively, two virtual worlds of the kind called massively multiplayer online role-playing games (hereafter referred to simply as MMOs). Both were high-quality science fiction virtual worlds in which thousands of real-world users could experience possible futures for themselves in outer space. And both were destroyed by their commercial publishers, despite being greatly admired by both scholars of virtual worlds and MMO players. Traditionally, when a book went "out of print," it was still available in libraries, and a drama or a symphony still existed on paper and could be performed whenever professionals or audiences wished. But MMOs and other online virtual worlds are ephemeral, and no practical way currently exists to revive one once it has been terminated. This chapter will explore all the major ramifications of this situation, especially the fact that the avatars who dwell in these worlds "die" when the cataclysm strikes.

The Lives of Avatars

When online virtual worlds first arose, initially as text-based "dungeons" and then as visually realistic three-dimensional environments, many observers assumed that the character operated by a user was an avatar of that person. In some ways, this was a profound assumption, giving some spiritual meaning to the virtual embodiment, because *avatar* is a Hindu religious term describing the common belief in ancient Indo-European cultures that gods could come to Earth in the form of mortal beings. Had Jesus been an Indo-European, he would have been described as a mere avatar of Jehovah. However, despite the delightfully profound connotations of the term *avatar,* it has tended to oversimplify people's conceptions of the identities of virtual beings. A considerable body of research demonstrates that many people do identify closely with their online representations, and that what happens to an avatar can deeply affect the person.[2] However, there is great individual variation, and when dedicated gamers have multiple avatars, each may be just a temporary role rather than an expression of the person's essence.

MMO companies tend not to use the word *avatar* but rather *character.* This reflects the fact that many video games and computer games have the user operate a character with a predefined name, background, and story who was conceptually quite separate from the user. When my daughters used to play Nintendo video games, they often operated a character named Mario who was an Italian man with a moustache, not a little American girl. When Sir Lawrence Olivier played Hamlet, to be sure he entered into Shakespeare's character yet remained in some sense Olivier, at the very least looking like the actor and speaking English rather than Danish. So there is no strict dividing line between an avatar and a character but something more like a dimension of variation. Yet looking more deeply into how avatars are currently used by expert players, we see even more forms of diversity.

Every MMO mentioned here is one I studied extensively, using standard methods of ethnographic and participant observation sociology, based on prior experience doing the same inside real-world subcultures.[3] In my extensive MMO research, I have invested something well over 7,000 hours in about a hundred avatars, each one different from the others. Fairly early on, I discovered that there were really two different ways one might invest meaning in them, what for want of better terms I call *function* and *emulation*. Simula Tion in *Star Wars Galaxies* was a functional avatar, and her very name is an abstraction, *simulation*. She was a kind of person implied by the *Star Wars* saga but not emphasized, a female Jedi knight. Function has two elements: (1) the abstract concept I wished to explore at that point in my research and (2) how the culture of the gameworld affects that goal. *Star Wars Galaxies* was set at a time in the saga when hardly any Jedi still existed, and the Rebellion was only just forming. Thus, Simula was somewhat ambivalent toward the ambiguous social forces swarming around her, inclined toward the Rebellion but unready to join it wholeheartedly. Algorithma Teq cared nothing for either political faction, because she was a robot engineer who loved only high-tech algorithms.

Bridgebain, in contrast, was an emulation based on my own grandfather William Seaman Bainbridge who had been a New York surgeon, world-traveling adventurer, and medical scientist. True, he performed a "function" in *Tabula Rasa*, exploring the exobiologist class of characters, learning all the biological science and advanced philosophy offered by that rather marvelous MMO. But that function was a direct expression of my grandfather's character. In Bridgebain and through him, I could reexperience my grandfather in adult terms, although I was only seven years old when I said goodbye to him as he lay on his deathbed. Indeed, "Bridgebain" was my grandfather's telegraph cable address as far back as 1923, and he had always been at the forefront of technological advance, living a science fiction life not unlike that in *Tabula Rasa*. Bridgebain belonged to the subclass of emulations I call Ancestor Veneration Avatars (AVAs).[4]

My first avatar in, arguably, the most influential MMO, *World of Warcraft* (WoW), was named Aristotle, and to some extent combined the two functions. The ancient Greek scientist and philosopher by that name was probably not an ancestor of mine, but all scientists belong to his heritage. My second avatar in that MMO, a priest named Maxrohn, was explicitly an AVA, based on my deceased uncle, Max Rohn, who had been an Episcopal priest. I do not know how often users invest their memories of a deceased person in an avatar, but, as of November 21, 2013, fully 51 avatars in *WoW* were named Gygax, undoubtedly memorializing Gary Gygax, the creator of *Dungeons and Dragons*, on which the original *Warcraft* game was largely based. When I held a major scientific conference inside *WoW* in May 2008, one of our field trips took us to the Shrine of the Fallen Warrior that memorializes Michel Koiter, one of the artists who created WoW but died of heart failure at age 19 just months before its original launch.

Technically, there are two kinds of avatars in virtual worlds: (1) those directly operated by players, and (2) nonplayer characters (NPCs) that employ simple artificial intelligence to behave as if they were extensions of people, but do not require real-time input from any human being. Currently, the number of active NPC memorials in MMOs is few, but they could become quite common. In the MMO *Dungeons and Dragons Online*, players are led through one of the subterranean tombs by the recorded voice of Gary Gygax, now stilled in the real world by death, not far from a memorial sculpture erected in his honor. Two active avatars in *WoW* memorialize players, Dak Krause, who died August 22, 2007, and Ezra Chatterton, who died October 20, 2008. Krause is represented by his former avatar, Caylee Dak, who completes a mission that centers on a poem about transcendence of death. Chatterton was a young boy dying of brain cancer who actually designed a mission about a lost dog and recorded the voice for the character who gives the mission to players.[5]

EVE Online is a remarkable MMO, in which advanced players take over the role of game master and assign themselves missions in competition against each other. The September 11, 2012, attack on the U.S. consulate in real-life Benghazi, Libya, is widely reported to have caused the deaths of four people, but one might say the correct number is five. Also murdered was Vile Rat, a cyberdiplomat primarily active in the virtual world *EVE Online* and the alter ego of Sean Smith, the slain Benghazi information officer; as Sean Smith's avatar, Vile Rat was the chief diplomat representing Goonswarm, the most significant "corporation" or guild of players, who even served on the elected advisory board through which players advise the game designers. *EVE Online* is set in an alternate galaxy consisting of thousands of solar systems, where four competing interstellar civilizations have emerged after a period of disorderly colonization from Earth. Despite its fantasy and science fiction qualities, *EVE Online* is a simulation of real human industry, society, and conflict. Currently about 400,000 people live parts of their lives inside it, and thus it has the potential to preserve aspects of them even after their demise in places less exotic than Benghazi.

We can imagine a time when all the thousands of NPCs in a virtual world are based on past players, each operated by artificial intelligence systems based on data about the real person's behavioral tendencies as recorded when that person played the game years before.[6] But already most of the MMOs make death a major theme of the action, and avatars often die themselves, then are resurrected, as part of ordinary gameplay. Thus, it is worth considering the fact that virtual worlds are themselves mortal, and some of the best of them have already died.

The Classical Civilizations

Ancient Greece and Rome continue to influence our world, and the extensive publications about the most prominent virtual worlds will preserve cultural memories of them, but it is certainly technically possible to keep a virtual world alive permanently. Six major and relatively successful gameworlds I have studied no longer exist, however, and descriptions of their fates will provide a good background for exploring more deeply the economic and social issues involved in the decline and fall of virtual civilizations:

> *Star Wars Galaxies* (2003–2011)
> *Tabula Rasa* (2007–2009)
> *The Matrix Online* (2005–2009)
> *City of Heroes* (2004–2012)
> *Warhammer Online* (2008–2013)
> *Pirates of the Caribbean Online* (2007–2013)

When *Star Wars Galaxies* (SWG) was launched in 2003, the virtual-world market had existed for about six years but was not yet mature. Therefore, the creators of SWG did not have a very good basis for judging which features were most conducive for commercial success, but their design decisions were also constrained by the *Star Wars* mythos and the point in fictional history where it seemed best to place SWG. They elected to set the action immediately after the conclusion of the original 1977 movie, just after Luke Skywalker had destroyed the Death Star, when the galactic civil war was in its early stages. This meant that Jedi knights were in short supply, and thus a player could not easily have a character of this elite type. There were relatively few story-based missions—generally called *quests* in MMOs—and the key idea was to live within the *Star Wars* universe. This assumption led to the creation of many tools the player could use to build things, including houses and many objects to place within them, in the context of a rather complex set of skill sets avatars could attain.

Over time, there were several additions to SWG, but the most significant and controversial occurred in 2005 with the New Game Enhancements that simplified the skill system and permitted easy creation of Jedi characters. Intended to attract new players (since fewer had subscribed than expected), these changes offended old players, and the net commercial result was minimal. I explored SWG for fully 618 hours after most of the additions had been made, and I found it really quite marvelous but requiring players to take the initiative in creating their own businesses and virtual towns, more a virtual world simulation than a game. The player population had shrunk considerably by the midnight when the publisher, Sony Online Entertainment, later shut SWG down. The deathblow was the withdrawal of rights to *Star Wars* intellectual property by their owner, Lucas Arts, which transferred the rights to BioWare and Electric Arts for their new MMO, *Star Wars: The Old Republic.*

This was far from an adequate replacement for SWG, because the new MMO emphasized story line quests rather than living somewhat realistically on virtual planets. Also, it was set in time thousands of years before the action of the movies, thus distancing the avatars from the beloved heroes. Indeed, on one of her SWG missions, Simula met an NPC representing Luke Skywalker, immediately after his own great mission.

Simula could be seen standing with dozens of other avatars outside the Mos Eisley Spaceport, at the exact instant SWG shut down, with a message near the center that said, "Connection to SWG lost!" Some of the players moved over to *Star Wars: The Old Republic,* but many connections between them were also permanently lost. When the MMO blogsite *Massively* polled its readers in September 2012 about which MMO was most worthy of resurrection, fully 59.4 percent of 4,458 respondents picked *Star Wars Galaxies.*[7]

Second place in the *Massively* poll was *Tabula Rasa* with 11.8 percent of the vote. Set primarily on two distant planets, *Tabula Rausa* is premised on a few humans surviving after an alien invasion of Earth and battling to regain their home world. The chief creator of *Tabula Rasa* was Richard Garriott, who had also played a leading role in the creation of one of the first MMOs, *Ultima Online,* back in 1997. The son of astronaut Owen Garriott, he was a committed advocate for an expanded space program and filled *Tabula Rasa* with imaginary groups that expressed many different reasons for space exploration and colonization. Richard Garriott was actually in space, visiting the International Space Station, when his publisher, NCSoft of Korea, decided to shut down his visionary virtual world.

In its annual financial report for 2007, NCSoft reported gross sales income of about $5,400,000 from *Tabula Rasa,* compared with $141,300,000 for *Lineage II,* its most successful MMO, and the company hoped *Tabula Rasa* would pass $15,000,000 in 2008.[8] A separate budget category apparently covered online subscriptions, and the report did not subtract costs from income for specific games, so we cannot be certain about the exact financial balance. But when *Tabula Rasa* failed to gain significantly in 2008, it was undoubtedly considered a financial drain on the company, given the costs of maintaining it and adding new material.

This example highlights a key problem for MMOs, which have recently become a major cultural genre. Unlike books (which can be preserved in traditional libraries) or recorded performances (which can be sold profitably even if they are limited to small audiences), MMOs currently have no survival mode. We can imagine a digital library for MMOs, one that would preserve the best ones for constant use by teachers and students for research and as virtual classrooms, following an educational analogy. A vacation resort analogy might work as well, gaining income from small numbers of paying visitors, as part of an archipelago of games that would not cost much to maintain. But three problems retard development of such an MMO digital library. First, no organization currently exists that is prepared to manage the extensive development effort to set one up. Second, the MMOs employ a range of different software systems, some dependent upon particular hardware, so there would be significant implementation and maintenance costs. Third, and perhaps most crucial, the game companies themselves do not want to relinquish the rights to the games, at the very least because a public MMO digital library would compete with their current commercial games for customers.

Rather further down in the *Massively* ranking, 5th place out of 14, was *The Matrix Online* with 3.5 percent of the votes. Based on the trilogy of *Matrix* movies, this MMO allowed players to experience living in *The City,* which was explicitly a simulation created by sinister computer technologies. Based loosely on postmodern philosophies that consider humans to be alienated from the artificial societies that surround them in modern capitalism, the *Matrix* mythos used computers as both a central metaphor and as the technology with which to create the artworks.[9] Like *Star Wars Galaxies, The Matrix Online* was published by Sony Online Entertainment, but in this case as with *Tabula Rasa*, economic considerations were paramount. Reportedly, the population of players had dropped below 500 shortly before termination, which is far too few even to support maintenance costs, let alone permit any expansions or even modest updates.[10] One could well imagine, if this MMO were included in an education digital library, that it could be used as the virtual classroom for online college courses such as urban sociology, postmodern philosophy, and social implications of technology.

The superhero-themed MMO *City of Heroes* was closed by NCSoft a month after the *Massively* poll, so it was not included but could well have won first place. The threat of its demise triggered widespread fan-initiated efforts to save it, then to resurrect it, none to this point successful. In its 2007 annual report, NCSoft said its annual sales were about $25,3000,000, but later reports saw this figure drop, and in the first quarter of 2012 it constituted only 2 percent of the company's sales. Closed along with the game was the 80-employee American subsidiary of NCSoft that had maintained it, Paragon Studios, an indication of the costs involved. Like *The Matrix Online, City of Heroes* offered a vast virtual urban environment, but emphasizing fantasy more than science fiction, and rather more complex and creative.

These four MMOs were published by two Asia-based companies, Sony and NCSoft, and illustrate the uncertain relationships between various companies. Sony had itself created SWG, but *The Matrix Online* had been developed by an independent game developer, Monolith Productions, which was in the process of being taking over by Warner Brothers when the MMO was released. *Tabula Rasa* was developed by Destination Games, which went out of business in 2009, and *City of Heroes* was designed by Cryptic Studios which was taken over in 2011 by the Chinese Company, Perfect World. Of course, this pattern is similar to that in television broadcasting, in which networks traditionally made short-term agreements with production companies. The big difference is that television programs go through reruns and under a wide range of business arrangements, while no such preservation mechanism exists for MMOs.

Warhammer Online was a high-quality fantasy MMO that pioneered new technical means for recruiting players to group battles, and it possessed stories having some philosophical depth. Unfortunately, in competition with several other high-quality fantasy MMOs, it lost ground. I used it primarily as the environment to experience operating an ancestor veneration avatar based on my father: he had served as an instructor in the horse cavalry during World War II, became a vice president of a major life insurance company, and died in an accidental home fire on May 14, 1965. (Life insurance, of course, is one of the most practical ways humanity deals with death, and he used to comment that strictly speaking it should be named *death insurance*. His life insurance policy funded my graduate education.) So, when reviving a deceased person as an AVA, eventually the question arises about how to end the experience properly, and I tend to leave each AVA in a situation very symbolic of the deceased person. In some alternative reality, perhaps the archived database of *Warhammer Online*, he sits proudly on his knight's horse even today.

Pirates of the Caribbean Online was based on the horror-comedy-adventure movies starring Johnny Depp as piratical Jack Sparrow, represented in the MMO by an NPC who sat drinking in a tavern, interacting with the players for some of the missions. The MMO had the wacky characteristics of the movies, and the player was able to pilot ships as well as swashbuckle on land. The style was childish, as if this MMO were explicitly designed for young players, yet controversially it included much gambling, including many opportunities to cheat while playing cards, which parents might find offensive. While the *Pirates of the Caribbean* film series is quite looney, it is set in a particular historical location, about the year 1700 around the British colony at Port Royal. So I decided to base my avatar on Lionel Wafer, a historical personage who actually lived crazy experiences in the Caribbean prior to 1700 and on whom I imagine Jack Sparrow's situation at the beginning of *Pirates of the Caribbean: Dead Man's Chest* was based. Yes, at one point Wafer really did become the witch doctor of an indigenous tribe, painting his body and wearing a large nose ring, looking, I imagine, just like Johnny Depp impersonating Jack Sparrow impersonating a tribal chief.[11] My avatar based on this remarkable historical personage did not achieve nearly so much, merely exploring many virtual islands, helping other players defeat an occasional attack by zombies, and assembling a collection of voodoo dolls.

Complex Life Histories

One sadly common life history for MMOs is an incomplete birth and what could be metaphorically called *infant mortality*. It is difficult to study such cases, because they are short-lived, but one method is for the researcher to volunteer to become a beta tester. Creating an MMO is an iterative process of design, implementation, and testing, initially with hired alpha testers and then with volunteer beta testers. Testers are usually under legal restrictions limiting how much they can report about an unfinished MMO, but volunteering is an effective research tactic. For example, I was a beta tester for *Faxion* (probably pronounced *faction*) that had a rather interesting conception. It was centered on a city called Purgatory, surrounded by seven zones representing the seven deadly sins, and it was poised between Heaven above and Hell below. After the testing period, the game was launched but lasted only three months. Another example was *Seven Souls Online*, which was an adaptation for the North American market of an Asian game, and it lived only briefly after being opened to the general public.

The most interesting example of an MMO that died after a shaky launch was *Gods and Heroes*, based on the mythology and culture of Ancient Rome, even including a nice representation of the Eternal City itself. I explored it thoroughly in an extensive closed beta, then I explored it again after it launched for the general public. The unfinished initial version was created by one small company, which went out of business, was acquired and brought closer to completion by another, was launched in a satisfactory condition but with room to expand, and then closed down in 2012 when it was clear there would not be a sufficient player base for this MMO to make a profit. In addition to the attractive classical architecture and missions based on ancient culture, in the final version each player owned a country estate that had been damaged in war but could be rebuilt by completing various missions in the wider world. *Gods and Heroes* is the one example I can argue should be preserved in an MMO digital library, despite never really having been commercially successful.

A Tale in the Desert, which is set in Ancient Egypt, is different from *Gods and Heroes* in that it was commercially successful but has followed a very different "life path" from the other MMOs described here. *Tale* involves no combat but extensive cooperation between players to build Egypt, a really marvelous alternative to the standard "hack and slash" fighting of most MMOs. Following an intentional plan, it has been launched six times sequentially, each constituting a *tale*, and each time starting from scratch, a birth followed by rebirths, requiring players to build houses, monuments, and other structures needed for a viable Ancient Egyptian community. I studied both Tale 4 and Tale 6, never finding the total population above 1,500, about 1 percent of what mass-market MMOs might consider marginally viable. However, *A Tale in the Desert* was created and operated by a small company, eGenesis, which may not have required the large populations of major MMOs, analogous to the difference between a small local grocery store and a chain of supermarkets. This MMO, also, should be preserved, if its developer is ever unable to support it.

Pirates of the Burning Sea was rather more commercially successful than *Gods and Heroes* and *A Tale in the Desert,* but it shares with them an historical orientation and considerable sophistication (which, sadly, are disadvantages for commercial MMOs while strengthening the case for preservation). Stylistically very different from *Pirates of the Caribbean Online,* this MMO is set in the same area but a few years later, 1720. While including some anachronisms, such as musicians playing string quartets for the general public rather earlier in the century than they became popular with European elites, many of the historical details are reasonably accurate and educationally inspirational. Created by Flying Lab Software, a small company that has since gone out of business, it was published by Sony Online Entertainment. Sony dropped this MMO at the beginning of 2013, but former personnel from Flying Lab formed a new company to sustain it.

A sense of the social solidarity of the community of players was suggested by the dozens of ships that sailed across the Caribbean, their sails colored black to represent mourning. This happened during an hour-long memorial service held on January 12, 2014, for a player who had died of leukemia and whose character's name was Truuth Bringer, ending with a brief service in the church at Port Royal. He had been a leader in the group of players called The Royal Alliance, whose members tended to be Americans or Australians, but which seemed to have been disbanded. Perhaps this memorial happened during Sony's withdrawal, which triggered some consolidation among player groups. Most MMOs distribute players across multiple internet servers, each hosting a distinct implementation of the entire virtual world, and population decline typically triggers server consolidation, which can disrupt social relations even as it encourages successful groups to merge. At the time of Truuth Bringer's memorial, there were only two servers, one primarily for North America and one primarily for Europe, with plans to merge them. My character belonged to a society called Order of the Temple, and one of its leaders sent all members a message the day before the memorial inviting them to participate. Other societies did the same, and it was very much a user-initiated activity.

The role of MMO players in preservation cannot be overemphasized. A striking example is *Uru: Myst Online,* which was an MMO descendent of the tremendously influential solo game *Myst* released in 1993. Very different from most popular video games of the 1990s and from today's MMOs, *Myst* was a set of puzzles within puzzles, the most puzzling being the overall environment and the ultimate goals for the player, all of which had to be discovered via exploration. It emphasized intellect rather than violence, real brains versus virtual brawn, and may thus have been attractive at that point in the history of computing when a fairly large number of people had become sophisticated users of personal computers but the World Wide Web had not yet become their homeland.

Uru: Myst Online dates from 2003, going through a chaotic series of near-launches but never quite becoming established. Celia Pearce has studied the remarkable process through which a dedicated community of *Uru* fans built their own spin-off areas in two nongame virtual worlds, *Second Life* and *There.com*.[12] *Myst*-related environments still exist in *Second Life*, but *There.com* shut down in 2010, only reopening in 2012 on a limited basis. The original creators reopened *Uru* itself in 2010, charging no fee but soliciting donations, and I was able to explore it fairly thoroughly in 2013. If the creators of an MMO are willing, or the entity currently holding the intellectual property rights agrees, a small-but-dedicated group of users could sustain a virtual world, so long as there was no need to add new computer program code or other features.

A rather more expensive version of a similar roller-coaster history is *Final Fantasy XIV*, which is an MMO from a major Japanese game company ?—as the name implies the 14th is a series of very popular video and computer games, sharing the same general mythology but set in different times and places. The series included one earlier MMO, *Final Fantasy XI* (*FFXI*), which launched back in 2002 and continues to receive updates even today. I was studying *FFXI* in 2010 when *FFXIV* launched, and I did censuses of *FFXI* players, by manually doing many focused searches of the online system for finding players to form teams, discovering that the new game did not decimate the population of the old one. As reviews of *FFXIV* were published over the early weeks of its existence, it became obvious that *FFXIV* was seriously flawed, perhaps even a failure.

In the middle of 2012, when I learned that *FFXIV* would be shut down with the hope of relaunching in better condition, I quickly studied it, sending one character throughout all its play areas and to the maximum experience level in one of the combat specializations. From November 11, 2012, until August 27, 2013, *FFXIV* was offline, as a new team of developers completed a very different new version. I participated in one closed beta test before the relaunch, then repeated a thorough exploration once *Final Fantasy XIV: A Realm Reborn* went public. All data about the earlier characters were preserved, so I employed the same character. This was good, because I had modeled him on my main professor in graduate school, behavioral sociologist George C. Homans, and was using his theoretical perspective as the vantage point for analyzing the relative costs and benefits offered to players, both before and after the transformation of *FFXIV*. To the amazement of reviewers, and delight of players, the revival proved to be marvelously successful. Sometimes a sickly child matures into a healthy adult, and science need not be limited to postmortems, but can learn also from observing miraculous cures.

Challenges and Opportunities

Preservation of MMOs faces many challenges, but there also will be several paths to success, so here we shall consider many of both in greater depth. Each MMO requires maintenance of a constantly changing database, for example updating the virtual locations of all avatars and the contents of their inventories of virtual possessions. This database must be on an internet server, or often on more than one if the player base is large or distributed geographically around the globe. Also essential are the users themselves, as each must have other people to interact with, and managing their active involvement requires maintenance of registration and communication systems outside the MMO itself. To this point in their history, MMOs have been designed for different graphics engines, database systems, and communication software. All these features increase the cost of maintenance, so preservation in working order of many MMOs will be costly.

As the previous section indicates, in some cases an MMO might find a unique method for continued life. A hypothetical-but-feasible example would be the revival of *Star Wars Galaxies* as the campus for a virtual college, in the context of the modern movement toward internet-based education, especially massively open online courses (MOOCs). The chief advantage of *Star Wars Galaxies* is that its design already incorporates tools for setting up facilities like those on a real-world college campus. The house shared by Simula Tion and Algorithma Teq had a large living room that could easily have been converted into a classroom. On the second floor was a domed area that could have been a seminar room. The house already contained a workshop where virtual goods, robots, and vehicles could be constructed, plus extensive storage space. Another room could serve as an office. Not far away was a huge town hall, belonging to the local community, which already was occasionally used as an auditorium. Also nearby was a local shuttleport, providing swift transportation across Tatooine and to starports where transportation to other planets was available.

When SWG shut down, four of my avatars had reached the maximum experience level of 80 and owned a total of two dozen houses or factories, a dozen spaceships including a yacht with rooms like a house inside, and a couple dozen robots. Not only did all four "people" die, but all this property was destroyed, without benefit of insurance protection. Not surprisingly, the formal user agreements for MMOs specify that the player does not actually "own" anything inside the MMO, and I wonder what the effect would be if governments prohibited that term in the contracts, allowing users to own their virtual property. This would prevent companies from shutting down MMOs, which in turn would require them to charge users higher fees and to set up a preservation mechanism, perhaps working with independent virtual insurance and real-estate maintenance companies that would be formed in the wake of such legislation.

An obvious issue is the intellectual property rights, such as those associated with *Star Wars*, and the contracts with game companies that currently are in force. Writing in *Communications of the Association of Computing Machinery* under the name of Rumilisoun, one of my female avatars in *Lord of the Rings Online*, I had advocated government support of a digital library for MMOs.[13] A picture in that magazine shows her lecturing the reader inside the Library of Elrond in Rivendell, a venue that suggested what such an archive might look like. At the beginning of 2014, *Lord of the Rings Online* received a renewal of its license to use intellectual property of the estate of J.R.R. Tolkien through 2017, but what about 2018?[14] There is a fascinating symbolism in this case. The Christianization of Europe had the effect of destroying much living culture that could be described as pagan and that could be highly valuable to us today in a post-Christian culture. In a few cases, such as the splendid work of Snorri Sturluson around the year 1200 in Iceland, such pre-Christian literature was preserved, if in altered form. This did not happen in Britain, and Tolkien's Hobbit stories were an attempt by a scholar of historical linguistics to duplicate Snorri's feat, imagining Britain's pre-Christian culture but Christianizing it in the process.

One plan would be for the Library of Congress, which has taken many leadership roles in translating historical information into forms suitable for sharing over the internet, to set up a limited digital library of MMOs. Legislative action could award a dozen initial places in the digital library, naming some of the MMOs described here as the equivalent of national treasures and authorizing the Library of Congress to operate one version of each, thereby redefining the intellectual property rights. Each year, one more could be added, for example the best one that was about to end its commercial existence. I might nominate *Dark Age of Camelot*, which is set in the late European Dark Ages and launched way back in 2001. Culturally, this is a very rich MMO, and one of the NPCs even represents Snorri Sturluson. It is not based on preexisting intellectual property as is *Lord of the Rings Online,* but it is similar in deriving much of its material from European folklore. *Dark Age of Camelot* continues to receive updates, but the population is much lower than years ago, and at some point in the next few years, the developers might be happy to find a permanent home for it.

It might be argued that the very idea of intellectual property rights is outdated, as, for example, the Pirate Parties International argues.[15] Millions of ordinary citizens pirate music recordings today, and one can argue that copyright favors low-quality pop stars and distribution companies, at the expense of excellent artists who lack commercial advertising. If musical recordings were no longer covered by copyright, performers could earn their incomes locally through live performances for which they were paid and achieve wider fame by sharing their recordings freely online.[16] An analysis of expensive productions like movies and television dramas would be different, but today anyone who wants to see a particular episode of *Game of Thrones* can follow links to pirated copies of all the episodes, available for free. Clearly, the new information technologies are undercutting old assumptions, but less so for MMOs because entering one requires not only the permission but the active help of the owners. I still have the original computer discs for *Tabula Rasa,* but they cannot recreate that MMO because I lack all the software and data that had been on NCSoft's servers.

Preservation has been an issue in many areas of the digital revolution. An especially challenging example is "Voices from the Rwanda Tribunal," a demonstration and research project at the University of Washington, that seeks the technical and organizational methods to sustain an intensely meaningful archive over many generations, potentially forever.[17] Currently supported in part by the National Science Foundation, a team led by Batya Friedman is working from a set of video interviews with participants in the International Criminal Tribunal for Rwanda, which sought justice through careful deliberation in the wake of the 1994 Rwandan genocide. Over time, such a living archive will not only grow with addition of more interviews and links to documents, but it will also serve as the focus for contemporary discussions and educational activities. Among the parallels to MMOs are the challenges in managing the current activities of participants, which at times may themselves raise ethical issues such as privacy violations and misrepresentations of fact.

The fact that "Voices from the Rwanda Tribunal" has become the focus of well-funded research reminds us that one of the key steps in the development of today's internet-based culture was the U.S. government's Digital Library Initiative, dating from 1994, which, among other things, supported research that resulted in Google.[18] Now, over a decade after the conclusion of the Digital Library Initiative, it may be time for a new concerted research program focusing on the technical, economic, and cultural issues about preserving MMOs, but including other parallel themes as well. A good first step was a 2010 white paper, "Preserving Virtual Worlds," that resulted from a workshop supported by the National Digital Information Infrastructure for Preservation Program of the Library of Congress.[19] The scope of this white paper was much broader than MMOs and included ordinary world-like solo-player games from the early history of the genre, so similar efforts focused on contemporary MMOs and on future-oriented topics would also be necessary as preparation for a new research funding initiative.

It is important to realize that major MMOs have very significant satellite activities that also need to be preserved, and they often can be preserved even when the MMO itself cannot. Each game has at least one wiki, set of forums, extensive backstory and instruction manual on their websites, and the like. On January 15, 2014, entering "Star Wars Galaxies" into YouTube generated about 30,600 hits; "City of Heroes" generated 50,300, and "The Matrix Online" gave 4,210. Entering "World of Warcraft" locates about 1,230,000 videos, while "A Tale in the Desert" finds only 343. These videos, like the text in forums and wikis, preserve aspects of players (a few of whom, like their MMOs, may have passed away). Among the most famous *WoW* videos is a violent attack on a serious memorial service for a deceased player, "Serenity Now bombs a World of Warcraft funeral," in its current main manifestation having been viewed 6,074,409 times.

Whatever method is used to support MMO preservation, a user community must be developed. Suppose that *Warhammer Online* were made part of a private digital library, supported by public contributions. I could imagine paying into an endowment so that my father's avatar could be transformed into one of the NPCs, perhaps a quest-giver standing in one of the army camps, or even an enemy warrior involved in one of the attacks that players must repel. Family members could log in every year on January 11, his birthday, meet at whatever virtual location he was placed, say a few words of remembrance, then socialize with each other. As the decades passed, some of us might join him, funded by additional endowments in perpetuity, considered a better investment than a traditional tombstone.

Conclusion

However seriously we take ideas like ancestor veneration avatars and virtual memorial services, MMOs have become an important part of social life for millions of people. The experience of an MMO does not last forever, just as attendance at a school or even employment by a company does not last forever. One might philosophically conclude that J.R.R. Tolkien was wrong to compose a song titled "The Road Goes Ever On" for his Hobbits to sing, because the path of each life leads to a cliff called Death. Yet Tolkien's works may survive for thousands of years, and it is technically possible to achieve that same immortality for the latest "total works of art," as Richard Wager called his grand operas, the MMOs. Achievement of that goal will require a concerted research effort, development of appropriate legislation and financial supports, and the enthusiasm of tens of thousands of members of the gamer community. The result may be even more than the very practical goal of preserving MMOs, but even a new form of transcendence of personal death for the people whose avatars dwell in these virtual worlds.

Notes

1. The views expressed in this chapter do not necessarily represent the views of the National Science Foundation or the United States.

2. Bonnie Nardi, *My Life as a Night Elf Priest: An Anthropological Account of World of Warcraft* (Ann Arbor: University of Michigan Press, 2010); Jim Blaskovich and Jeremy Bailenson, *Infinite Reality: The Hidden Blueprint of Our Virtual Lives* (New York: William Morrow, 2011); Nick Yee, *The Proteus Paradox: How Online Games and Virtual Worlds Change Us-and How They Don't* (New Haven, CT: Yale University Press, 2014).

3. William Sims Bainbridge, *Online Multiplayer Games* (San Rafael, CA: Morgan and Claypool, 2010); *Online Worlds: Convergence of the Real and the Virtual* (London: Springer, 2010); *The Warcraft Civilization* (Cambridge, Massachusetts: MIT Press, 2010); *The Virtual Future: Science-Fiction Gameworlds* (London: Springer, 2011); *eGods: Faith versus Fantasy in Computer Gaming* (New York: Oxford University Press, 2013).

4. William Sims Bainbridge, "Ancestor Veneration Avatars," in *Handbook of Research on Technoself: Identity in a Technological Society*, ed. Rocci Luppicini (Hershey, PA: Information Science Reference, 2013); "Perspectives on Virtual Veneration," *The Information Society* 29, no. 3 (2013): 196–202; "Transavatars," in *The Transhumanist Reader*, ed. Max More and Natasha Vita-More (Chichester, West Sussex, UK: Wiley-Blackwell, 2013), 91–108.

5. Martin Gibbs, Jopji Mori, Michael Arnold, and Tamara Kohn, "Tombstones, Uncanny Monuments and Epic Quests: Memorials in World of Warcraft," *Game Studies* 12, no. 1 (2012).

6. William Sims Bainbridge, *Personality Capture and Emulation* (London: Springer, 2014).

7. Justin Olivetti, "Leaderboard: MMO Most Worthy of Resurrection," *Massively,* September 24, 2012, massively.joystiq.com/2012/09/24/leaderboard-mmo-most-worthy-of-resurrection/ (accessed January 14, 2014).

8. global.ncsoft.com/global/ir/earnings.aspx (accessed January 12, 2014).

9. Jean Baudrillard, *Simulacra and Simulation* (Ann Arbor: University of Michigan Press, 1994).

10. Mike Foster, "GDC Europe 2013: SOE Talks Game Shutdowns, The Matrix Online," *Massively,* August 19, 2013, massively.joystiq.com/2013/08/19/gamescom-2013-soe-talks-game-shutdowns-the-matrix-online/ (accessed January 14, 2014).

11. Lionel Wafer, *A New Voyage and Description of the Isthmus of America* (Cleveland, OH: Burrows, 1903).

12. Celia Pearce and Artemesia, *Communities of Play: Emergent Cultures in Multiplayer Games and Virtual Worlds* (Cambridge, MA: MIT Press, 2009).

13. Rumilisoun, "Rebirth of Worlds," *Communications of the ACM* 53, no. 12 (2010): 128.

14. Justin Olivetti, "Lord of the Rings Online Renews License through 2017," *Massively,* January 14, 2014, massively.joystiq.com/category/lord-of-the-rings-online (accessed January 14, 2014).

15. Brad Hall, ed., *No Safe Harbor: Essays about Pirate Politics* (undisclosed location: United States Pirate Party, 2012).

16. William Sims Bainbridge, "Privacy and Property on the Net: Research Questions," *Science* 302 (2003):1686–87.

17. Batya Friedman and Lisa P. Nathan, "Multi-Lifespan Information System Design: A Research Initiative for the HCI Community," in *Proceedings of CHI 2010* (New York: ACM Press, 2010), www.tribunalvoices.org/? (accessed January 15, 2014).

18. Michael Lesk, "The Digital Library Initative," in *Leadership in Science and Technology,* ed. W. S. Bainbridge (Thousand Oaks, CA: Sage, 2012).

19. Jerome P. McDonough, Robert Olendorf, Matthew Kirschenbaum, Kari Kraus, Doug Reside, Rachel Donahue, Andrew Phelps, Christopher Egert, Henry Lowood, and Susan Rojo. 2010. "Preserving Virtual Worlds," www.ideals.illinois.edu/handle/2142/17097 (accessed January 15, 2014).

Bibliography

Aceti, Lanfranco. "Eternally Present and Eternally Absent: The Cultural Politics of a Thanatophobic Internet and Its Visual Representations of Artificial Existences." *Science, Technology and Society* (forthcoming; abstract available at http://research.sabanciuniv.edu/23350/ last accessed July 14, 2014).

Althaus-Reid, Marcella. *From Feminist Theology to Indecent Theology: Readings on Poverty, Sexual Identity and God.* London: SCM Press, 2004.

Althaus-Reid, Marcella. *Indecent Theology: Theological Perversions in Sex, Gender and Politics.* New York: Routledge, 2000.

Altheide, David L. "Identity and the Definition of the Situation in a Mass-Mediated Context." *Symbolic Interactionism* 23, no. 1 (2000): 1–27.

Amira, Dan. "NPR's Scott Simon Is Live-Tweeting His Mother's Death and Making Everyone Cry." *New York Magazine,* July 29, 2013. ymag.com/daily/intelligencer/2013/07/npr-scott-simon-live-tweeting-mothers-death.html. Accessed March 24, 2014.

Anderson, Paul. "What Is Web 2.0? Ideas, Technologies and Implications for Education." *JISC Technology and Standards Watch* 1, no. 1(2007): 1–64.

Ansell-Pearson, Keith. *Viroid Life: Perspectives on Nietzsche and the Transhuman Condition.* New York: Routledge, 1997.

Arendt, Hannah. *On Revolution.* New York: Penguin Books, 1965.

Aries, Philippe. *The Hour of Our Death.* Translated by Helen Weaver. New York: A. A. Knopf, 1981.

Aries, Philippe. *Western Attitudes toward Death: From the Middle Ages to the Present.* Vol. 3. Translated by Patricia M. Ranum. Baltimore: Johns Hopkins University Press, 1975.

"Arlington National Cemetery Will Be Open If the Federal Government Shuts Down." *The Official Website of Arlington National Cemetery,* September 30, 2013. http://www.arlingtoncemetery.mil/news/NewsItem.aspx?ID=376a2906-6584-4468-89e5-0c697e28f662. Accessed May 12, 2014.

Ashton, Kevin. "That 'Internet of Things' Thing, in the Real World Things Matter More than Ideas." *RFID Journal,* June 22, 2009. http://www.rfidjournal.com/articles/view?4986. Accessed April 18, 2014.

Bainbridge, William Sims. "Ancestor Veneration Avatars." In *Handbook of Research on Technoself: Identity in a Technological Society,* edited by Rocci Luppicini, 308–21. Hershey, PA: Information Science Reference, 2013.

Bainbridge, William Sims. *eGods: Faith versus Fantasy in Computer Gaming.* New York: Oxford University Press, 2013.

Bainbridge, William Sims. *Online Multiplayer Games.* San Rafael, CA: Morgan and Claypool, 2010.

Bainbridge, William Sims, ed. *Online Worlds: Convergence of the Real and the Virtual.* London: Springer, 2010.

Bainbridge, William Sims. *Personality Capture and Emulation.* London: Springer, 2014.

Bainbridge, William Sims. "Perspectives on Virtual Veneration." *The Information Society* 29, no. 3 (2013): 196–202.

Bainbridge, William Sims. "Privacy and Property on the Net: Research Questions." *Science* 302 (2003): 1686–87.

Bainbridge, William Sims. "Transavatars." In *The Transhumanist Reader,* edited by Max More and Natasha Vita-More, 91–108. Chichester, West Sussex, UK: Wiley-Blackwell, 2013.

Bainbridge, William Sims. *The Virtual Future: Science-Fiction Gameworlds.* London: Springer, 2011.

Bainbridge, William Sims. *The Warcraft Civilization.* Cambridge, MA: MIT Press, 2010.

Banks, R., D. Kirk, and Sellen. "A Design Perspective on Three Technology Heirlooms." *Human-Computer Interaction* 27 (2012): 63–91.

Bannon, L. J. "Forgetting as a Feature, Not a Bug: The Duality of Memory and Implications for Ubiquitous Computing." *CoDesign* 2, no. 1 (2006): 3–15.

Barthes, Roland. *Camera Lucida: Reflections on Photography.* Translated by Richard Howard. New York: Macmillan, 1981.

Basulto, Dominic. "The Existential Angst of the Facebook Timeline." *Big Think,* December 19, 2011.

Bataille, Georges. *Visions of Excess: Selected Writings 1927–1939.* Vol. 14. Manchester, UK: Manchester University Press, 1985.

Battlestar Wiki. http://en.battlestarwiki.org/wiki/Main_Page. Accessed May 12, 2014.

Baudrillard, Jean. *Simulacra and Simulation.* Ann Arbor: University of Michigan Press, 1994.

Baym, Nancy K. *Tune in, Log On: Soaps, Fandom, and Online Community.* Thousand Oaks, CA: Sage, 2000.

Bazin, André, and Hugh Gray. "The Ontology of the Photographic Image." *Film Quarterly* 13, no. 4 (1960): 4–9.

Becker, Ernest. *The Denial of Death.* New York: Free Press, 1973.

Bell, G., and J. Gemmell. *Total Recall: How the E-memory Revolution Will Change Everything.* New York: Penguin Books, 2009.

Bellah, Robert N. *Habits of the Heart: Individualism and Commitment in American Life.* Berkeley: University of California Press, 2008.

Benner, Joanna, and Aaron Smith. "72% of Online Adults Are Social Networking Site Users." *Pew Research Internet Project,* August 5, 2013. http://pewinternet .org/Reports/2013/social-networking-sites.aspx. Accessed April 18, 2014.

Berger, Peter L. *The Sacred Canopy: Elements of a Sociological Theory of Religion.* 1st ed. Garden City, NY: Doubleday, 1967.

Bergman, O., and S. Tucker. "It's Not that Important: Demoting Personal Information of Low Subjective Importance Using GrayArea." In *Proceedings of the International Conference on Human Computer Interaction, ACM,* 269–78, 2009.

Beyer, Gerry W., and Naomi Cahn. "When You Pass on, Don't Leave the Passwords behind: Planning for Digital Assets." *Probate & Property* 26, no. 1 (2012): 40–43.

Blaskovich, Jim, and Jeremy Bailenson. *Infinite Reality: The Hidden Blueprint of Our Virtual Lives.* New York: William Morrow, 2011.

Bloons. Designers Chris Harris and Stephen Harris. Ninjakiwi.com, 2007. Video Game.

Boellstorff, Tom. *Coming of Age in Second Life: An Anthropologist Explores the Virtually Human.* Princeton, NJ: Princeton University Press, 2008.

boyd, danah. "Social Network Sites as Networked Publics: Affordances, Dynamics, and Implications." In *A Networked Self: Identity, Community, and Culture on Social Network Sites,* edited by Zizi Papacharissi, 39–58. New York: Routledge, 2011.

Brasher, Brenda. *Give Me that Online Religion.* San Francisco: Jossey-Bass, 2001.

Brooks, David. *The Social Animal: The Hidden Sources of Love, Character, and Achievement.* 1st ed. New York: Random House, 2011.

Brown, Jennifer E. "News Photographs and the Pornography of Grief." *Journal of Mass Media Ethics* 2, no. 2 (1987): 75–81.

Brubaker, Jed R., and Gillian R. Hayes. "'We Will Never Forget You [Online]': An Empirical Investigation of Post-Mortem Myspace Comments." In *Proceedings of Computer Supported Cooperative Work CSCW,* 123–32, 2011.

Brubaker, Jed R., Gillian R. Hayes, and J. P. Dourish. "Beyond the Grave: Facebook as a Site for the Expansion of Death and Mourning." *The Information Society* 29, no. 3 (2013): 152–63.

Brubaker, Jed R., F. Kivran-Swaine, L. Taber, and G. R. Hayes. "Grief-Stricken in a Crowd: The Language of Bereavement and Distress in Social Media." In *Proceedings of the International Conference on Weblogs and Social Media,* 42–49, 2012.

Brubaker, Jed R., and Janet Vertesi. "Death and the Social Network." Presented at the CHI 2010 Workshop on HCI at the End of Life: Understanding Death, Dying, and the Digital, Atlanta, GA, USA, 2010.

Buck, Stephanie. "How 1 Billion People Are Coping with Death and Facebook." *Mashable,* February 13, 2013. http://mashable.com/2013/02/13/facebook-after-death/. Accessed May 8, 2014.

Campbell, Heidi A., ed. *Digital Religion: Understanding Religious Practice in New Media Worlds.* New York: Routledge, 2013.

Campbell, Heidi. *Exploring Religious Community Online: We Are One in the Network.* New York: Peter Lang, 2005.

Campbell, Heidi A. *When Religion Meets New Media*. New York: Routledge, 2010.

Cann, Candi. *Virtual Afterlives: Grieving the Dead in the Twenty-first Century*. Lexington: University Press of Kentucky, 2014.

Cann, Candi. "Virtual Memorials: Bereavement and the Internet." In *Our Changing Journey to the End: Reshaping Death, Dying, and Grief in America*, edited by Christina Staudt and J. Harold Ellens. 2 vols, Vol. 1, 193–206. Santa Barbara, CA: Praeger, 2013.

Carretero, Jesus, and Daniel García. "The Internet of Things: Connecting the World." *Personal and Ubiquitous Computing* 17 (2013): 545–59.

Carroll, B., and Katie Landry. "Logging On and Letting Out: Using Online Social Networks to Grieve and to Mourn." *Bulletin of Science, Technology & Society* 30 (2010): 341–49.

Carroll, Evan, and John Romano. *Your Digital Afterlife: When Facebook, Flickr and Twitter Are Your Estate, What's Your Legacy?* Berkeley, CA: New Riders, 2011.

Carson, Denise. *Parting Ways: New Rituals and Celebrations of Life's Passing*. Berkeley: University of California Press, 2011.

Caruso, David B., and David Porter. "WTC Memorial Magnificent, but at a Steep Price." *Yahoo News*, September 10, 2012. http://news.yahoo.com/wtc-memorial-magnificent-steep-price-132938429.html. Accessed May 12, 2014.

Cashmore, Pete. "Facebook Recommends Reconnecting with Ex-Lovers, Dead Friends." *Mashable*, October 25, 2009. http://mashable.com/2009/10/25/facebook-reconnect/. Accessed May 12, 2014.

Castells, Manuel. *The Rise of the Network Society*. Cambridge, MA: Blackwell, 2000.

Castronovo, Russ. *Necro Citizenship: Death, Eroticism, and the Public Sphere in the Nineteenth-Century United States*. Durham, NC: Duke University Press, 2001.

Cheong, Pauline Hope, Peter Fischer-Nielsen, Stefan Gelfgren, and Charles Ess, eds. *Digital Religion, Social Media and Culture*. New York: Peter Lang, 2012.

Cherished Lives.com, March 4, 2009. http://www.cherishedlives.com/. No longer active.

Chidester, David. "Rituals of Exclusion and the Jonestown Dead." *Journal of the American Academy of Religion* 56, no. 4 (1988): 681–702.

Chomsky, Noam, and Edward Herman. *Manufacturing Consent: The Political Economy of the Mass Media*. New York: Pantheon, 1988.

Closer. Dir. Mike Nichols. Columbia Pictures, 2004.

Colcord, Chris. "Facebook and Existentialism." *Fort Wayne Reader*, December 19, 2012.

Coleman, Beth. "Everything Is Animated: Pervasive Media and the Networked Subject." *Body & Society* 18 (2012): 79–98.

Consalvo, Mia. "There Is No Magic Circle." *Games and Culture* 4, no. 4 (2009): 408–17.

Contra. Konami (1988). Video Game.

Crawford-Mason, Clare, Dolly Langdon, Melba Beals, Nancy Faber, Diana Waggoner, Connie Singer, Davis Bushnell, Karen Jackovich, and Richard K. Rein. "The Legacy of Jonestown: A Year of Nightmares and Unanswered Questions." *People Magazine*, November 12, 1979. http://www.people.com/people/article/0,20075018,00.html. Accessed May 12, 2014.

Csikzentmihalyi, Mihaly. *Flow: The Psychology of Optimal Experience.* New York: Harper Perennial, 1990.

Curl, James Stevens. *The Victorian Celebration of Death.* Detroit, MI: Partridge Press, 1972.

Czerwinski, M., D. Gage, J. Gemmell, C. Marshall, M. Pérez-Quiñonesis, M. Skeels, and T. Catatci. "Digital Memories in an Era of Ubiquitous Computing and Abundant Storage." *Communications of the ACM* 49, no. 1 (2006): 45–50.

Davies, Charlotte Aull. *Reflexive Ethnography: A Guide to Researching Selves and Others.* 2nd ed. London and New York: Routledge, 2008.

Davies, Douglas. *Death, Ritual, and Belief: The Rhetoric of Funerary Rites.* London: Continuum, 2002.

Dawson, Lorne L., and Douglas E. Cowan, eds. *Religion Online: Finding Faith on the Internet.* New York: Routledge, 2004.

Debnath, Neela. "Review of Black Mirror 'Be Right Back.'" *The Independent,* February 11, 2013. http://blogs.independent.co.uk/2013/02/11/review-of-black-mirror-be-right-back/. Accessed April 18, 2014.

Debray, Regis. *Transmitting Culture.* New York: Columbia University Press, 2000.

DeGroot, Jocelyn M. "'For Whom the Bell Tolls': Emotional Rubbernecking in Facebook Memorial Groups." *Death Studies* 38, no. 2. (2014): 79–84.

Dennis, Jeanne. "Death and Dying: Living and Dying in 140 Characters." *Huffington Post,* September 6, 2013. http://www.huffingtonpost.com/jeanne-dennis/scott-simon-mother_b_3866213.html. Accessed April 18, 2014.

Derrida, Jacques. *Archive Fever: A Freudian Impression.* Translated by Eric Prenowitz. Chicago and London: University of Chicago Press, 1995.

Derrida, Jacques. *Specters of Marx: The State of the Debt, the Work of Mourning and the New International.* London: Routledge, 2006.

Dervin, Fred, and Tanja Riikonen, eds. *Digital Technologies of the Self.* Newcastle, UK: Cambridge Scholars, 2009.

DesMarais, Christina. "Facebook's Instagram Says It Has 90 Million Monthly Active Users." *PC World,* 2013.

DeSpelder, Lynne Ann, and Albert Lee Strickland. *The Last Dance: Encountering Death and Dying.* 9th ed. New York: McGraw-Hill Higher Education, 2011.

Diderot, Denis. *Rameau's Nephew/D'alembert's Dream.* London: Penguin UK, 1976.

van Dijck, José. "Digital Photography: Communication, Identity, Memory." *Visual Communication* 7, no. 1 (2008): 57–76.

van Dijck, José. *Mediated Memories in the Digital Age.* Stanford, CA: Stanford University Press, 2007.

Dobler, R. "Ghosts in the Machine: Mourning the MySpace Dead." In *Folklore and the Internet: Vernacular Expression in a Digital World,* edited by T. Blanj. Logan: Utah State University Press, 2009.

Doka, Ken. *Disenfranchised Grief: Recognizing Hidden Sorrow.* Lanham, MD: Lexington Books, 1989.

Dourish, Paul, and Adrian Friday, eds. *UbiComp 2006: Ubiquitous Computing.* Irvine, CA: Springer, 2006.

Dow, S., J. Lee, C. Oezbek, B. MacIntyre, J. D. Bolter, and M. Gandy. "Exploring Spatial Narratives and Mixed Reality Experiences in Oakland Cemetery." In *Proceedings of the 2005 ACM SIGCHI International Conference on Advances in Computer Entertainment Technology (ACE '05)*, 51–60. New York: ACM, 2005.

Duggan, Maeve, and Joanna Brenner. "The Demographics of Social Media Users-2012." *Pew Research Internet Project*, February 14, 2013. http://www.pewinternet.org/2013/02/14/the-demographics-of-social-media-users-2012/. Accessed May 8, 2014.

Duggan, Maeve, and Aaron Smith. "Social Media Update, 2013." *Pew Research Internet Project*, December 30, 2103. http://www.pewinternet.org/2013/12/30/social-media-update-2013/. Accessed May 8, 2014.

Eakin, Paul John. *How Our Lives Become Stories: Making Selves*. Ithaca, NY: Cornell University Press, 1999.

Ecstasy of Order: The Tetris Masters. Dir. Adam Cornelius, and Perf. Thor Aackerlund. Amazon Digital Services, Inc., 2011. http://www.hulu.com/watch/429491. Accessed February 18, 2014.

Eisenberg, Anne. "Bequeathing the Keys to Your Digital Afterlife." *The New York Times*, May 25, 2013. http://www.nytimes.com/2013/05/26/technology/estate-planning-is-important-for-your-online-assets-too.html?_r=0.

Egelman, S., A. J. B. Brush, and K. M. Inkpen. "Family Accounts: A New Paradigm for User Accounts within the Home Environment." In *Proceedings of Computer Supported Cooperative Work*, 669–78. New York: ACM Press, 2008.

Eliade, Mircea. *The Sacred and the Profane: The Nature of Religion*. New York: Harcourt, 1959.

Everett Yuehong Zang. "Mourning." In *A Companion to Moral Anthropology*, edited by Didier Fassin, 264–83. Chichester, UK: Wiley-Blackwell, 2012.

Eyal, Keren, and Jonathan Cohen. "When Good Friends Say Goodbye: A Parasocial Breakup Study." *Journal of Broadcasting & Electronic Media* 50, no. 3 (2006): 502–23.

Final Fantasy IX. Dir. Hiroyuki Ito, Prod. Hironobu Sakaguchi, and Shinji Hashimoto. Square, 2000. Video Game.

Finley, Klint. "Hypersigils Reconsidered." *Technoccult*, February 18, 2010. http://technoccult.net/archives/2010/02/18/hypersigils-reconsidered/. Accessed May 8, 2013.

Fitzpatrick, Kathleen. *Planned Obsolescence: Publishing, Technology, and the Future of the Academy*. New York: New York University Press, 2011.

Foot, Kirsten, Barbara Warnick, and Steven M. Schneider. "Web-Based Memorializing after September 11: Toward a Conceptual Framework." *Journal of Computer-Mediated Communication* 11, no. 1 (2005): 72–96.

Ford, Paul, and Matt Buchanan. "Death in a Crowd." *The New Yorker*, February 4, 2014. http://www.newyorker.com/online/blogs/elements/2014/02/how-social-media-wrote-its-eulogy-for-philip-seymour-hoffman.html. Accessed May 8, 2014.

Fouque, Victor, and Nicephore Niepce. *The Truth Concerning the Invention of Photography: Nicéphore Niépce, His Life, Letters, and Works.* New York: Arno Press, 1973.

Fowler, Bridget. *The Obituary as Collective Memory.* New York: Routledge, 2007.

Friedman, B., P. H. Kahn Jr., and A. Borning. (2006). "Value Sensitive Design and Information Systems." In *Human-Computer Interaction in Management Information Systems: Foundations,* edited by P. Zhang and D. Galletta, 348–72. Armonk, NY: ME Sharpe, 2006.

Friedman, Batya, and Lisa P. Nathan. "Multi-Lifespan Information System Design: A Research Initiative for the HCI Community." In *Proceedings of CHI 2010.* New York: ACM Press, 2010.

Garces-Foley, Kathleen, and Justin Holcomb. "Contemporary American Funerals: Personalizing Tradition." In *Death and Religion in a Changing World,* edited by K. Garces-Foley. Armonk, NY: ME Sharpe, 2005.

Garde-Hansen, Joanne, Andrew Hoskins, and Anna Reading, eds. *Save As. . . . Digital Memories.* Basingstoke, UK: Palgrave Macmillan, 2009.

Garfinkel, S., and D. Cox. "Finding and Archiving the Internet Footprint." Invited paper presented at the First Digital Lives Research Conference, London, February 2009.

Gavitt, Renée. "Discerning Paradoxical Binaries within Digital Memorials: Youth's Struggle for Transitory Permanence on Facebook." Bennington College, 2011.

Gawronski, Bertram, Galen V. Bodenhausen, and Andrew P. Becker. "I Like It, Because I Like Myself: Associative Self-Anchoring and Post-Decisional Change of Implicit Evaluations." *Journal of Experimental Social Psychology* 43 (2006): 221–32.

Geertz, Clifford. *The Interpretation of Cultures: Selected Essays.* New York: Basic Books, 1973.

Gemmell, Jim, Gordon Bell, and Roger Lueder, R. "MyLifeBits: A Personal Database for Everything." *Communications of the ACM* 49, no. 1 (2006): 88–95.

Gershon, Ilana. *The Breakup 2.0: Disconnecting over New Media.* Ithaca, NY: Cornell University Press, 2010.

Getty, E., J. Cobb, M. Gabeler, and C. Nelson. "I Said Your Name in an Empty Room: Grieving and Continuing Bonds on Facebook." In *Proceedings of the SIGCHI Conference on Human Factors in Computing Systems,* 997–1000, 2011.

Gibbs, Martin, Craig Bellamy, Michael Arnold, Bjorn Nansen, and Tamara Kohn. "Digital Registers and Estate Planning." *Bulletin of Retirement and Estate Planning Bulletin* 16, no. 3 (September 2013): 63–68.

Gibbs, Martin, Joji Mori, Michael Arnold, and Tamara Kohn. "Tombstones, Uncanny Monuments and Epic Quests: Memorials in World of Warcraft." *Game Studies* 12, no. 1 (2012). http://gamestudies.org/1201/articles/gibbs_martin. Accessed May 8, 2014.

Giddens, Anthony. *Capitalism and Modern Social Theory: An Analysis of the Writings of Marx, Durkheim and Max Weber.* Cambridge, UK: Cambridge University Press, 1971.

Gilbert, Kathleen R., and Michael Massimi. "From Digital Divide to Digital Immortality: Thanatechnology at the Turn of the 21st Century." In *Dying, Death, and Grief in an Online Universe: For Counselors and Educators,* edited by Carla Sofka, Illene Noppe Cupit, and Kathleen R. Gilbert, 16–27. New York: Springer Publishing, 2012.

Glater, Jonathan. "50 First Deaths: A Chance to Play (and Pay) Again." *New York Times Online,* March 4, 2004. http://www.nytimes.com/2004/03/04/technology/50-first-deaths-a-chance-to-play-and-pay-again.html. Accessed May 8, 2014.

Goffman, Erving. *Encounters; Two Studies in the Sociology of Interaction.* Indianapolis: Bobbs-Merrill, 1961.

Goffman, Erving. *Interaction Ritual; Essays on Face-to-Face Behavior.* 1st ed. Garden City, NY: Anchor Books, 1967.

Green, James W. *Beyond the Good Death: The Anthropology of Modern Dying.* Philadelphia: University of Pennsylvania Press, 2012.

Greenfield, Adam. *Everyware: The Dawning Age of Ubiquitous Computing.* San Francisco: New Riders Publishing, 2006.

Grider, Nicholas. "'Faces of the Fallen' and the Dematerialization of US War Memorials." *Visual Communication* 30, no. 6 (2007): 265–79.

"The Grimmies." Society of Professional Obituary Writers.com, 2014. http://www.societyofprofessionalobituarywriters.org/the-grimmies.html. Accessed May 12, 2014.

Gumpert, Gary. *Talking Tombstones and Other Tales of the Media Age.* Oxford: Oxford University Press, 1988.

Habermas, Jürgen. *Jürgen Habermas on Society and Politics: A Reader,* edited by Steven Seidman. Boston, MA: Beacon Press, 1989.

Habermas, Jürgen, Michael Reder, Josef Schmidt, and Ciaran Cronin. *An Awareness of What Is Missing: Faith and Reason in a Post-Secular Age.* Cambridge, UK, and Malden, MA: Polity, 2010.

Hall, Brad, ed. *No Safe Harbor: Essays about Pirate Politics.* Undisclosed location: United States Pirate Party, 2012.

Hall, Catherine, and Michael Zarro. "Social Curation on the Website Pinterest .com." *Proceedings of the American Society for Information Science and Technology* 49, no. 1 (2012): 1–9.

Hallam, Elizabeth, and Jenny Hockey. *Death, Memory, and Material Culture.* New York: Bloomsbury, 2001.

Hallam, Elizabeth, Jenny Hockey, and Glennys Howarth. *Beyond the Body: Death and Social Identity.* New York: Routledge, 1999.

Hamblin, James. "Selfies at Funerals." *The Atlantic,* October 29, 2013. http://www.theatlantic.com/health/archive/2013/10/selfies-at-funerals/280972. Accessed May 8, 2014.

Harrison, Ryan, and Nick Morgan. "Super Mario 64 Walkthrough." IGN.com, January 1, 2006. http://www.ign.com/faqs/2006/shindou-super-mario-64-rumble-pak-vers-walkthrough-566275. Accessed May 8, 2014.

Heidegger, Martin. "Building Dwelling Thinking." In *Poetry, Language, Thought.* New York: Harper & Row, 1971.

Hellekson, Karen. "A Fannish Field of Value: Online Fan Gift Culture." *Cinema Journal* 48, no. 4 (2009): 113–18.

Hess, Aaron. "In Digital Remembrance: Vernacular Memory and the Rhetorical Construction of Web Memorials." *Media, Culture & Society* 29, no. 5 (2007): 812–30.

Hesse, Monica. "NPR's Scott Simon Takes Twitter to a New Frontier: His Mother's Hospital Bed." *The Washington Post,* July 29, 2013. http://www.washingtonpost.com/lifestyle/style/nprs-scott-simon-takes-twitter-to-a-new-frontier-his-mothers-hospital-bed/2013/07/29/44cc67ea-f86f-11e2-8e84-c56731a202fb_story.html. Accessed May 8, 2014.

Hieftie, Kimberly. "The Role of Social Networking Sites in Memorialization of College Students." In *Dying, Death, and Grief in an Online Universe: For Counselors and Educators,* edited by Carla Sofka, Illene Noppe Cupit, and Kathleen R. Gilbert. New York: Springer, 2012.

Hockey, Jenny, Jeanne Katz, and Neil Small. *Grief, Mourning, and Death Ritual.* Philadelphia: Open University Press, 2001.

Hockey, Jenny, Carol Komaromy, and Kate Woodthorpe, eds. *The Matter of Death: Space, Place and Materiality.* London: Palgrave Macmillan, 2010.

Hogg, Alec. "Mandela through Social Media-How Twitter Is Talking about Madiba with Video." Biznews.com, December 13, 2013. http://www.biznews.com/keke-lekaba/. Accessed April 18, 2014.

Horton, Donald, and R. Richard Wohl. "Mass Communication and Para-Social Interaction." *Psychiatry* 19 (1956): 215–29.

Hoven, E. van den, C. Sas, and S. Whittaker. "Introduction to This Special Issue on Designing for Personal Memories: Past, Present, and Future." *Human-Computer Interaction* 27, no. 1–2 (2012): 1–12.

Hoven, E. van den, W. Smeenk, H. Bilsen, R. Zimmermann, S. de Waart, and K. Koen van Turnhout. "Communicating Commemoration." In *Proceedings of the Simulation Technology Conference.* November 20–21, 2008.

"How to Throw a Series Finale Party." *Videojug.* http://www.videojug.com/film/how-to-throw-a-series-finale-party. Accessed May 12, 2014.

Huizinga, Johan. *Homo Ludens: A Study of the Play-Element in Culture.* Boston: Beacon Press, 1955.

Hum, Noelle J., Perrin E. Chamberlin, Brittany L. Hambright, Anne C. Portwood, Amanda C. Schat, and Jennifer L. Bevan. "A Picture Is Worth a Thousand Words: A Content Analysis of Facebook Profile Photographs." *Computers in Human Behavior* 27, no. 5 (2011): 1828–33.

Hume, Janice. *Obituaries in American Culture.* Jackson: University of Mississippi Press, 2000.

Hutchings, Emma. "New Facebook App Lets You Say Goodbye after Your Death." *PSFK,* January 10, 2012. http://www.psfk.com/2012/01/facebook-death-app.html. Accessed September 29, 2013.

Hutchings, Tim. "Wiring Death: Dying, Grieving and Remembering on the Internet." In *Emotion, Identity and Death: Mortality across Disciplines,* edited by Douglas Davies and Chang-Won Park, 43–58. Farnham, UK: Ashgate Publishing, 2012.

Innis, Harold A. *Changing Concepts of Time*. Toronto: University of Toronto Press, 1952.

Innis, Harold A. *Empire and Communications*. Toronto: University of Toronto Press, 1950.

Jalland, Patricia. *Death in the Victorian Family*. New York: Oxford University Press, 1996.

Jenkins, Henry. *Textual Poachers: Television Fans and Participatory Culture*. New York: Routledge, 2013.

Johnson, Marilyn. *The Dead Beat: Lost Souls, Lucky Stiffs, and the Perverse Pleasures of Obituaries*. New York: Harper Collins, 2006.

Jones, Kevin T., Kenneth S. Zagacki, and Todd V. Lewis. "Communication, Liminality, and Hope: The September 11th Missing Person Posters." *Communication Studies* 58, no. 1 (2007): 105–21.

Juul, Jesper. *Half-Real: Video Games between Real Rules and Fictional Worlds*. Cambridge, MA: MIT Press, 2005.

Juul, Jesper. "The Magic Circle and the Puzzle Piece." In *Conference Proceedings of the Philosophy of Computer Games 2008*, edited by Stephan Günzel, Michael Liebe, and Dieter Mersch, 56–67. Postdam, Germany: Potsdam University Press, 2008.

Kahneman, Daniel, Jack L. Knetsch, and Richard H. Thaler. "Experimental Tests of the Endowment Effect and the Coase Theorem." *Journal of Political Economy* 98, no. 6 (1990): 1325–48.

Karaganis, Joe, ed. *Structures of Participation in Digital Culture*. New York: Social Science Research Council, 2008.

Karppi, Tero. "Death Proof: On the Biopolitics and Noopolitics of Memorializing Dead Facebook Users." *Culture Machine* 14 (2013). http://www.culturemachine.net/index.php/cm/article/viewArticle/513. Accessed May 8, 2014.

Kasket, Elaine. "Being-Towards-Death in the Digital Age." *Existential Analysis* 23, no. 2 (2012): 249–61.

Kelly, Max. "Memories of Friends Departed Endure on Facebook." *Facebook*, October 26, 2009. https://www.facebook.com/notes/facebook/memories-of-friends-departed-endure-on-facebook/163091042130. Accessed May 12, 2014.

Kelty, Christopher. "Geeks, Social Imaginaries, and Recursive Publics." *Cultural Anthropology* 20, no. 2 (2005): 185–214.

Kern, Rebecca, Abbe E. Forman, and Gisela Gil-Egui. "R.I.P.: Remain in Perpetuity: Facebook Memorial Pages." *Telematics and Informatics* 30 (2013): 2–10.

Kilduff, Marshall, and Ron Javers. *The Suicide Cult*. New York: Bantam Books, 1978.

Kim, Joohan. "Phenomenology of Digital-Being." *Human Studies* 24 (2001): 87–111.

Kirby-Diaz, Mary, ed. *Buffy and Angel Conquer the Internet: Essays on Online Fandom*. Jefferson, NC: McFarland, 2009.

Kirk, D. S., and A. Sellen. "On Human Remains." *ACM Transactions on Computer-Human Interaction* 17, no. 3 (2010): 1–43.

Kirk, D. S., S. Izadi, A. Sellen, S. Taylor, R. Banks, and O. Hilliges. "Opening up the Family Archive." In *Proceedings of Computer Supported Cooperative Work, ACM,* 261–70. February 6–10, 2010.

Kitsch, Carolyn, and Janice Hume. *Journalism in a Culture of Grief.* New York: Routledge, 2008.

Klass, Dennis, Phyllis R. Silverman, and Steven L. Nickman, eds. *Continuing Bonds: New Understandings of Grief.* Washington, DC: Taylor & Francis, 1996.

Knorr Cetina, Karen. "The Synthetic Situation: Interactionism for a Global World." *Symbolic Interactionism* 32, no. 1 (2009): 61–87.

Kohn, Tamara, Martin Gibbs, Michael Arnold, and Bjorn Nansen. "Facebook and the Other: Administering to and Caring for the Dead Online." In *Responsibility,* edited by G. Hage, 128–41. Melbourne, Australia: University of Melbourne Press, 2012.

Kotenko, Jam. "This Casket Streams Spotify So You Can Keep On Shuffling into the Afterlife." *Digital Trends,* September 10, 2013. http://www.digitaltrends .com/social-media/you-can-get-a-coffin-to-play-your-funeral-songs-via-spotify/#ixzz2qcaPW8Q3. Accessed May 8, 2014.

Kundera, Milan. *The Unbearable Lightness of Being.* Translated by Michael Henry Heim. New York: Harper Perennial, 1999.

Lambert, Alexander. *Intimacy and Friendship on Facebook.* Basingstoke, UK: Palgrave MacMillan, 2013.

Lee, Newton. *Facebook Nation: Total Information Awareness.* New York: Springer, 2013.

Lennon, John, and Malcolm Foley. *Dark Tourism.* London: Continuum, 2000.

Lesk, Michael. "The Digital Library Initative." In *Leadership in Science and Technology,* edited by W. S. Bainbridge. Thousand Oaks, CA: Sage, 2012.

Lindley, S. "Before I Forget: From Personal Memory to Family History." *Human-Computer Interaction* 27 (2012): 13–36.

Lipton, Mark. "Forgetting the Body: Cybersex and Identity." In *Communication and Cyberspace: Social Interaction in an Electronic Environment,* edited by L. Strate, R. Jacobson, and S. B. Gibson, 335–49. Cresskill, NJ: Hampton, 1996.

Luck, Morgan. "Crashing a Virtual Funeral: Morality in MMORPGs." *Journal of Information, Communication and Ethics in Society* 7, no. 4 (2009): 280–85.

Lustig, Nathan. "2.89m Facebook Users Will Die in 2012, 580,000 in the USA." *Nathan Lustig: Staying Out of the Cubicle.* June 6, 2012. http://www.nathanlustig .com/tag/facebook-death-rate/. Accessed May 12, 2014.

Luxton, David D., Jennifer D. June, and Jonathan M. Fairall. "Social Media and Suicide: A Public Health Perspective." *American Journal of Public Health* 102, no. S2 (2012): S195–S200.

Manovich, Lev. *The Language of New Media.* Cambridge, MA: MIT Press, 2001.

Marketing Charts Staff. "The Demographics of Instagram and Snapchat Users." Marketing Charts, October 29, 2013. http://www.marketingcharts.com/wp/ online/the-demographics-of-instagram-and-snapchat-users-37745/. Accessed May 9, 2014.

Marsh, Sarah. "Store Your Loved One's Ashes in a 3D-Printed Urn in the Shape of Their Head." Wired, July 27, 2012. http://www.wired.co.uk/news/archive/ 2012-07/27/cremation-urn-3d-head. Accessed May 9, 2014.

Martin, Daniel D. "Identity Management of the Dead: Contests in the Construction of Murdered Children." *Symbolic Interactionism* 33, no. 1 (2010): 18–40.

Martinussen, Einar Sneve, and Timo Arnall. "Designing with RFID." In *Proceedings of the 3rd International Conference on Tangible and Embedded Interaction,* 343–50, 2009.

Marwick, Alice, and Nicole B. Ellison. "'There Isn't Wifi in Heaven!': Negotiating Visibility on Facebook Memorial Pages." *Journal of Broadcasting & Electronic Media* 56, no. 3 (2012): 378–400.

Marx, Karl, and Friedrich Engels. *The Marx-Engels Reader,* edited by Robert C. Tucker. 2nd ed. New York: Norton, 1978.

Massimi, Michael, and Ronald Baecker. "Dealing with Death in Design: Developing Systems for the Bereaved." In *Proceedings of the International Conference on Computer Human Interaction,* 1001–1010, 2011.

Massimi, Michael, and Ronald Baecker. "A Death in the Family: Opportunities for Designing Technologies for the Bereaved." In *Proceedings of the International Conference on Computer Human Interaction,* 1821–30, 2010.

Massimi, Michael, and A. Charise. "Dying, Death, and Mortality: Towards Thanatosensitivity in HCI." In *Proceedings of the International Conference on Computer Human Interaction,* 1–10, 2009.

Massimi, Michael, W. Moncur, and W. Odom. "Memento Mori: Technology Design for the End of Life." In *Proceedings of the International Conference on Computer Human Interaction,* 2759–62, 2012.

Massimi, Michael, W. Odom, R. Banks, and D. Kirk. "Matters of Life and Death: Locating the End of Life in Lifespan-Oriented HCI Research." In *Proceedings of the International Conference on Computer Human Interaction,* 987–96, 2011.

Matyszczyk, Chris. "Does Facebook Need a Cemetery?" CNET, November 21, 2013. http://www.cnet.com/news/does-facebook-need-a-cemetery/. Accessed May 9, 2014.

Mayer-Schönberger, Viktor. *Delete: The Virtue of Forgetting in the Digital Age.* Princeton, NJ: Princeton University Press, 2009.

McClean, Paul. "An Existentialist Critique of Facebook." Young Freethought, November 18, 2010. http://www.youngfreethought.net/2010/11/existentialism-facebook_18.html. Accessed May 9, 2014.

McGehee, Fielding. "The Campaign for the New Jonestown Memorial: A Brief History." the jonestown report 13 (2011). http://jonestown.sdsu.edu/?page_id=34364. Accessed May 12, 2014.

McLuhan, Marshall. *Understanding Media: The Extensions of Man.* New York: McGraw-Hill, 1964.

Mendoza, Dorinne. "A Son Tweets His Goodbyes." CNN, July 29, 2013. http://www.cnn.com/2013/07/29/living/parents-scott-simon-storify/. Accessed May 9, 2014.

Miller, Daniel. *Tales from Facebook.* Cambridge, UK and Malden, MA: Polity Press, 2011.

Miller, Daniel. "What Will We Learn from the Fall of Facebook?" *UCL Social Networking Sites & Social Science Research Project,* November 24, 2013. http://

blogs.ucl.ac.uk/social-networking/2013/11/24/what-will-we-learn-from-the-fall-of-facebook/. Accessed May 9, 2014.

Miller, Nancy K. "Representing Others: Gender and the Subjects of Autobiography." *differences* 6, no. 1 (1994): 1–27.

Mitchell, Amy, and Emily Guskin. "Twitter News Consumers: Young, Mobile, and Educated." *Pew Research Journalism Project,* November 4, 2103. http://www.journalism.org/2013/11/04/twitter-news-consumers-young-mobile-and-educated/. Accessed May 9, 2014.

Mollick, Sharon. "Mapping the Dead." Presentation at the ESRI Conference. 2005. http://proceedings.esri.com/library/userconf/proc05/papers/pap1008.pdf. Accessed May 9, 2014.

Moncur, W., J. Bikker, E. Kasket, and J. Troyer. "From Death to Final Disposition: Roles of Technology in the Post-Mortem Interval." In *Proceedings of the International Conference on Human Computer Interaction,* 531–40, 2012.

Moncur, W., and A. Waller. (2010). "Digital Inheritance." In *Digital Futures' 10,* October 11–12, 2010, Nottingham, UK.

Moore, K., and J. C. McElroy. "The Influence of Personality on Facebook Usage, Wall Postings, and Regret." *Computers in Human Behavior* 28, no. 1 (2012): 267–74.

Moore, Rebecca. "The Stigmatized Deaths in Jonestown: Finding a Locus for Grief." *Death Studies* 35, no. 1 (2011): 42–58.

Moore, Rebecca. *Understanding Jonestown and Peoples Temple.* Westport, CT: Praeger, 2009.

Moore, Rebecca, and Fielding M. McGehee III, eds. *The Need for a Second Look at Jonestown.* Lewiston, NY: The Edwin Mellen Press, 1989.

Moran, Chuk. "Playing with Game Time: Auto-Saves and Undoing despite the 'Magic Circle.'" *The Fibreculture Journal* 16 (2010). http://sixteen.fibreculturejournal.org/playing-with-game-time-auto-saves-and-undoing-despite-the-magic-circle/. Accessed May 9, 2014.

Morewedge, Carey K., Lisa L. Shu, Daniel T. Gilbert, and Timothy D. Wilson. "Bad Riddance or Good Rubbish? Ownership and Not Loss Aversion Causes the Endowment Effect." *Journal of Experimental Social Psychology* 45, no. 4 (2009): 947–51.

Mosco, Vincent. *The Digital Sublime: Myth, Power, and Cyberspace.* Cambridge, MA: MIT Press, 2004.

Moss, Miriam. "Grief on the Web." *Omega: Journal of Death & Dying* 49, no. 1 (2004): 77–81.

Muse, Gabrielle. *Death in the Digital Age-Managing Online Accounts When a Loved One Dies.* Riverview, FL: Idea Adapter, 2011.

My Cemetery.com, 1994. http://www.mycemetery.com. Accessed May 12, 2014.

Nabokov, Vladimir. *The Original of Laura.* New York: Random House, 2013.

Nardi, Bonnie. *My Life as a Night Elf Priest: An Anthropological Account of World of Warcraft.* Ann Arbor: University of Michigan Press, 2010.

Nathan, L. P., B. Friedman, P. Klasnja, S. K. Kane, and J. K. Miller, J. K. "Envisioning Systemic Effects on Persons and Society throughout Interactive System Design." In *Proceedings of Designing InteractiveSystems,* 1–10, 2008.

Norman, Donald A. *Emotional Design: Why We Love (or Hate) Everyday Things.* New York: Basic Books, 2005.

NPR Staff. "Scott Simon on Sharing His Mother's Final Moments on Twitter." *National Public Radio.* July 30, 2013. http://www.npr.org/blogs/alltechconsid ered/2013/07/30/206987575/Scott-Simon-On-Sharing-His-Mothers-Final-Moments-On-Twitter. Accessed May 9, 2014.

Odom, W., R. Banks, D. Kirk, and R. Harper. "Technology Heirlooms? Considerations for Passing Down and Inheriting Digital Materials." In *Proceedings of the International Conference on Human Computer Interaction,* 337–46, 2012.

Odom, William, Roger Harper, Abigail Sellen, David Kirk, and Richard Banks. "Passing On & Putting to Rest: Understanding Bereavement in the Context of Interactive Technologies." In *Conference on Human Factors in Computing Systems,* 1831–40, 2010.

O'Gorman, Marcel. "What Is Necromedia?" *Intermédialités: Histoire et théorie des arts, des lettres et des techniquesIntermediality/History and Theory of the Arts, Literature and Technologies* 1 (2003): 155–64.

O'Hara, K., M. Tuffield, and N. Shadbolt. "Lifelogging: Issues of Identity and Privacy with Memories for Life." In *Proceedings of Identity and the Information Society,* 28–30, May 2008.

O'Leary, Stephen D. "Cyberspace as Sacred Space." In *Religion Online: Finding Faith on the Internet,* edited by Lorne L. Dawson and Douglas E. Cowan. New York: Routledge, 2004.

Ottoni, Raphael, Joao Paulo Pesce, Diego Las Casas, Geraldo Franciscani Jr., Wagner Meira Jr., Ponnurangam Kumaraguru, and Virgilio Almeida. "Ladies First: Analyzing Gender Roles and Behaviors in Pinterest." In *Proceedings of ICWSM.* 2013.

Pac-Man. Midway, 1980. Video Game.

Palahniuk, Chuck. *Fight Club.* New York: W. W. Norton & Company, 1996.

Parks, Malcolm R., and Lynne D. Roberts. "'Making Moosic: The Development of Personal Relationships On-Line and a Comparison to Their Off-Line Counterparts." *Journal of Social and Personal Relationships* 15, no. 4 (1998): 517–37.

Pearce, Celia, and Artemesia. *Communities of Play: Emergent Cultures in Multiplayer Games and Virtual Worlds.* Cambridge, MA: MIT Press, 2009.

Peters, John Durham. *Speaking into the Air: A History of the Idea of Communication.* Chicago: University of Chicago Press, 2000.

Petrucci, Armando. *Writing the Dead: Death & Writing Strategies in the Western Tradition.* Stanford, CA: Stanford University Press, 1998.

Piazza, Jo. "Audiences Experience 'Avatar' Blues." CNN.com, January 11, 2010. http://www.cnn.com/2010/SHOWBIZ/Movies/01/11/avatar.movie.blues/. Accessed May 12, 2014.

Pollak, Sorcha. "Swedish Man Designs Surround-Sound Coffin." *Time,* January 20, 2013. http://newsfeed.time.com/2013/01/20/swedish-man-designs-surround-sound-coffin/#ixzz2gRt4gBGL. Accessed May 9, 2014.

Potter, Tiffany, and C. W. Marshall, eds. *Cylons in America: Critical Studies in Battlestar Galactica.* New York: Continuum, 2008.

Ratcliffe, Tracey. "Death and the Persistent Identity: Implications for Managing Deceased Online Identities and Digital Estates." Conference presentation for CommUnity Online Conference on Networks and Communities, 2012.

Recuber, Timothy. "The Prosumption of Commemoration: Disasters, Digital Memory Banks, and Online Collective Memory." *American Behavioral Scientist* 56, no. 4 (2012): 531–49.

"Remember Laura: A Laura Roslin Community." *LiveJournal.* http://remember-laura.livejournal.com/. Accessed May 12, 2014.

Riechers, Angela. "The Persistence of Memory Online: Digital Memorials, Fantasy, and Grief as Entertainment." *Digital Legacy and Interaction: Post-Mortem Issues,* edited by Cristiano Maciel and Vinicius Carvalho Pereira. Berlin: Springer, 2013.

Roberts, Pamela. "Here Today and Cyberspace Tomorrow: Memorials and Bereavement Support on the Web." *Generations* 28, no. 2 (2004): 41–46.

Roberts, Pamela. "The Living and the Dead: Community in the Virtual Cemetery." *OMEGA-Journal of Death and Dying* 49, no. 1 (2004): 57–76.

Roberts, Pamela, and Lourdes A. Vidal. "Perpetual Care in Cyberspace: A Portrait of Memorials on the Web." *Journal of Death and Dying* 40, no. 4 (2000): 521–45.

Romano, John, and Evan Carroll. *Your Digital Afterlife: When Facebook, Flickr, and Twitter Are Your Estate, What's Your Legacy?* San Francisco: New Riders, 2010.

Ruby, Jay. "Post-Mortem Portraiture in America." *History of Photography* 8, no. 3 (1984): 201–22.

Rumilisoun. "Future Tense: Rebirth of Worlds." *Communications of the ACM* 53, no. 12 (2010): 128–ff.

Russell, Cristel Antonia, and Barbara B. Stern. "Consumers, Characters, and Products: A Balance Model of Sitcom Product Placement Effects." *Journal of Advertising* 30, no. 1 (2006): 7–21.

Sahlins, Marshall. *Historical Metaphors and Mythical Realities: Structure in the Early History of the Sandwich Islands Kingdom.* Ann Arbor: University of Michigan Press, 1981.

Sartre, Jean-Paul. *Being and Nothingness; An Essay on Phenomenological Ontology.* New York: Washington Square Press, 1966.

Sas, C., and S. Whittaker. "Design for Forgetting: Disposing of Digital Possessions after a Breakup." In *Proceedings of the SIGCHI Conference on Human Computer Interaction,* 1823–32, 2013.

Satterfield, T. "In Search of Value Literacy: Suggestions for the Elicitation of Environmental Values." *Environmental Values* 10, no. 3 (2001): 331–59.

Schröering, Heather. "Posthumous Posting: On Death, Dying and Facebook." *Echo Magazine,* 2013: 56–59.

Schuster, Eva. *Das Bild vom Tod: Darstellungen aus der Graphiksammlung der Heinrich-Heine-Universität Düsseldorf.* Aurel Bongers, 1992.

Sellen, A., and S. Whittaker. "Beyond Total Capture: A Constructive Critique of Lifelogging." *Communications of the ACM* 53, no. 5 (2010): 70–77.

Shavit, Vered. *Digital Dust: Death in the Digital Era & Life after Death on the Net: Digital, Virtual and Online Aspects of Current Death.* 2012–2014. http://digital-era-death-eng.blogspot.co.il/. Accessed May 25, 2014.

Skylar, F., and S. F. Hartley. "Close Friends as Survivors: Bereavement Patterns in a "Hidden" Population." *Journal of Death and Dying* 21, no. 2 (1990): 103–12.

Smith, Jonathan Z. *Imagining Religion: From Babylon to Jonestown.* Chicago: University of Chicago Press, 1982.

Snood. Designer David M. Dobson. Snood World, 1996. Video Game.

"Social Networking Fact Sheet." *Pew Research Internet Project.* http://www.pewinternet.org/fact-sheets/social-networking-fact-sheet/. Accessed May 9, 2014.

Socolovsky, Maya. "Cyber-Spaces of Grief: Online Memorials and the Columbine High School Shootings." *JAC* 24, no. 2 (2004): 467–89.

Sofka, Carla J., Illene Noppe Cupit, and Kathleen R. Gilbert, eds. *Dying, Death, and Grief in an Online Universe.* New York: Springer, 2012.

Sontag, Susan. *On Photography.* New York: Anchor, 1990 [1977].

de Souza e Silva, Adriana, and Jordan Frith. "Locative Mobile Social Networks: Mapping Communication and Location in Urban Spaces." *Mobilities* 5, no. 4 (2010): 485–505.

Space Invaders. Midway, 1978. Video Game.

Stark, Andrew. "Forever-Or Not." *The Wilson Quarterly* 30, no. 1 (2006): 58–61.

Steinhart, Eric Charles. *Your Digital Afterlives: Computational Theories of Life after Death.* Basingstoke, UK: Palgrave, 2014.

Steinkuehler, Constance. "The Mangle of Play." *Games and Culture* 1, no. 3 (2006): 199–213.

Stillman, Ari. "Mapping Mapss: Intertextuality across Territories." Unpublished paper. University of Chicago, 2013.

Stokes, Patrick. "Ghosts in the Machine: Do the Dead Live on in Facebook?" *Philosophy & Technology* 25, no. 3 (2012): 363–79.

Sturken, Marita. *Tourists of History: Memories, Kitsch, & Consumerism from Oklahoma City to Ground Zero.* Durham, NC: Duke University Press, 2007.

Suler, John. "The Online Disinhibition Effect." *CyberPsychology & Behavior* 7, no. 3 (2004): 321–26.

Sumiala, Johanna. *Media and Ritual: Death, Community, and Everyday Life.* New York: Routledge, 2013.

Super Mario 64. Dir. Shigeru Miyamoto. Nintendo, 1996. Video Game.

Super Mario Bros. Dir. Shigeru Miyamoto, and Prod. Shigeru Miyamoto. Nintendo, 1985. Video Game.

Super Mario Bros. 3. Dir. Shigeru Miyamoto, Takashi Tezuka, and Prod. Shigeru Miyamoto. Nintendo, 1990. Video Game.

Takacs, Stacy. *Terrorism Tv: Popular Entertainment in Post-9/11 America.* Lawrence: University Press of Kansas, 2012.

Talbot, Michael. *The Holographic Universe.* New York: HarperCollins, 1991.

Tambling, Jeremy. *Becoming Posthumous: Life and Death in Literary and Cultural Studies*. Edinburgh: Edinburgh University Press, 2001.

Taylor, Charles. *The Ethics of Authenticity*. Cambridge, MA: Harvard University Press, 1992.

Tetris. Nintendo, 1989. Video Game.

Thomas, Lisa, and Pamela Briggs. "An Older Adult Perspective on Digital Legacy." In *Proceedings of the 8th Nordic Conference on Human-Computer Interaction*, 2014 (forthcoming).

Thompson, John B. *The Media and Modernity: A Social Theory of the Media*. Stanford, CA: Stanford University Press, 1995.

Tomb Raider. Core Design, 1996. Video Game.

Tomb Raider 2. Core Design, 1997. Video Game.

Trottier, Daniel. *Identity Problems in the Facebook Era*. Hoboken, NJ: Taylor and Francis, 2013.

Turner, Victor. *The Ritual Process: Structure and Anti-Structure*. Chicago: Aldine Publishing, 1969.

Twenge, Jean M., and W. Keith Campbell. *The Narcissism Epidemic: Living in the Age of Entitlement*. New York: Free Press, 2009.

Veale, Kylie. "Online Memorialisation: The Web as a Collective Memorial Landscape for Remembering the Dead." *Fibreculture* 3 (2004). http://three.fibre culturejournal.org/fcj-014-online-memorialisation-the-web-as-a-collective-memorial-landscape-for-remembering-the-dead/. Accessed May 9, 2014.

Vercillo, Kathryn. "QR Codes on Tombstones Provide Info about the Deceased." Dial-a-phone, March 16, 2011. http://www.dialaphone.co.uk/blog/2011/03/16/qr-codes-on-tombstones-provide-info-about-the-deceased/. Accessed May 9, 2014.

Virtual Graveyard. 2009. http://virtualgrave.eu/. Accessed May 12, 2014.

Wafer, Lionel. *A New Voyage and Description of the Isthmus of America*. Cleveland: Burrows, 1903.

Wagner, Rachel. *Godwired: Religion, Ritual and Virtual Reality*. New York: Routledge, 2012.

Walter, Tony. "A New Model of Grief: Bereavement and Biography." *Mortality* 1, no. 1 (1996): 7–25.

Walter, Tony. *The Revival of Death*. London: Routledge, 1994.

Walter, Tony, Rachid Hourizi, Wendy Moncur, and Stacey Pitsillides. "Does the Internet Change How We Die and Mourn? Overview and Analysis." *Omega* 64, no. 4 (2011): 275–302.

Wang, Y., G. Norcie, S. Komanduri, A. Acquisti, P. G. Leon, and L. Cranor. "I Regretted the Minute I Pressed Share: A Qualitative Study of Regrets on Facebook." In *Proceedings of Symposium on Usable Privacy & Security*. 2011.

Warner, Michael. *Publics and Counterpublics*. Cambridge, MA: Zone Books, 2005.

Watkins, Gregory J., ed. *Teaching Religion and Film*. New York: Oxford University Press, 2008.

Weinberger, David. *Small Pieces Loosely Joined: A Unified Theory of the Web*. Cambridge, MA: Perseus, 2002.

Weiser, Mark. "The Computer of the 21st Century." *Scientific American* 265, no. 3 (1991): 66–75.

Whittaker, S., O. Bergman, and P. Clough. "Easy on that Trigger Dad: A Study of Long Term Family Photo Retrieval." *Personal and Ubiquitous Computing* 14, no. 1 (2010): 31–43.

Williams, Amanda L., and Michael M. J. Merten. "Adolescents Online Social Networking Following the Death of a Peer." *Journal of Adolescent Research* 24, no. 1 (2009): 67–90.

Williams, Rhiannon. "Social Media Users Warned to Prepare for Digital Afterlife." *The Telegraph,* October 21, 2013. http://www.telegraph.co.uk/technology/news/10393996/Social-media-users-warned-to-prepare-for-digital-afterlife.html. Accessed May 12, 2014.

Willis, Peter, Timothy Leonard, Anne Morrison, and Steven Hodge, ed. *Spirituality, Mythopoesis and Learning.* Mt. Gravatt, Australia: Post Press, 2009.

Wittmer, Matthew D. "Memorializing Mount Carmel Center East of Waco, Texas." Stormbound.org, June 1, 2013. http://www.stormbound.org/waco.html. Accessed May 12, 2014.

Yee, Nick. *The Proteus Paradox: How Online Games and Virtual Worlds Change Us—And How They Don't.* New Haven, CT: Yale University Press, 2014.

Zhang, Ying, and Ayelet Fishbach. "The Role of Anticipated Emotions in the Endowment Effect." *Journal of Consumer Psychology* 15, no. 4 (2005): 316–24.

Zhao, Shanyang. "The Digital Self: Through the Looking Glass of Telecopresent Others." *Symbolic Interactionism* 28, no. 3 (2005): 387–405.

Zhao, Shanyang, Sherri Grasmuck, and Jason Martin. "Identity Construction on Facebook: Digital Empowerment in Anchored Relationships." *Computers in Human Behavior* 24 (2008): 1816–36.

Žižek, Slavoj. *The Sublime Object of Ideology.* New York: Verso, 1989.

About the Contributors

Erica Hurwitz Andrus is a lecturer at the University of Vermont where she teaches courses in comparative religion and religion and popular culture. She received her PhD from the University of California, Santa Barbara, writing her dissertation on the relationship between southern Protestant evangelicalism and the culture of bluegrass music. Her current projects include research on the religion of Dudeism, and the mythology and ritual aspects of Lego Bionicles.

Michael Arnold is a senior lecturer in the History and Philosophy of Science Program in the School of Historical and Philosophical Studies, at the University of Melbourne. His ongoing teaching and research activities lie at the intersection of contemporary technologies and our society and culture. In recent years, Michael's research projects include (1) a comparative study of social networking in six locations across the Asia-Pacific, (2) several studies of high-speed broadband in the domestic context, (3) a study of ethical and governance issues associated with the electronic health record, (4) a study of digital storytelling by young aboriginals, and (5) a study of digital commemoration.

Michael Arntfield is assistant professor of digital and emerging media in the Department of English and Writing Studies at Western University in London, Canada. He also teaches at the university's Centre for American Studies and in the School for Advanced Studies in the Humanities, and has a wide array of interdisciplinary interests and publications encompassing digital environments. Having previously served as a police detective for over 15 years, his PhD research focused on police slayings, including online narratives of specific murders and digital memorials written for fallen officers.

William Sims Bainbridge earned his doctorate in sociology from Harvard University with his first book, *The Spaceflight Revolution* (Wiley-Interscience), a social history of the space program. He joined the National Science Foundation (NSF) in 1992 to run its sociology program, but soon became centrally involved in the Digital Library Initiative, and moved to NSF's computer science directorate in 2000. Especially relevant books include *Dimensions of Science Fiction* (Harvard University Press), *The*

Sociology of Religious Movements (Routledge), *God from the Machine: Artificial Intelligence Models of Religious Cognition* (AltaMira), *The Warcraft Civilization* (MIT Press), and *eGods: Faith versus Fantasy in Computer Gaming* (Oxford University Press). He is currently exploring the scientific use of avatars based both on deceased relatives and on deceased social theorists in massively multiplayer online gameworlds.

Pam Briggs holds a chair in applied psychology at Northumbria University, where she explores identity, trust, privacy, and disclosure issues in social media. Her current projects address trust issues in peer-to-peer health care; the influence of social media in message dissemination during pandemics; location-based services and technologies; and cybersecurity identity management and digital personhood.

Candi K. Cann has written several book chapters on internet memorialization, and is the author of a book on contemporary mourning practices in the popular realm, *Virtual Afterlives: Grieving the Dead in the Twenty-First Century.* An assistant professor of religion in the Baylor Interdisciplinary Core at Baylor University, her research focuses on contemporary memorialization of death, and the ways in which new forms of remembering the dead create and make meaning for those in mourning.

Heidi Ebert is a researcher in Toronto, Canada. She was one of the first graduates of the University of Waterloo's Master's program in Experimental Digital Media. Her research interests include digital identity, social media practice, and Christianity in pop culture.

Martin Gibbs is a senior lecturer in the Department of Computing and Information Systems at the University of Melbourne. His current teaching and research interests lie at the intersection of science and technology studies (S&T), and human-computer interaction, and are focused on the sociable use of interactive technologies. He is the coeditor of the book *From Social Butterfly to Engaged Citizen,* a new work on new technologies and civic engagement, recently published by the MIT Press.

Denisa Kera is a philosopher and designer, working as assistant professor at the National University of Singapore and a fellow of the Asia Research Institute. Her work brings together studies in science, technology, and society (STS), science communication, and interactive media design. She uses design methodologies and prototypes based on open hardware as tools for deliberation and public participation in science and technology.

Tamara Kohn is associate professor in anthropology in the School of Social and Political Sciences at the University of Melbourne. Her research and teaching interests include transcultural communities of practice, the anthropology of the body and senses, death studies, and mobility. Recent publications include *The Discipline of Leisure* (Coleman and Kohn, eds.), and "Crafting Selves on Death Row" (in Davies and Park, eds. *Emotion, Identity and Death*).

A. David Lewis is an adjunct assistant professor with MCPHS University and has recently served on the faculty of Northeastern University, Bentley University, Tufts University, and Merrimack College. He is the coeditor of *Graven Images: Religion in Comic Books and Graphic Novels* (Bloomsbury, 2010), with Christine Hoff Kraemer, and author of *American Comics, Literary Theory, and Religion: The Superhero Afterlife* (Palgrave, 2014). Additionally, he has been named coeditor of Palgrave's forthcoming *Contemporary Religion and Popular Culture* series with Eric M. Mazur.

Stephen Mazzeo has had a two short stories and a poem published. He is an adjunct professor at two community colleges in the Philadelphia area; a founding editor of *Obsession Literary Magazine*; and production editor for *Marathon Literary Review*. He holds an MA in English, an MA in humanities, and an MFA from Arcadia University.

Rebecca Moore is professor of religious studies at San Diego State University. She has written and published on new religious movements, where she has concentrated on interpreting a group called Peoples Temple and the events at Jonestown, Guyana, which occurred in November 1978. This effort can be seen on the website http://jonestown.sdsu.edu, and in the book *Understanding Jonestown and Peoples Temple* (Praeger, 2009).

Christopher M. Moreman is associate professor and chair of the Department of Philosophy at California State University, East Bay, where he teaches courses in comparative religion. His research revolves around issues of death, the afterlife, and popular culture. Recent publications include the three-volume edited collection, *The Spiritualist Movement: Speaking with the Dead in America and around the World* (Praeger, 2013) and *Beyond the Threshold: Afterlife Beliefs and Experiences in World Religions* (Rowman & Littlefield, 2010).

Bjorn Nansen is a research fellow in the Department of Computing and Information Systems at the University of Melbourne. He is a researcher of digital media and culture, with interests in technology adoption and innovation, screen and interface ecologies, family and children's media use, material culture studies, and critical theory of technology. His current research projects investigate young children and interactive media, broadband in the home, and digital commemoration.

Daniel Schall is the director of the Writing Center at Arcadia University. His research encompasses a wide range of traditional and developing trends and discussions in writing and popular culture. His creative studies are also focused on emerging and established experimental writing, including multimodal and asemic texts. His most recent work, "Philadelphiamble," was published in *Streetnotes* from the University of California (Davis) in early 2014.

Erinn Staley is a visiting lecturer at Wellesley College. She received her PhD in religious studies, with a graduate qualification in women's, gender, and sexuality studies at Yale University. Her research interests include intersections of religion, body, gender, health, and popular media. Recent and forthcoming publications concern intellectual disability and mystical theology; disability and the notion of disruption; and ecclesial practices and radical theology.

Ari Stillman is currently an MA candidate in Social Sciences at the University of Chicago and holds a previous MA in Religious Studies from Vanderbilt University. His research focuses on the offline consequences of online interaction, the impact of anonymity on communication, and the significance of past experiences on forming identity and commitment. His work has been published in *Religion Dispatches* and *The Revealer*.

Lisa Thomas is a senior researcher based in the Psychology and Communication Technology (PaCT) research group at Northumbria University, UK. Her research draws on psychological perspectives, examining social media, technology design, and the impact new systems may have on diverse groups. She is currently working on the ReelLives project, exploring "digital personhood" and film-creation. After a PhD exploring perceptions of location-based services, she also worked on a multidisciplinary "IMPRINTS" project, understanding perceptions of future identity management enhancing technologies with vulnerable communities.

Index

Note: page numbers followed by n indicate notes.